Open Minds

To my parents, Peter and Audrey,
who taught me fairness,
my wife, Amanda,
who keeps me on my toes
(especially when my head is in the clouds)
and my children, Tom, Olivia and Venetia,
who assume all places of work are like St. Luke's.

Open Minds

21st Century Business Lessons
and Innovations from St. Luke's

Andy Law

THOMSON
™
TEXERE

Australia · Canada · Mexico · Singapore · Spain · United Kingdom · United States

THOMSON

Open Minds
Andy Law

Printed and bound in Great Britain by T.J. International Ltd.
ISBN 1-58799-046-6

1 2 3 4 5 6 7 09 08 07 06 05 04

For more information, contact TEXERE, 622 Third Avenue, 10th Floor, New York, NY 10017. Or you can visit our website at www.etexere.com.

Composed by: Selwood Systems, Midsomer Norton

A CIP catalogue record for this book is available from the British Library.

Contents

Ten Ways To Create A Revolution In Your Company

① Ask yourself what you want out of life.

② Ask yourself what really matters to you.

③ Give all your workclothes to Oxfam and wear what you feel is really you.

④ Talk to people (even those you don't like) about 1 and 2.
(*You should be feeling very uncomfortable now. You may even be sick. This is normal.*)

⑤ Give up something you most need at work (desk, company car, etc.).

⑥ Trust everyone you meet. Keep every agreement you make.
(*You should be feeling a little better now.*)

⑦ Undergo a group experience (anything goes, parachuting, holidaying).

⑧ Rewrite your business plan to align all of the above with your customers.

⑨ Draw a line on the office floor and invite everyone to a brave new world.

⑩ Share everything you do and own fairly with everyone who crosses the line.

(You should be feeling liberated. Soon you will have, in this order, the following: grateful customers, inspired employees, friendly communities, money.)

Acknowledgements

There are so many people to thank for helping me write this book. I guess I should thank Martin Liu of Orion Publishing first. After all, it was his idea to do it. Having said that, I could not have written it if my wife Mandy had not given me some space in a house that saw the arrival of our third child, Venetia, just at the point I decided to start writing.

In many senses this book is the work of everyone at St. Luke's, but David Abraham filled in detail where I had been negligent and provided direction throughout.

Some I had burdened with reading early drafts, including my wife, Chris Southey, Jenny Alexander and Neil Thomson. Together they reassured me it was at least readable.

I shall be eternally grateful to everyone who has proffered a view or given me insight. Particularly I should thank, John Drummond, Charles Handy, Vernon Jennings, Gerry Labourne, Charles Leadbeater, Ruth Lederman, David Mills, Geoff Mulgan, Richard Pascale, Rhoda Pitcher, Anita and Gordon Roddick, Steve Russell, Dr Bart Sayle, Peter Simpson, Elaine Sternberg, Franceska van Dijk, The Reverend Crispin White, Simon Zadek and Theodore Zeldin, who may or may not know how much they have had a hand in the development of St. Luke's.

Dramatis Personae

As you will discover, this book is about people. It is about the collection of people that make up a business. The people below all played a major role in inventing St. Luke's.

David Abraham
An operator in a conventional company, who became a leader in an unconventional one.

Roger Alexander
A Lawyer and (surely?) a Greek philosopher, who became attracted to a New Way.

Dave Buonaguidi (Bono)
A Creative Director, who became a Trustee, and reinvented himself in a new creative domain.

Jody Burrows
A TV Producer, who became an expert on pensions and a Trustee of a company she owned.

Jay Chiat
An inspirational boss on high, who became a trusted friend by our side.

Lucinda Chiesman

A Mum, who became a Hubster, then became a Mother again (of the office).

Colin & Seyoan

A Creative Team, who wrote ads and who became a creative team that did much more.

Mari Cortizo

A small Strategist, who became a big Strategist and healed many in the process.

Libby Cuthbert

A temp, who became an employee and then an owner.

Lynn Ellis

A quiet Accounts Clerk, who became an Account Handler and then a vociferous Trustee of her own company.

John Grant

A Strategic Planner with a brain the size of a planet, who piloted new creative thinking in Deep Space.

Tim Hearn

A Copywriter and winner of awards, who gave it all up and became a Creative Director and winner of something much more valuable.

Andrew Hill

A Media Planner, who became a media entrepreneur. (Not as simple as it sounds.)

Paul Johnson (Jonners)

An Accounts Clerk, who became a Creative Services Director and leader of an entrepreneurial group.

Sally Kelso

An innocent Secretary, who became Head of IT and an expert in a leading edge company.

Andy Law
A Managing Director at the top of the pyramid who became a Chairman in an altogether differently shaped company.

Andy Lockley
A Copywriter, who became a Trustee and directed the course of an advertising agency he owned.

Kate Male & Ben Bilboul
A couple of obvious players in their last jobs, who became the first St. Luker's and anything but obvious.

Jan Martin
A nice person who worked in the Accounts Department, who became an even nicer person when her fellow owners voted her a Trustee.

Fred Meyer
A Madison Avenue big (Swiss) cheese, who came up smelling of roses.

Clare Nash
An Advertising Executive, who became a business innovator and subsequently changed her life.

Sarah Naughten (Naughty)
A Secretary, who became an accomplished Account Handler and Trustee of a company she owned.

Kerry Newman
A Secretary, who became an Account Handler, then a Mother and then returned to midwife the business of the Trustees.

Kola Ogundipe
A Copywriter, who opened Pandora's Box of New Media and jumped right in.

Andy Palmer
An Account Director no one knew very much about, who became a Trustee everyone knew a great deal about.

Dave Pemsel, Tim Hunt & Neil Henderson
A trio of strong Account Directors, who became a strong trio of owner entrepreneurs.

Rachael Plant
A Secretary, who became an Office Manager and then transformed herself into an Account Manager.

George Porteous
A Secretary, who became an accomplished Account Handler and Trustee of a company he owned.

Naresh Ramchandani
A Creative Director in advertising who became a Creative Producer in something entirely different.

Jay Ryan
A quiet girl on the front desk who became a Radio Producer and proficient public speaker.

Sarah Sanderson
A feisty Account Handler, who fought her corner hard and who then became one of the first Trustees and started fighting corners for other people.

Andy Smith (Smudger)
A regular bloke in Print Production, who then ran the department (and St. Luke's) like a regimental sergeant-major and who later became an entrepreneur in something he invented with others.

Robbie Sparks
The Father of the House and an ever so 'umble typographer who became a most trusted Trustee of a company he owned.

Kate Stanners
An Art Director, who became a Creative Director and an inspiration to us all.

Phil Teer
A tall Strategist, who gained in stature and became a giant of cultural marketing.

Neil Thomson
An Accountant in a grey suit, who became a social entrepreneur in jeans and a T-shirt.

Julian Vizard
A Designer, who became an Art Director, who became a Creative Director (without saying a word to anyone).

Tessa Wire
A TV producer and one-man band, who became a Department Head, Group Leader and design guru.

James Wood
A junior 'runner', who became a highly respected TV producer, but remained a hippy throughout all his changes.

Al Young
A Copywriter, who became a Creative Director and improved his soul in the process.

Charlotte Zamboni
A Client Services Director, who left to have a baby and returned to give birth to a whole new career.

and

Crowd, Vendors, Soldiers, Messengers, Attendants, Handmaiden and Watchmen:
Karen Anderson, Chris Bagust, Cathy Baker, Fraser Barker, Freddie Baveystock, Sam Beschizza, Celine Billy, Alistair Campbell, Penny Carling, Annika Carstedt, Mike Chadwick, Tom Childs, Rebecca Clarke, Gidon Cohen, Shanie Connard, Holly Day, Andy Dear, Ken Dixon, Andy Drugan, Samantha Dunn, Vanessa Elliot, Simon Friedberg, Vince Gant,

Angela Gaunt, Suzanne Gaunt, Martyn Gaylard, Veronica Gibson, James Gillham, Jason Goldsmith, Jason Gormley, Bill Griffin, Suzanne Hails, Rose Hamilton, Ava Hitchings, Michelle Hynes, Andrea Ingarfield, Matt Janes, Verity Johnston, Angela King, Mark Lambourne, Mark Lewis, Roddy Lodge, Jessica Lovell, Sarah Madge, Sophie Martin, Sue McGrath, Steve McKenzie, Jonathan Mitchell, Jo Moore, Ed Morris, Jenny Moss, Michael Mwavula, Daniel Norris, James Parr, Graham Parsons, Jaqueline Quinn, Natasha Rampley, John Robson, Juliet Soskice, Debra Stephens, Jonathan Wakeham, Denise Webber.

Preface

Who are you who are reading this book?

A businessman on a plane? A businesswoman in a hotel, maybe?

An academic assessing the real nature of work today?

A business commentator, who enjoys finding rich pickings among the constantly emerging new business ideas?

Or are you a student, learning about life after study which consumes most of our waking hours?

How do you see yourself? Do you categorise yourself at all?

For example, are you better or worse than the person in the seat/room/car next to you? Are you less valuable? Less important? More interesting? More creative? Are you 'just' a mum? Or a dad? A partner, a brother, a sister, a friend? Are you something very special and private that no one really knows about?

I'll tell you how I see you. You're either a woman or a man. And you're living your life how best you can. And you are the earth's most valuable asset today.

Yes, *you*. You, reading this book are valuable and undoubtedly underused. You are the greatest, maybe the last untapped energy resource on the planet.

Yet this energy of yours is plied daily into a world of work which is all tied up in knots because, as it changes to meet the requirements of the future, it can't shake off habits from the past. It's a world in which 'Industrial Age' ritual has collided messily with 'Information Age' rites and created a frustrating soup of liberation and anxiety.

For evidence of this, look no further than your place of employment. I don't know where you work, but I know this. Your office will most likely be a squared-off brick and glass edifice partitioned into rectangles of various sizes according to a fashion determined many years ago. I also know that it will house, amongst other things, some quite magical technology – modems and computers that were unimaginable only 20 years ago.

Two worlds have met and there has not been a gradual evolution from one to the other. And for humans like you and me, this meeting has created new vocabularies (teleworking, Internet, downsizing, HTML, ISDN, knowledge economy, Repetitive Strain Injury, ME) the concepts of which, let alone the words themselves, need a lot of explanation. These new words sit alongside older ones (boss, 9–5, redundancy, bonus, company car, profit), concepts we readily understand and which live in the language of every workplace.

The rules of the past business regimes still tirelessly dog us so that the world of work we inhabit today is strikingly similar to the world our grandparents knew. Yet the world of life is running at a pace we think only our grandchildren will comprehend. Have you noticed how increasingly we adults defer to our children's greater knowledge and skills – particularly in the use of technology but also in other things like the absorption of images and multimedia messages?

And who am I? What person is writing this book? Not an academic, not a social observer. Not a doom-merchant wrapping each development of our species into a prophesy of fear or disaster. Nor a futurist offering tantalising glimpses of what might be.

In fact I'll tell you a secret right now, right up front. I can't tell the future. If I could I'd have presidents, kings, queens and chairmen (as well as you who would most likely want to know next week's winning lottery numbers) queuing to meet me. Actually no one can tell the future. So don't buy into theorists that claim to be able to.

I'm certainly neither a guru nor a management consultant.

I'm not on the sidelines at all. I'm right in the thick of it.

I'm a man in business. In the advertising business actually.

But I'm a businessman who has chosen to experiment with a group of like-minded experimenters. I'm someone who has chosen to discover whether all the tools we have at our disposal today can make our work lives – such a fundamental part of life itself – more enriching, thought-provoking, interesting, rewarding, fun for everyone.

I'm someone who challenges whether business today should bear any relationship at all to business of twenty, ten or even five years ago.

This book is nothing more than a peek into the experiment at work at St. Luke's, a creative communications company that mainly produces advertising, but makes documentaries and short films as well.

This book does not proffer a General Universal Theory of work, it is not a business handbook and it will not seek to prove itself within any domain other than that which I and my colleagues personally know about.

What you'll discover, I hope, is a wonderful company. A company that has chosen to change the 'DNA' of business. St. Luke's furiously seeks a new, better, more fulfilling and fairer role for business in the lives of its employees – who are all also its shareholders – and in the lives of the people it touches whether purposely or inadvertently.

But you'd be mistaken if you thought it was a 'nicey-nicey' company or a bunch of hippies trying to create Utopia. (We've been accused many times of both, although only two of us, myself and Robbie Sparks – 'The Father of the House' we call him – are old enough to have been hippies.)

In searching for a new role for business the people in St Luke's have turned their backs on just about every established aspect of conventional business life. So that St Luke's isn't just a new sort of advertising agency, it's a different kind of company altogether.

It has eschewed conventional hierarchy in favour of the flattest possible organisational layout and the craziest ever decision-making process (but it works . . . now).

Those who would have been seen as senior managers by their peers in the advertising industry have forgone the traditional and more obvious forms of company ownership in favour of total ownership by everyone who is in the company today (and tomorrow), within a co-operative framework.

All personal computers have been thrown out of the office and have been replaced by public workstations used by anyone at anytime. No one has a desk of their own; you can work in any part of the building that suits you. Or outside of the building if that suits you better.

It has even handed over the office space itself to its customers, or 'clients', as it comes to terms with how a truly collaborative business organism should look and behave. Each client has their own creative communications centre, fitted out with their requirements specifically in mind.

Spurning advertising industry convention, it does not enter the lavish awards ceremonies, yet as I write, it's work is rated by some industry observers as the most imaginative in the business.

Why, you might ask, do we do all this?

My critics say it's for show, that it's some kind of permanent PR stunt (we are an advertising agency after all!). If it is (which it isn't), then it has been a very expensive one, because our annual report will show that we have all put our money where our mouths are and have actually done the things we say we have done. An independent Social and Environmental Audit will also attest to the fact that we 'walk the talk'.

Those more cautiously watchful say it's an ad agency, it's creative, and it is obvious that a system like ours can work for us 'absolutely fabulous' folk. Not so. Ad agencies are strangely very conservative. This is not a jibe, they are by and large filled with very talented people, but they have not changed or developed for over 40 years. Not since (so the story goes) someone called Bill Bernbach, an American, reconfigured his human resources in a more creative way. (He put the writers from the attics next to the illustrators from the basements and created what is now known as 'The Creative Team'.)

I suppose the bottom line is that we believe in St Luke's and we believe our ideas can change more people than just us lucky bunnies.

No, it's not a stunt. It's a movement. It's a movement of people who'd like to point out some basic facts of life that are staring us in the face each time we brush our hair, clean our teeth and go to work every morning.

Humans are creative, fun and inquiring; yet work for so many is monotonous, complex and dreary.

Humans are individual and versatile; yet at work we discover we are all expendable and carefully placed in a well-manicured organogram.

I'm not at all surprised that *Homo sapiens* and Work are unhappy bedfellows. The average corporation now lives half as long as the average human, which means that most of us will have been part of a company that is thrashing around in its death throes at some stage in our lives.

Businesses are dying around us, everywhere and in every sector, and in their own special death throes they search for any treatment money can buy: from selling to the highest bidder, cutting costs to the bone (or further), whizz-kid MDs, to management gurus and spiritual advisers. Maybe when things get really desperate they will use all of these.

There's a new remedy every year (for example, downsizing, integration, empowerment), but as all of us in business know, if these remedies really worked we would all be taking them as instant cure-alls. The truth is that businesses are immensely complex – and getting more so.

Businesses now contend with more forces than ever before – legal pressures, consumer watchdogs, media stalking, aberrant individuals, financial, social, environmental and ethical auditors, the Church, the State, the international community. You name it, businesses have met it. Head on. These demanding and increasing pressures makes businesses tense places to be in and humans are the flesh and blood that feel the agonies of business first and most.

The power business has over our lives is awesome. It can promote us or dump us. It can offer self-esteem or lack of dignity. It can frighten and coerce us. It can stretch our imaginations. It can destroy families and it can sponsor and build marriages. It can support evil governments and it can enliven economies. It can create unbearable stress and it can invent wonderful new products and services.

In short, it can treat you as well or badly as it chooses, yet we devote our lives unthinkingly to it and donate almost all of our knowledge and learning and creativity and sweat without any regard to its true value.

Most of what we do in our working lives we do for others and their profit. That just doesn't seem right and the further we at St. Luke's explore, the more we look back to the world we have left behind stupefied that so many must behave in such a way.

We often describe ourselves to each other as pioneers in a wagon train. We have no real idea of where we are going (so little of what has come about was actually planned), but we keep moving because we know that round the next corner will be something wonderful and undiscovered or unexamined.

Despite all the changes we have made, we estimate that we have achieved only a small percentage of the innovation we could achieve.

That's why we keep on developing new ideas.

And that's why St. Luke's has a perpetual vision – to Open Minds.

And because it has opened its own and the minds of those who have come to know it, I hope that this book contributes to the pursuit of that vision and that you, the reader, husband, wife, employer, human are changed by it in some way.

No, I hope more.

Doesn't it strike you as odd that in your house now, or the one you grew up in, you have, for sure, these three books: a bible of your religion, a map of your area and a dictionary of your language?

Three huge reference books, which each, in their own way, direct you.

Yet there is no reference book about the activity you will start in your early twenties and end up pursuing into old age – work.

Yes, there are business books, but they tend to be management texts; ideas and experiences from one leader or guru to the next. This book won't, of course, be as inspirational as a bible, nor will it be as practical as a map. And it won't be as comprehensive as a dictionary. But it might start a thought process in your mind. It might prime you to ask yourself some questions.

Like, am I truly valued?

Is my real potential being genuinely realised?

Is my sweat equity properly recognised?

Is my work life making me a better person?

My aim with this book is to show a different way for everyone in employment. I hope it will encourage you to think about work and where it leads us. I hope it will in some small way redevelop the landscape of our working lives. This book, then, really is for you and the person you are sitting next to right now.

Introduction:
The World Of Advertising

Now hang on a minute. I'm writing this for you and maybe you'll be aware of the 'ins and outs' of the advertising business and maybe you won't. The only advertising agency you'll be sure to have heard of is Saatchi & Saatchi, unless you either know someone in advertising or are in the business yourself. You will probably only know of Saatchi & Saatchi because of their ads for the Conservative Party but I'll wager you don't know what other clients they produce adverts for. In fact you probably don't know what really goes on inside any ad agency at all.

What you've got to know is that advertising is like a village community. It's a small bespoke business in which everyone knows everyone else, even though there are hundreds of advertising agencies (although probably only 50 of them produce the bulk of the advertising that you or I would see every day).

Its trade paper, *Campaign*, which comes out every Thursday, is full of village gossip. Walk into any agency and you will find everybody from the Chairman down poring over its pages, desperate to find out what's going on, or better, to read a story about themselves.

The majority of advertising agencies begin their lives as a collection of essentially self-motivated entrepreneurs who want to get together, form a company, do some nice work and make a million bucks.

Once formed, almost every agency is named after its founders. You're right, it's not very imaginative. I mean, for a business that works hard to create images and brand names, the people in it do not expend much energy doing it for themselves. So, Messrs Smith, Jones, Brown and White get together and call themselves, wait for it ... Smith Jones Brown White, or SJBW for short. In London today we have, for example, AMV, BBH, BMP, BBDO, BDDH, GGT, CDP, JWT, O&M, TBWA, DDB, FCB – and there are hundreds more that sound just the same. The other technique is to have such long or complicated names that only the first or occasionally first two are mentioned (you can imagine the scramble to get your name in first); hence, Lowes, for Lowe Howard-Spink; Howell Henry, for Howell, Henry, Chaldecott, Lury.

The advertising business is much less crazy than you would think. Apart from the Copywriters (who write the words) and the Art Directors (who set the visual style), both of whom tend to dress as wildly as they can, most people in advertising dress conventionally and could be mistaken for working for management consultants, law firms, account-ants, or any desk-bound commercial business you can think of. In an almost conscious effort to be accepted as regular businesspeople, advertising executives ape the fashion and behaviour of these less creative, but certainly more conspicuously 'professional' occupations.

Customers of advertising agencies are known as 'clients' and their advertising contract with the agency is called an 'account'. The people who meet and deal with the clients are the Account Managers and the people who research and analyse consumers like you and me are the Account Planners.

As the account goes through various stages of development from a formal written document outlining the problem, to a rough sketch, to (say) a finished film, it is said to be 'trafficked' through the system. Traffic Managers do this job. TV Producers and Print Production actually make the advertisement, be it TV or cinema commercial, poster, newspaper, magazine or radio.

Advertising is not an easy business to get into and it's not an easy business to survive in. Furiously meritocratic, it weeds out weak per-formers early on and actively sponsors bright young things. This makes the working environment tough, political, pressured and, of course, precious.

It's a business that has always ranked highly in the various lists of most stressful jobs and there is a 'work hard play hard' mentality in most agencies. That's because it's not uncommon for an advertising budget to be in excess of £10 million. The stakes are thus extremely high. Produce a successful ad and your client's sales could double. Do something very wrong (which fortunately doesn't often happen) and you could cost your client mega-bucks and lose the business.

The people who work in advertising are a lot of fun. Usually they are very bright; fast talking and hard thinking are the order of the day. Because the work is stressful, the rewards are high. Most agencies have as many get-togethers as they can muster, at the local pub or in bars and clubs. Everyone is known by their first name, or even their nickname, which if they haven't got they get given pretty fast. Nicknames are a good sign: it means people really know each other well. In fact, I bet if you looked at the performance of companies where nicknames were more prevalent, they would out-perform those competitors who talk to each other more formally!

Expense-account lunches in ritzy restaurants, like Conran's Pont de la Tour or The Ivy, are the norm and most Friday nights are 'get pissed nights'. Salaries are much higher than the average and company cars, from Ferraris to Porsches to the humble BMW, abound. Advertising is a land of Armani suits and posh watches. The image it projects is affluence.

The familiarity engendered between people in ad agencies reaches an all time high when the agency tenders – 'pitches' – for a new account. Most clients invite at least four agencies to pitch and the will to win, with only a 25 per cent chance of doing so, keeps people up all night, every night, seven days a week. The team spirit is usually very good although emotions will run high. Winning provides a surge of energy to the company; losing can cause introspection and lack of morale. The pitch stakes are therefore very high.

Each agency vies with all the others all the time. No matter which agency you are with, all the others will be downgraded in some way. They will be less 'creative', less happy, less successful. You will transfer your loyalty, though, at the drop of a hat if you get offered a big job with more money somewhere else. And needless to say this happens a lot. People move around whenever they can to cash in as high a price for their services as they possibly can.

Every agency likes to think it has a unique way of doing things. I worked for three different agencies who all professed to be uniquely producing Relevant, Distinctive and Effective advertising. The truth is, almost all advertising agencies do things the same way. The internal systems are very similar, if not identical, agency to agency. What differentiates them is the work they produce.

Some agencies are known to be 'creative'*. This means they regularly produce work which wins advertising awards and which is, mostly, liked by consumers. Work such as Boddington's (the Cream of Manchester), or Hamlet Cigars (Happiness Is A Cigar Called Hamlet) is considered to be 'creative'.

But there are many more agencies who are content to produce work which, well, just *works*. The soap powder ads you see, work. Supermarket ads *work*. Some of those ads that drive you mad, *work*.

It's much harder to produce advertising which is truly creative: it has to be of very high quality, it has to be imaginative, and it has to *work*. Playing in the small arena of creative agencies is tougher than just churning out workmanlike ads.

London has long held a special place in world advertising. It is known to be a place of creative excellence. To be a premier creative agency in London is to be a premier creative agency in the world.

So here we have it. The world of advertising. A charismatic, frenetic, hardworking, precarious business, full of clever, fun people who vie with each other constantly! This world is alluded to throughout the book, so if you find yourself getting lost in its intricacies, just refer back to these pages: I hope you will make some sense of it!

---

* Advertising has hijacked the word 'creative'. Whereas to you, an artist or furniture designer would be 'creative', to an ad man an advertisement your peers like, or one that is very funny, is considered 'creative'.

PART ONE

In the Beginning . . .

① The Phone Call

So this is what happened.

In 1995 I was the Managing Director of the advertising agency Chiat/Day London, a subsidiary of a large and famous American advertising agency with offices in Los Angeles, New York and Toronto.

At 7.00 a.m. on the morning of Monday, 30 January 1995, I received a phone call from Jay Chiat, Chairman of the agency. I'll describe Jay to you in more detail later, but all you need to know at this stage is that he was in Vancouver, so he must have been calling late – I guess it was 11.00 at night. Later it occurred to me that he must have spent that weekend making all sorts of phone calls, to all sorts of people around the world, and that I must have been one of the last he would have made.

His call to me went like this.

'Hi, Andy, its Jay. You know we've been talking about the sale of the company, well we've sold it, and I'm telling you in person because I know you disagreed with it when we talked about it before Christmas and I know you'll be unhappy.'

'Unhappy?' I said. 'I'm in shock.'

'Of course you're in shock, I told you you'd be unhappy.' (Jay had this great way of reconfirming back to you what you had just said.) 'Well it's happened,' he went on, 'we're selling to Omnicom, its strategic. We're merging with TBWA. Your job is to meet with the guys at TBWA straightaway and work out with them the best way of joining forces. They're so happy it's you guys, by the way, they think you're fantastic ... we're not selling out, it's strategic ... it's to do with Nissan ... stick with it, you are personally in a great position. You'll make stacks out of a very preferential senior stock option. Mind you, Andy, this is confidential. We're tied up in crap legal tape. You gotta know this is a big deal and lawyers and accountants are crawling all over it. So don't speak to anyone about it except the guys at TBWA I told you about.'

Jay went on, never pausing, never letting me get in with a counter-comment. I felt then that he was embarrassed about the conversation. In fact, I felt he was more unhappy than I was and steamrollering it through me was some kind of defence mechanism. As the conversation drew to a close, it was clear that the essence of my brief from him was to take the maximum amount of business with the minimum amount of people.

This was Madison Avenue at work. No, it was more; it was so obvious, conventional, well, ordinary in fact. It was big business making a big business manoeuvre. We've all read about it or seen it on TV. It was, no doubt, one of many similar big business decisions taken that January day around the world. Decisions made by a few people that affect many others. Decisions that make people like you and me redundant. Decisions that treat people like you and me as names on a telephone list. They are decisions often taken by one person and then, maybe, endorsed by a few more.

But it was actually happening to me and Jay was right. I was very unhappy. And for good reason.

I and my colleagues had spent two years rebuilding a crumbling business in London after a series of senior management hirings and firings. I'll tell you the full story. I have to. It's full of clues as to why we did what we did. It demonstrates how, although we didn't realise it at the time, Life Before The Phone Call was to have been a rehearsal for something much more significant. I'll tell you about how I and others came into Chiat/Day and what a crazy time we had, then you'll under-stand why what happened at ten past seven that January morning, immediately after I'd put the phone down to Jay and talked it through with my wife, had to happen.

② A Way In . . .

Chiat/Day, an American advertising agency, began life in 1968, when two young maverick advertising men in Los Angeles who liked one another's work, Guy Day and Jay Chiat, decided over lunch that they should start working together. Think about it. This was 1968, it was the West Coast of America, Timothy Leary, Flower Power and all that. It was the age of Woodstock. It was Hippie Heaven. It was the perfect environment to set up a different kind of ad agency.

The two ad men had the idea of a company that lacked all the normal business bullshit. They were creative people in a highly charged creative culture; their urge to be different drove every decision they made. The style of Chiat/Day was forged in this climate and was to live in the agency until its very last day. The people that worked there knew they were different. They were special because Chiat/Day was special. When you speak to them now it's as if they were in a weird religious cult, or certainly something that was more than just a company. They saw themselves as the Pirates, everyone else in advertising was the Navy.

In its time Chiat/Day acquired a fearsome reputation in the USA for innovation. It did not just make innovative advertisements, it also used innovative working practices. It was one of the first companies to work in open-plan offices (today most ad agencies are still not open plan). It also pioneered more collaborative ways of working with clients, including them in some of the early stages of advertising development. This was more radical than it sounds. Advertising agencies don't like to present an idea to the client until they are 100 per cent happy with it, and when they do present the idea they defend it to the hilt using whatever persuasion tactics they can call upon. It is this style of working that gives us the clichéd image of the smooth-talking, bow-tied ad man.

When Chiat/Day launched the Apple Mac in 1984 for Apple Computers, Jay confiscated all electronic typewriters from the office and replaced them overnight with Apple Macs. In 1989, Chiat/Day installed an international e-mail system, one of the first in the world, and in 1993 it built a state-of-the-art, Frank Gehry designed 'virtual office' on Venice Beach in Los Angeles and, a couple of years later, an astonishing multi-coloured designer office in Battery Park, New York.

Chiat/Day was the toast of ad agencies the world over. It was everything ad men wanted to be: creative, unconventional, arrogant, successful. Its swagger was its trade mark. 'If you can't be bothered to work on Saturday,' Jay would say, 'don't bother to come in on Sunday.' The zest for work and the zeal for the agency got it the reputation of 'Chiat/Day/and Night'. This agency was the greatest show on earth.

Chiat/Day London was established in October 1989, after Chiat/Day had acquired Mojo, an Australian advertising agency famous for creating Australian jingles. Mojo had tried unsuccessfully to conquer the UK advertising market and its tiny office off Oxford Street in London offered Jay Chiat his longed wished for chance to establish a beach-head and conquer the UK himself. (Not many of his colleagues back in the USA shared this desire by the way!)

The first thing Jay did was to move out the Mojo team. He wanted a clean slate and he wanted people he could trust, people he knew and people who were good.

A group of us were assembled from established and well-known advertising agencies in the UK and from Chiat/Day New York. We felt like Kelly's Heroes. All of us were good in our field. Together we'd make a formidable force. It was a superstar team.

Be that as it may, deciding to set up Chiat/Day in London was a big risk for all of us. We all had 'reputations' and we were all surviving the recession of the late 80s, which was ultimately to wipe out thousands of jobs in advertising.

I was working for Collett Dickenson Pearce (CDP). Wow, to hear people back then talk about CDP. It was known as 'the cathedral of advertising' and it had been running its most famous ads – for Hamlet Cigars (Happiness Is A Cigar Called Hamlet) – for nearly 25 years. This advertising agency was a place to have on your CV. Its wild, tempestuous, brilliant creative genius was the Irishman John O'Donnell. He knew what would be effective, particularly on television, and he knew he had to protect ideas he really believed in, even if he made enemies along the way. I learned from him that discomfort in the development of ideas was inevitable, and would remember this ten years later as we wrestled with the construction of a company based on a unique idea.

And I was doing great at CDP. By the time I was approached to join Chiat/Day I was the youngest person (31) on the CDP International Board (the 'inner sanctum'), on a fat salary and with more perks than I knew what to do with, including personal secretary, leather sofa, drinks cabinet and TV in my luxurious corner office.

I chose to give all this up and join Chiat/Day because I knew, by reputation (or advertising folklore, if you like) that Jay Chiat was an extraordinary man, who had built an extraordinary company. He was a rule-breaker with a brutal way of dismissing old-fashioned ideas and dull advertising. Joining Chiat/Day was a chance of a lifetime.

It was Jay who inspired the phrase 'Innovate Or Die' which appeared on the company T-shirts back in 1992 and who, in pursuit of creative excellence, also crafted the phrase that was to become the mantra of Chiat/Day: 'Good Enough Is Not Enough'. He was a man who liked to rattle you and who encouraged bold thinking and who, after his agency was accorded the title 'Agency Of The Decade' in 1989, was heard to remark, 'Congratulations everyone, now get back to work'. No plaudits, awards or titles were ever more important than the creative output of his company.

If I have ever done anything faintly innovative, it is because I felt as if I had Jay Chiat sitting on my shoulder goading me to 'take it further, to go the extra mile'. He will not know it, but he has been, and will be, a fundamental part of the building of St. Luke's.

When I first met Jay he was immaculately dressed as an Italian aristocrat might be. His white, too perfect hair, sat atop a bronzed face that had the air of long-term exposure to benign climates. He spoke softly and, unusually for an American, had a terrific sense of irony. He was, in fact, more European than most Americans that I had met. Although not a tall man (less than six foot), he was clearly fit and his presence filled the room. He was a natural Chairman. Dignified, knowledgeable and witty. I have never known how old Jay is. In his sixties, certainly, but in his mind he is as old as whatever is totally new. He seems to have arrested the march of time with a hunger for whatever tomorrow holds. The entrance foyer to his house in New York had two Damien Hurst pieces before anyone had ever heard of the artist and his mad cow-halving extravaganzas.

I jumped. I left the cosy world of a 200-person company and a Board Director's rich trappings for ten people and an orange box.

And I suppose I have been hinting at the real reason as to why, haven't I? CDP was a successful company, but it was just like every other company I had worked for. It had little interest in anything outside the close confines of the Board of Directors and was internally focused on its own systems for the production of work. What's more, it was having a golden patch, but it would go into decline. I knew it. Most of all, despite being successful throughout the 80s, its sense of itself was based almost entirely on a past mythology. Throughout the eight years I was there, employees still spoke fondly and passionately of a time when the company was run by a charismatic and gifted ad man called Frank Lowe, who left a year before I joined. They did not speak so fondly or passionately of their current management line up. Everyone revelled in the past.

Like so many companies today its structure and purpose had been taken straight out of a book. It was nothing more than a replica of an existing version. It had no values, I felt, other than the personal financial success of the senior management, whose Porsches and Ferraris filled the basement car park. My perception was that it was driven by fear, greed and ego although it professed a deep-seated desire to continue its creative provenance. This was evident in the daily routine of the agency which constantly battled and balanced the twin desires of money versus creative status as if they were mutually exclusive.

I had bought shares in CDP, but when I left the share value had hardly increased because of a 'technical detail' in the paperwork. And I'd paid for those shares, so I felt I'd lost money. Actually I felt as if I had paid the company for the benefit of me working there!

So naturally I was thrilled to take the job at Chiat/Day. In fact, I felt honoured and flattered that I was considered Chiat/Day material.

Chiat/Day was new, decidedly un-British and pathologically anti-convention. For sure I felt this was the greatest career move I could ever make. The day I signed my contract I phoned all the friends and relatives I knew, eager for them to bathe in the reflected glory of me taking this Great Job.

Sadly, the thrill was not to last long.

Things began well enough. Cooped up in an office so small we could just about answer each other's phones without moving from our desks, we were punchy and not a little arrogant. Under the direction of our Managing Director, Marie-Terese Rainey (who liked to be called MT for short), we soon straightened out what little business there was of the old Mojo regime, firing those clients that didn't aspire to our standards and winning nice new ones like HMV Music Stores and Neutrogena, the soap and shampoo people.

MT cut a glamorous figure. Scottish, good looking and highly intelligent she was, according to Jay, 'the smartest person' he'd ever employed. She had a kind of 40s glamour to her, with long flowing hair *à la* Faye Dunaway and that manicured look you only get from being cosseted in the best Manhattan beauty salons. In 1990 she was voted 'Advertising Woman Of The Year' in the USA and indeed everything about her was impressive, from her intellect, to her clothes, to her stunning designer apartment. (A story was told at the time she landed in the UK to take up the London job. At the airport, she ordered two taxis: one for her, the other for her suitcases of designer clothes!) MT had been working with Chiat/Day in the USA since 1984 and was very involved in the famous launch of the Apple Mac – the first real personal computer ever produced. By training she was a Planner – that is to say, she was a strategist who analysed consumers' trends and behaviour – and her mantelpiece at home groaned with awards for her outstanding work.

But MT was the Managing Director, so we also had a Planning Director, Heather Harris, a fiery redhead from Yorkshire with a Bette Midler-meets-Ruby Wax air, who also came over from New York. MT and Heather were friends, but I often wondered whether being schooled in the same discipline gave Heather problems. MT couldn't resist taking the lead in key planning issues – she was brilliant at it.

Then there were the Creative Directors, Ken Hoggins and Chris O'Shea. They had previously worked at the prestigious Lowe Howard-Spink agency. Ken was a big bluff Northerner with a beer-barrel chest and Chris was an Essex man, with a wizened, wily face and goatee beard. Ken drew the pictures and Chris wrote the copy.

The Finance Director was Jerry Wales. A softly spoken, tall and handsome man who lived in a small flat in Thames Ditton with a cat and not much else. He was hard-working and diligent but a worrier who would look dour and wring his hands if the word 'risk' was ever mentioned. He would rarely express himself in more than two or three sentences, but at the weekend he would take to the sea in his sailing boat, set a course for the wildest location and throw caution to the wind.

The seventh member of the management team was Julian Martin. He was The Businessman. He was hard-talking and deal-making every step of the way. An Australian, he was happy to call a spade a spade and had little time for the Brits and their pussy-footing around sensitive issues. He was a buttoned-down man in a buttoned-down shirt with the face, features and 'let's-get-to-work' look of Agent Skinner from the TV series *The X-Files*.

And me. What was I to bring to the team? My knowledge of the UK market for starters. MT and Heather were out of touch, having worked in the USA in the booming 80s, and Julian had never worked in the UK. I was also known as a 'creative' account handler. It was true that I only enjoyed the high-risk creative advertising solutions and was never any good with purely workmanlike answers. Indeed I was someone who focused on getting the creative solution at any cost, often at the expense of securing the commercial details on my accounts, much to the frustration of my more organised seniors!

My creative credentials for Chiat/Day were impeccable. In 1987, for example, every account I worked on was awarded a Gold award at some creative award ceremony somewhere. I felt, then, part of a creative process, with creative people I really admired and clients who wanted to be made famous.

Creativity was where my heart lay, but at Chiat/Day I was hired not to be in the front line, convincing clients to be braver (that was Julian's job), but in the background, wooing and winning new clients. I was, officially, the Business Deveopment Director.

Our greatest moment came soon. In the summer of 1990, after a long pleading letter from me and a whole series of meetings, we were asked to handle the advertising for the Midland Bank. It was unheard of that a small American company, with such a wild creative strategic intent, should be appointed to such a grand and long-standing British institution. Behind the decision at the bank were two brilliant marketeers, Kevin Gavaghan and Peter Simpson. They saw in us something strikingly new and different and felt the bank would benefit from our fresh approach.

The creative approach they bought was daring and innovative. That means it was also risky and untried, but they went with it. It featured a hidden camera observing people reacting to the true value of money. A shopper who buys a CD for £14.99 demands her penny change, for example, while the shopkeeper pretends to think it's not worth giving. It was a tremendous break in tradition for a bank to run such honest, observational work and it suited the recessionary times perfectly.

Things could not have gone better for us in year one. We were the golden team, it seemed. Jay felt confident enough to rehouse us out of our tiny little office and into a site he was developing at great cost on Shaftesbury Avenue that would match the prestitious offices in the USA.

We started hiring people like mad to run the bank and help us grow and took on board a young account director I had worked with at CDP, called David Abraham. At this point you should know more about David.

David worked with me at CDP and after we had won the Midland Bank assignment, in the autumn of 1990, I persuaded him to join Chiat/Day. He was the brightest advertising executive of his generation and at 26 had the ability to run large pieces of business that most companies would not entrust to anyone under 40. Oxford educated, David was not only administratively sound but was also a superb intellect. I knew he had just the right combination of skills to work with the likes of Peter Simpson. He was also as much a friend as a colleague and we both knew we complemented each other's skills. His attention to detail was as copper-bottomed as my ability to see the creative solution. I convinced MT that he was the right man for the job.

To persuade David to join I took him to the site the office was going to move to. It was the top floor of Berkshire House, opposite the Shaftesbury Theatre and above the Oasis swimming pool. Its location was fabulous and its views across London were sensational. The up and coming Italian designer, Stephano de Martino was commissioned by Jay to make it an office every bit as funky as the ones in LA and New York.

When we arrived at the office the interior was still under construction. David and I donned hard hats and climbed to a high vantage point. He was impressed. He took on board the idea that Chiat/Day was a different kind of company and he was amazed to see that the differences were self-evident not just in the way we developed work with our clients, but also in the use of technology, and, as we could see from where we stood, the way the office was to be designed. He saw the idea that every facet of the office was one of creative imagination.

It was a wonderful office, open plan, with luminous plastic screens, tables that raised into the air, a sunken discussion pit full of carpet fish and weird rooms like The Iceberg, The Edge and The Ledge. People talked about it for months afterwards and architects and designers wrote about 'The Office Of The Future' and the creative genius of Chiat/Day. Jay's bid for London credibility was paying off.

We had started the year ranked 142 in the Top 300 list of agencies; 12 months later we had moved up to 69, adding 17 staff and more than doubling our turnover. Our clients included HMV Music Stores, Neutrogena, Cable & Wireless Telecommunications, the Australian Tourist Commission, Qantas (the Australian airline), Reebok sports shoes and, of course, Midland Bank.

We had 'arrived on the UK advertising scene with a splash', *Campaign* magazine wrote. And our work was getting talked about, particularly the work for Neutrogena which featured a little known model called Kate Moss, and the Australian Tourist Commission, which was to run the longest ever print ad displaying the huge panoply of the Australian landscape. We started to collect plaudits and awards early. So far so good.

But what outsiders, even Jay, couldn't see were the deep internal rifts that had begun to appear by Christmas of 1990.

On the contrary, Jay was full of admiration for what we seemed to be achieving. He was proving the moaning minnies back in LA wrong. When he saw us winning business like Midland Bank he knew his London office would be the jewel in the crown. By way of support and as a big thank you, he sent everyone in London an original red Huffy bike, the sort you see the post boys ride in small-town America. It was generous, unexpected and original. It was just the sort of creative statement Jay liked to make.

The problem with the office wasn't anything to do with the new rush of employees, or the clients. It was to do with us, the management. I believed we were dysfunctional and unfocused. We were what we were – a group of individuals thrown together to make something work. We had no shared vision for the company and no agreed way of working. Yes, we were all in our own ways experienced and passionate about the company, but in reality we did not work well together. In fact, it transpired that each of the seven senior managers had in their mind their own particular understanding of what Chiat/Day meant. The result was that very little happened with the business after 1990, because our efforts were not harnessed in the same direction.

I was as much a part of the problem as anyone else and soon found it difficult to enjoy the risk I had taken. The Creative Directors took issue with the way the development of their work was so open, with so many people making an input. They had real difficulty with the system, imported from the USA, whereby creative ideas in their very earliest form would be discussed by the whole team working on the account, including the client.

But this was the famous Chiat/Day way!

It became a fascinating issue for me. We were in London, a town renowned around the world for producing top quality advertising. Was the way London worked, in its rather quaint, formal way, with creative people protected from the clients and the demands of business – and even timetables – the only way that top-end creativity could be produced? If so, this experiment at Chiat/Day was looking like a waste of time.

In March 1991 things came to a head.

After months of bitter disputes the Creative Directors resigned. MT, wanting to assert the Chiat/Day method, had been convinced a single Creative Director was necessary and had offered Ken Hoggins the job. He declined and preferred to leave with his partner and seek a fresh start. (They went on to found their own successful agency, Banks, Hoggins, O'Shea.) *Campaign* put the news on its front page and quoted MT as saying: 'The style and system in place was not consistently producing the best work, so we decided on a more streamlined system which makes the lines clearer.' Although the advertising village become momentarily excited by the news, Ken and Chris' departure scarcely caused a ripple.

Internally, however, it led to a great deal of questioning about how creativity and creative people should be handled in the future. My experience at CDP had taught me to go with creative people and give them time to develop. Ken and Chris's departure raised a lot of questions about our working methods in general. I began to doubt that good creative people could bend to a more inclusive way of developing their work. Ken and Chris were 'old school', like the people I'd left behind at CDP, but they had a proven track record. Maybe Chiat/Day was destined to be only an American concept. Maybe this sort of change would not work in the UK.

But we had to keep going. To admit that Chiat/Day's success in the USA was not possible in the UK was to admit our own failure. We all still passionately believed that we could create something wonderful in our market following the same textbook that Jay handed out in the States. After much internal musing and navel gazing we simply concluded that we had hired the wrong Creative Directors.

Without many options, a team we had hired only a week earlier were appointed Creative Directors. Kes Gray and Jonathan Greenhalgh didn't want to be Creative Directors, mind you, they just wanted to create, without the onerous duties of meeting clients or administering internal reviews. Kes and Jonathan were a 'hot team', famous for producing the Carling Dambusters commercial at their previous agency WCRS, and as 1991 rolled out they were able to produce and oversee some high-quality work, most notably the 'recycled advertising campaign' for Ecover, the environmentally friendly detergent.

Heather Harris also left during 1991 to set up her own consultancy; she was looking for a change of career and a new way of life. She found both with her research consultancy which she ran from a cottage in Oxfordshire. Only four of the original seven were left – after only 18 months.

In fact apart from David and myself, not one of the 25 people who was in the company at this stage is with us today. It was a transient, migrant set of camp followers.

With the addition of the high-profile First Direct account, 1991 had began well, but as the year rolled on there were to be a number of disappointments. HMV left, to get a cheaper, faster service, followed closely by the Australian Tourist Commission and Qantas. Cable & Wireless failed to spend any money as internally they debated the value of advertising. Reebok was swayed into giving more of its business to Lowe Howard-Spink. All of a sudden we were not so much the flavour of the month. There were few pitches, although the agency managed to win Ecover and the American Express Gold Card.

The work we produced for Ecover ranks amongst the best work I have been associated with. Devised by a maverick creative team, Dave Shane and Kiki Kendrick, it utilised genuine old Procter & Gamble commercials from the 1950s and recycled them, with a new dubbed voice-over to advertise Ecover.

Then the creatives went further. They invited anyone from the agency who was willing to go to a disused warehouse in South London and cut up old posters (like Gordon's Gin posters, or those for Silk Cut and Burger King). Established artists and students were invited to recycle them into posters for Ecover. It was a brilliant idea and for a while it applied a real creative focus and can-do spirit to the agency. The national press got wind of the idea and Ecover's owner, Robin Bines, was able to enjoy thousands of pounds of free publicity just by journalists writing about the advertising idea. Working with Ecover satisfied a latent desire to produce work with a social benefit – something that was to be at the heart of what we did at St. Luke's.

Two other important people arrived in 1991: the ultra-cool, streetwise Tessa Wire, who joined in April as Head of Television Production and the big and beery Andy Smith (Smudger), who joined the Print Production and Traffic department in October. They joined an agency that was fast losing consistency and direction, but they too, like me, saw that there was still an opportunity to create something very different. More importantly, they both took the same attitude, independently, which was that the agency might not be 100 per cent right, but it could be changed from within.

Not surprisingly our Lords and Masters in the USA were somewhat agitated. We were a big investment and soon they began to get the idea that it wasn't paying off. Gradually throughout 1991 senior American executives from the USA began to appear and more and more questions were being asked. Jay's decision to make such a heavy commitment in the highly competitive London market was being openly debated and he came under pressure from sceptical senior managers in the USA who never backed the idea in the first place.

In the middle of 1991, MT and I went to Los Angeles for the opening of the new Chiat/Day office. Conceived by Frank Gehry as a 'monument to vision', it featured a pair of giant binoculars as the entrance portico and inside felt the epitome of super-cool Los Angeles. It was a big building for the low offices on Venice Beach. It was imposing. It was the biggest and the best in the neighbourhood. The party was a classic Chiat/Day affair. Hundreds of people and a showbiz feel to the catering and entertainment. Jay, with his prestigious guests, continually did the rounds all night. For some, Jay had built an everlasting statement to his vision of the future. For others he had built himself a mausoleum.

Going to Los Angeles and seeing the office and meeting other Chiat/Day people was a good reminder of just what high standards we could attain. We saw some impressive advertising for Nissan and for Energiser batteries.

We also met some impressive people. MT knew them all, of course, but for me to meet Bob Kuperman (Kupe), the short, bearded, pony-tailed CEO of the LA office and Lee Clow, the even more bearded, almost biblical, creative supremo, was a real thrill. These were people who were fictionalised in the popular series *30 Something*. In the final, cliff-hanging episode of the series, the hero was to be offered the plum advertising job – as Creative Director of Chiat/Day, of course!

The office was not just on Venice Beach, it was part of the life of Venice Beach. The agency worked for free for the local environmental agency on a clean-up programme called 'Heal The Bay' and employees would be allowed, on full pay, to give up some of their time for charity work.

Everything about the office and the people was inspirational.

In stark contrast to the glitz of LA, the staff Christmas Party in London was a dismal affair. There were about 30 of us and we booked a drab Mexican restaurant somewhere in a not very fashionable part of London to have our Christmas lunch. To boost numbers we invited various business associates along. This only added to the sense of alienation internally and we limped into 1992.

The team that Jay put together began first to work to their own agendas and then, with the departure of three key people out of the seven, completely fragmented. Like a divorcing couple we put on a brave public face. Morale dropped to an all-time low. Kes and Jonathan stuck it for a year, then, midway through 1992, they bailed out. The creative culture and the responsibilities took their toll, although they tried harder and more successfully than their predecessors to work in 'the Chiat/Day way'.

The press started writing about the 'revolving door' of Chiat/Day management. Things looked bleak.

③ A Way Out . . .

I n the spring of 1992, I was shown a way out. Along with two others. It was a total breath of fresh air and just what I needed. It came in the form of a letter from Bob Kuperman.

Dear Andy

Jay personally feels that our business is going to change rapidly in the next ten years and that we must anticipate and understand those changes if we are to continue as a leader in our business. He has asked that a task force study and construct what the Advertising Agency of the Future might look like and make recommendations to him and the World Board of Directors on the steps we need to take to stay out in front.

I, David Abraham and Jerry Wales accepted like a shot. We were bursting with pride that Jay had selected us. Along with others from offices in LA, New York, Toronto, Auckland and Sydney we felt like astronauts, hand-picked for a very special mission.

Jay was getting increasingly worried that Chiat/Day was losing its way. It was heavily dependent on a single big client, Nissan, the Japanese car maker. What's more, after the boom of the 1980s, clients were looking for new ideas that might bypass the more conventional and expensive ways of communicating to customers. Direct marketing and telesales were growth businesses. Infomercials in the USA were becoming more prevalent. New electronic media like the Internet were emerging. Jay felt

Chiat/Day could get stuck in the past. He wanted to focus on the future and invent something totally new. This is what I wanted to hear!

While the London office was struggling with the present, the three of us were whisked off to 'invent the future'. I was still in charge of winning new business for the office but was increasingly becoming involved in any sensitive meetings we might have with senior clients. At the same time, David oversaw Midland Bank and Jerry was Finance Director. The Managing Director, MT, was not invited to join the group, and if that didn't annoy her, having three key executives swanning around the USA 'inventing' certainly did.

The group had its first meeting in Los Angeles in April 1992, the day after a jury in Santa Monica had acquitted some LA police officers of beating Rodney King, a black motorist. The black ghettos were rioting and half the city seemed to be going up in smoke. There was a real fear of anarchy and years of pent-up frustration boiled over onto the streets. Although the riots started in the poorer areas of Los Angeles, families from the more affluent parts of town began panicking and even evacuating their homes as the rioters started to move out towards them. This riot fast became a statement about the 'haves' and the 'have nots'.

Not surprisingly the Virgin plane I was on, from Heathrow to LA, was half empty. As the plane came into LA airport we could clearly see the devastation below. There were fires, burnt-out buildings and derelict cars everywhere. Once the plane had arrived at its gate an FBI agent came on board. What she said did nothing to quell our mounting apprehension.

'Los Angeles is a dangerous city,' she intoned. 'When you leave the airport go directly to your destination. If you have no specific destination stay within the airport and report to the police. Most major roads have road blocks and looters. Your plane was shot at as it came in to land; do not underestimate the mood of this town. There is a twelve-hour curfew from seven p.m. 'til seven a.m. You will be arrested if you are found on the street during curfew. Move from this plane swiftly and in an orderly fashion.'

I have never left a plane or raced through immigration faster than I did that day. I went straight to the Loews Hotel on Ocean Boulevard (thankfully not closed down by looters) and met with David who had been in the USA with his family for a week already, and had endured earthquakes prior to the riots.

In the hotel bar that night we watched as the National Guard and

LAPD mingled with crowds, their weapons lain casually on the tables while they sipped ludicrous looking (non-alcoholic) cocktails and awaited their orders. In the main lobby of the hotel a Miss Universe competition was taking place and scantily dressed beauties were lolling around everywhere mingling with fashion photographers and various LA luvvies. On the TV in the bar we watched on the live 'as-it-is-happening-now' news channel someone dragged from a truck and kicked to death by a gang of crazed rioters, as the world outside was turned upside down.

This was a long way from London. This was LA. This was 'La-La land'. This was where we were to start inventing the future. It was bizarre and it was going to get stranger still.

The Future Group christened itself The Chrysalis Committee. We saw ourselves as being part of a process of change. We boldly asserted that we could change Chiat/Day as dramatically and beautifully as a caterpillar changes into a butterfly.

We became a fully functional team, facilitated by an American 'business therapist' called Rhoda Pitcher. Rhoda taught us how to step outside of our comfort zones and truly invent. At times it all seemed too much like a Californian love-in; it was like Woodstock meets Wall Street – wild moments of deep human understanding broken occasionally by worrying glimpses of the money the company needed to make.

The meetings were intense and we knew it would take more than one session to interrogate every avenue and reach sound conclusions. Jay had given us a big brief; we were determined to answer it fully.

You can't really imagine what it was like. One month we'd be in Los Angeles, in the middle of the Rodney King riots, the next minute we'd be in peaceful Sonoma Valley where Jack London wrote *White Fang* and where all the good American wines come from. Then we'd go to Toronto and spend one meeting sailing gracefully across Lake Ontario. Other meetings were in New York, in the searing heat of the summer and in the frozen depths of the winter. The group discussed meeting in London next, then Sydney. We had the freedom to think and we greedily took advantage of it as if this future project were the only thing that mattered.

I loved it. It was fresh, it was about the future. The handpicked astronauts were bright and challenging. And Rhoda really made me think differently. The whole experience changed me and I realised that changing a company was a perpetual process, driven by a high ideal – like a long voyage of discovery, not a one-off plan that could be easily packaged and presented.

I ended up chairing the group, and the more the group met and dreamt of the future, the more I looked back at the past and grew bored with it and the more I noted that the London office was somewhere to be left far behind.

A huge document entitled 'Something Else Is Going On' was produced and deep within it lay some wonderful thinking. The author of the document was David Abraham and the wonderful thinking concerned the way businesses relate to society. It looked at the way that governments around the world were neglecting consumers and observed that businesses were having to shoulder the responsibility of looking after consumers, their complaints and their lives whether they wanted to or not. It proposed the notion that business should be more ethical and play what we called a Total Role In Society (TRS). We were convinced that if a company were to act as a more responsible citizen, it would more easily avoid the embarrassment of running an expensive ad at the same time as receiving some adverse publicity. We coined this regular occurrence 'Combined Inactivity', whereby the paid-for ad would be cancelled out by the bad actions of a company. We could point to businesses like The Body Shop and Ben & Jerry's as examples of companies who sought, successfully we felt, a more responsible role in society and who were profiting properly from it.

David and I got very excited about this and although the document was ultimately to be shelved by the group we were to spend hours and hours debating a new economic model for business. We talked about Stakeholders (three years before Tony Blair was to use the term) and we talked about the need for business to act properly and be decent and honest. We dreamt of a world where business would not cheat people like Robert Maxwell cheated the pensioners. On the contrary, we imagined a world where business would put something back and stop treating its employees, their families and their neighbours like nobodies.

In the penultimate meeting of the Chrysalis Committee we talked about Chiat/Day being a force for global good; it would be a company that would make money by doing good. The group could see Chiat/Day acting as consultants working with companies that needed to reassess the way they interacted with society. It was a fabulous idea. We would be like company marriage-guidance counsellors, repairing broken relationships and then communicating to staff and customers just how good a citizen they had become.

Then we went back to our day jobs.

Or rather, we were sent back to our day jobs. The group presented its findings to the Chairman/Founder, adding that the first company to be 'fixed' was Chiat/Day itself. The agency, worldwide, was dysfunctional, the group said, it was full of secrets, bogged down by myths of past glories and top heavy with overpaid dinosaurs who wouldn't change even if you offered them double the money to do so. Jay thought we'd been navel gazing and hit the roof. We hadn't given him any ideas he could act upon. He wanted an action list of ten brilliant things to do, not a pseudo-psychological portrait of his company – even if it was true.

At the final meeting in New York, the demoralised group was told to salvage and reconstruct just the consultancy idea as a way of getting to meet Chairmen and Managing Directors of large companies with something new to say. (This is a tried and tested – and generally unsuccessful – way of getting to the big chiefs in companies in the vain hope that, while listening to some new business theory, they can be persuaded to swing the advertising account your way.) The Chrysalis Committee began to disband and another team took on the task of creating a new consultancy arm.

With such a high level and constant exposure to the Chiat/Day offices in the USA, David, Jerry and I were painfully aware of what, by contrast, the London office had become – an expensive folly.

Concerned at the lowering morale and business success of the London office, and besieged by requests to close it down from senior managers in LA and New York, Jay did three things.

He sent over his trusted and loyal creative lieutenant Marty Cooke to replace Kes and Jonathan. Marty had turned round the Toronto office when it was going through hard times and bought with him boundless energy and some raw, sometimes refreshingly naive creative thinking. MT fiercely opposed his appointment, but by then Jay had had enough and wanted 'his own man' in place.

Secondly, he began to search for advertising agencies in London with whom we could join forces. We still had, after all, the much prized

Midland Bank account, which David Abraham had successfully defended and retained despite a concerted effort by Saatchi & Saatchi to snatch it away.

Thirdly, he paid for all 30 of us to fly to New York and join their Christmas Party ... 'There he goes again,' we thought. 'Just when we thought he'd had enough of us all he sends us on the Christmas Party of a lifetime.' The party was fabulous. Held in a smart warehouse in the fashionable Tribeca area of New York, where Robert de Niro has a restaurant, we partied like it was the Christmas Party to end all Christmas Parties.

The next day, during a respectably late brunch at Jay's house (a beautiful red-brick converted Dutch fire station nestling between some monstrous skyscrapers off Lexington Avenue) we talked about the future. The London office had not worked out. MT had not presided over a sound management or a consistent creative output. The London market had not responded the way Jay had hoped. On the table were a handful of ideas. All of them concerned merging the office with a friendly force in London. Present at the brunch was Adelaide Horton, Jay's 'Mrs Fixit'. We knew things were getting serious and the end was in sight.

The London market was mystified by us. On the one hand, the line up of people, some early prestigious new business wins and the reputation of Chiat/Day could not have suggested anything other than long-term success and prosperity. On the other, the management changes, inconsistent creative work and more recent lack-lustre performance in winning new clients signalled serious faults.

After three years of solid support, *Campaign* magazine was finding it difficult to find anything positive to say and in its 1992 year-end summary gave Chiat/Day London one final chance. '1993 is the year for Chiat/Day to put its talents to work,' it wrote. It was to be an auspicious pronouncement.

When I look back now at those crazy times they have a dreamlike, unreal quality. The meetings in America were in weird and wonderful places. Grown men would start crying as a vision of the future touched a previously unexposed nerve. But almost two years after it was disbanded I realised what a mistake that kind of 'Task Force' mentality is. We were creating a micro-culture for ourselves and were not changing the company. We were creating the aspirations for a new place for the company to go, but provided no means of getting there.

The Chrysalis Committee was a failure. Instead of recreating Chiat/Day, it stood by and witnessed its slow death.

David and I were called upon to advise the new group who were charged with setting up the TRS Consultancy and so found ourselves in the early spring of 1993 shuttling to and from the USA.

On those plane trips David and I pursued the ideas we had developed and which Jay had rejected. We remained convinced that we had discovered something highly motivating and spent hours scoping out the sort of company that could operate in a different dimension, one that could recognise it had a larger gift to its employees and stakeholders than merely a salary or shareholder return.

One sunny Saturday morning in late May, a Federal Express delivery arrived on my doorstep at home. It was a large box. I signed for it and noted it was from Los Angeles. Inside was a silver box, oval in shape. Its lid was inlaid with the most beautiful piece of porcelain salvaged from an antique vase from either the Ming or Ching Dynasties. I opened it carefully. Inside was a letter and three large butterfly pupae.

'These are Monarch chrysalids,' the letter began. 'The chrysalis is the pupal state of development (third of four) of butterflies, and is the stage during which the butterfly emerges.'

The letter went on to explain in great detail how I should unpack my chrysalids and how I should rear the Monarch butterflies and give them their freedom.

There was a card at the bottom of the box.

Thanks for all the hard work and for
helping us figure out the future.

Love

Jay and Kupe.

Within a week the butterflies emerged and became very attached to my son Tom until one day they flew away.

Many weeks later our neighbour, who had spent a few years in the USA teaching, said, 'You know, I saw the strangest thing the other day. I swear I saw three huge Monarch butterflies, the size of small birds, flitting through my garden. They're only found in the 'States. Weird.'

The gift, to each of the original Chrysalis members, was weird indeed. But it was as surreal and intangible, yet extraordinary and innovative as the Chrysalis project itself was.

It was Jay's unique thank you.

④ Air Miles

Things in London continued to go from bad to worse. MT felt she could wrestle control of the agency from the Americans and steer it to the success she always dreamed of. I loved Chiat/Day, but felt unable to sign up to a merger and had come to a dead end with MT. Our disagreements were almost all about style of management, so in early January I asked to be transferred out of London. It was MT's company, I felt, and it was unfair of me to keep destabilising things by suggesting a different direction.

Three weeks later I was in Auckland as their hot summer was slowly descending into a warm autumn. If for a moment I thought I was being banished to the furthest, most uncivilised corner of the globe for leading the ill-fated Chrysalis Committee, my fears were soon dispelled. Chiat/Day in Auckland was a very 'buzzy' place and the work it produced was of high quality. The office was on the top floor of an old wool-packing depot on the harbour and retained its sense of industry and honest hard work.

When I walked in I was hit with an immediate impression of vitality. There was music playing, people talking loudly in vast open-plan spaces and a constant clatter of shoes on the polished wooden floor. The people I met were young, eager and enthusiastic and had an irreverence that suggested they were ready to upset New Zealand's cosy advertising codes. This office looked like fun.

Jay offered me the post of CEO, but before I could accept, Chiat/Day Sydney asked me to pay them a visit.

I flew to Sydney straightaway.

In Sydney it was put to me that there was a much bigger job to be done in developing the whole of South East Asia. I took one look at Sydney, a vibrant, colourful, cosmopolitan city stretched out on one hell of a long, lovely beach, thought about the job and started house-hunting immediately.

Julian Martin, a native Australian, turned up in Sydney while I was there. He too was frustrated with the London office and felt unfairly left out of the Chrysalis project. He was in the process of landing a big job with Chiat/Day in Sydney as well. I liked Julian, mainly for his ballsy style and bawdy sense of humour. I thought the idea of the two of us ending up together in Sydney complementing each other and working closely together looked a good idea.

Things were looking up and while I was there I achieved a lot of basic 'admin', like looking for schools and places to live. My wife Amanda, who was not a little concerned at being transported to the other side of the world (she was four months pregnant with our second child) had found a family to rent our house in Wimbledon on a rolling yearly basis – we had no idea how long we would be away – and was packing up our belongings and arranging Christmas and christenings Down Under with nearest and dearest.

In all I spent two weeks Down Under and was delighted with the prospect of a major change in my life. Such was the energy for change that the Chrysalis Committee generated in me that staying put in London under almost any circumstances seemed a very dull option.

The night before I was due to fly back to London, I received a phone call from Jay Chiat.

'You're in the wrong continent,' he told me.

'What do you mean?' I replied.

'We've just sold all our Australian and New Zealand offices.'

On the plane coming back, I managed to fill the 24-hour journey with only one thought. I had burned my bridges in London, and had the carpet taken from underneath my feet in Australia. I was jobless and, with a rental agreement on my house about to be signed, almost homeless too.

By the time I arrived back in London, Jay had another idea. This time he wanted me to work in Los Angeles. Interestingly he wanted me to try out some of the Chrysalis thinking on the company's largest client – Nissan Cars. This was typical Jay. One minute our work was a waste of time, the next it was to be test driven with the most important client we had.

I flew to LA.

I liked the people at Nissan in Los Angeles. They really did want to try out some new thinking and were ready for whatever system I recommended. I phoned my wife to say we can rent out our house after all, so call in the removal men. 'This is the real thing,' I said. 'We're moving to LA.'

I spent a few days looking for property to rent and agreeing a new contract before returning to London.

After what seemed an eternity travelling I went back to the London office. In the lift going up to the office I was surprised to meet Jay Chiat.

'What are you doing here?' I asked.

'How was LA?' he replied.

'Fine,' I said. 'I'm going to enjoy it.'

'Shame,' said Jay. 'I'm relieving MT of her duties and you're to take over as Managing Director of the London Office.'

⑤ A New Job

'Don't do it,' said Frank Lowe. 'It's a non-job. You'll just be clearing up MT's mess. Chiat/Day in London is finished, get out while you can. Actually, Jay's getting old and Chiat/Day in the States isn't going anywhere either.' I was visiting Frank Lowe at his spectacular Italianate house in Chelsea. He'd just flown in from the USA and he met me in his silk dressing gown and slippers.

I had met him a few times before. Remember I told you he was the guy that everyone at CDP used to talk about. He haunted the corridors of CDP; he was the inspiration for the agency and his successors never lived up to the reputation which he bequeathed to the company. He had gone on to build a prestigious advertising agency of his own, established along the same lines as CDP. He was enormously successful and while many people will have heard of the Saatchi brothers and their cunning business and political acumen, it is, to my mind, Frank Lowe who set the creative standards for London advertising that the rest of the world so admires.

I was visiting Frank on the advice of Isabel Bird, who ran London's top advertising headhunting firm. She had placed me in all my jobs and played a key role, behind the scenes, in my joining Chiat/Day. If I was to be Managing Director of Chiat/Day, a job I never sought, I should look around the marketplace, she felt, and meet people to get an idea of what the job might entail. That way I would be clearer about what I needed to do with the company and whether I actually wanted to do it or not.

As it happens Frank was looking for someone to run his European network. We briefly talked about it, but it became clear that I would have been totally wrong for a job like that. It was too corporate, too defined, too established for me, someone who urgently wanted to shake things up.

I left the meeting with Frank both agreeing with him about Chiat/Day London and wanting to prove him wrong.

It was true the office was not in good shape. Julian Martin was not offered any other jobs by Jay in Chiat/Day and was encouraged to go to Sydney and work with the new owners. He was furious at this and resolved to find something that he wanted to do, rather than be shunted in and out of jobs that others wanted him to do. He left Chiat/Day in June and actually did end up in Australia, working for an advertising agency in Melbourne.

The superstar team had completely died. The office was on its knees, but some important initiatives had been taken to prevent total collapse. Firstly, David Abraham had put together a rescue plan with three other colleagues. He had been increasingly worried about MT's grip on the company and the commonly held view by the employees was that, exasperated by the lack of support for her in the UK and the USA, she was planning to leave and set up her own company. His rescue plan included looking at new Managing Directors if MT did bale out. Amongst the list of names, unknown to me, was mine.

The Americans became aware of the rescue plan and Jay flew over to meet with David and his three colleagues – the suave Tom Knox, the son of a High Court Judge, bookish, rakish and ambitious; the scruffy Richard Warren, loud and very much the naughty public school boy, who teased the women and drunk hard with the lads; and Mike Skagerlind, earnest and honest, with likeable boyish charms, who as the senior planner now took over as Planning Director. Jay was impressed by their dedication, their entrepreneurial flair, their feistiness and their passion for the agency. These were the qualities he knew had built Chiat/Day. He was also mightily impressed by their intellects. Three of them had attended Oxford, were erudite, well read and obviously bright. He christened them 'The Oxford Cabal' and for a while they represented Jay's only real hope of salvaging his company's reputation in London. At the very least The

Oxford Cabal had put together a workable business plan and had delayed the move, much favoured by many back in the USA, of merging, or even selling, the London office – assuming the right ad agency could be found.

Then there was Marty Cooke. Apart from directing the agency's creative output and calming down jumpy clients, his brief was to observe and take note of the strengths and weaknesses of the London office. He quickly realised and reported the importance of David and The Oxford Cabal, as well as others like Tessa Wire who was in charge of producing TV commercials; Sarah Sanderson, a feisty Yorkshire Account Director; Andy Smith – 'Smudger' – who oversaw all print production; Paul Johnson – 'Johnners' – Smudger's number two, who joined just in time for the amazing New York Christmas extravaganza; and Rachael Plant – 'Planty' – the office manager, who joined just too late for it!

And Sally Kelso, who started the same day as me as a secretary and who, with a phenomenal amount of self-will, grit and determination, trained herself so thoroughly in computer technology that at the tender age of 24 she became our Head of IT. These people, though unaware at the time, grew to become a major part of the St. Luke's story. They are people who took the opportunity to transform themselves and take up challenges that previously they may well have shied away from.

Marty was a nice, enthusiastic man, with boundless energy and a perpetual big beaming smile. Although 40 and greying fast, he bought a youthful vigour to the agency. But he was not going to remain long – he had been promised the plum job of Creative Director of Chiat/Day New York – and in a race against time he and I had to find a new Creative Director, bringing the number to four in as many years.

As it happened we found two. Naresh Ramchandani and Dave Buonaguidi ('Bono'). Their reputations preceded them. Like Kes and Jonathan they were 'hot creatives', with famous award-winning work for Maxell Tapes and Fuji Film under their belts. Unlike Kes and Jonathan, I was to discover they relished tearing up the rule book and working in a totally new way.

I first met Dave and Naresh in the bar of The Mountbatten, a dinky little hotel on Seven Dials in the heart of Covent Garden with that sort of mock-Edwardian feel that fools no one except Americans on vacation and gullible Japanese. The bar groaned under highly polished mahogany and brass, with every wall-space filled with etchings of 'London Past'. It was unusually dark in the bar and looked as if it was there purely to

countenance clandestine meetings between middle-aged lovers, businessmen or police informants.

I had to look hard to find them, but discovered them in a corner right
at the back. I had only the briefest description of them, but it was
obviously them because they stood out from the regular clientele. Naresh
was the smaller of the two and was earnest, intelligent and phlegmatic.
Bono was taller and, with his shock of curly hair and an excitable, cheeky,
devil-may-care tone, seemed in every way a natural counterweight to
Naresh. The truth is they complemented each other perfectly.

This was going to be my first big decision after taking the helm. I knew
that if I appointed the wrong creative people the market would not give
Chiat/Day another chance. Frank Lowe's words had haunted me since
I'd taken over in early June. I felt as if everyone was waiting for the final
failure.

Dave and Naresh talked ... and talked and talked. They were bursting
with enthusiasm and had a hundred and one brilliant and innovative
ideas on how to improve the work and develop the agency. It seemed
like there was almost no risk they weren't prepared to take. They were
energetic and they were young. They represented a new, unfussy, ego-
less generation who had a natural disdain for the way things were
previously done, particularly in the greedy, bourgeois 80s.

They were just what we needed. Marty could safely return to the U.S.

A couple of weeks later, the three of us met with Jay in a Japanese
restaurant in St James' that was so expensive the menu didn't have prices
on. Jay liked them.

'What's the job of a Creative Director entail?' asked Naresh.

'To make sure no bad ads get out', said Jay.

Dave and Naresh joined in August 1993 and later that month Jay
returned for another check-up on his fragile London concern.

He took a group of us to Bertorelli's, a smart restaurant loved by late-
night opera goers, being right next to the Opera House in Covent Garden.
We were all there, David and The Oxford Cabal, Bono, Naresh and me.

'Now you're running Chiat/Day,' he smiled, 'what are you going to
do, tread water?' He was like a stereotypical Jewish mother, praising and
reprimanding us in the same breath and making us feel guilty for a
misdemeanour not yet perpetrated. He launched his revamped agency,
in fact, with a sharp reminder of the culture that we belonged to and
were signing up to.

Actually, I felt very clear about what the office needed to do. Inspired by the Chrysalis experience, bolstered by Dave and Naresh's overt creativity and challenged by our past reputation, I set out a long-term plan to breathe life back into the company.

As if to tempt fate I gave an interview to *The Wall Street Journal*, explaining my ideas for the office, my continued endorsement of the Chrysalis thinking and my devotion to technology and what it could achieve in new forms of media as well as office and home life. The *Journal* ran the headline:

Chiat/Day, Daring To Be Hip, Weds High-Tech To New Age

The article reported that I believed in 'the hierarchy of ideas', which meant that if someone has a great idea, no matter what department they might belong to, they must be able to put that idea on the table. It reported that we were keen to recruit people with skills not common to the advertising business, because we wanted to experiment with creative ideas that came from unconventional places. We were daring. And I guess we were quite hip, with our talk of 'new media', 'interactive television' and 'non-hierarchical team structure'.

Jay's brief to me had been far simpler than that – make the work better. And with that, and some good advice from Bob Kuperman, who I'd come to like and respect throughout the Chrysalis period ('cancel the trade papers, duck below the parapet, concentrate on your own people, ignore the competition'), I embarked upon a new career as Managing Director of an Advertising Agency.

David Abraham and I revisited all the Chrysalis work we had done and were resolved to introduce the core beliefs about the role of business in society. We began to look at the emerging new media, particularly interactive media, and hired John Crowley as our first-ever Media Director.

Within two months, Dave and Naresh had hired Alan Young, Julian Vizard and Kola Ogundipe, three outstanding creative talents who loved to break rules and disturb with unexpected ideas. They also started experimenting with creatives outside of London, to bring in new ideas, and hired a wild team from Holland that became known simply as 'The Dutch'.

Alan Young and the Boots 17 team introduced the notion of 'girl power' to Boots for their '17' range of cosmetics. You may remember the cinema ads featuring girls taming men with their dazzling eyes and lips. '17', the end-line advised, 'is not make-up, it's ammunition.' And all this a good three years before any of us had heard of *The Spice Girls*.

These creatives enjoyed meeting and sparring with clients and worked naturally in collaboration with anyone who wanted to jump on board their fast new track. Working with them was wonderful.

The agency began to buzz.

⑥ 1994 – A Golden Year

J ay phoned me at 10.00 p.m. from Los Angeles on 2 January: 'Do you want to work for Prince Charles?'

'Um, yes, OK then,' I answered.

'Good. Meet with Jeremy White. I met him here in LA. He's a Brit who's going to be CEO of the Prince's Youth Business Trust. He's reorganising their communications and needs our help.'

So began a year's association with Prince Charles's Prince's Youth Business Trust and an invaluable insight into the work being done by the great and the good in business to help young people get a start in life. It's an initiative that passes many people by, but I must tell you that it is very successful. I learned about the existing establishment that was delivering a link between business and society and discovered groups like Business In The Community and London First who have been involved in issues of corporate responsibility for many years.

I was greatly encouraged by what they did, but I was also eager to take the debate further. What I saw was business as it has always been, behaving in a self-enlightened philanthropic way. Business has done this formally since the turn of the century when Rowntree, for example, went as far as building houses for its workers.

What I wondered was whether businesses themselves could actually change the way they behaved so as to belong, fundamentally, to all levels of society, rather than stand on the outside and give donations, however generous and effective they might be. I wondered too about the rights and wrongs of large charitable donations given out by companies who in the same financial year laid off workers, sometimes, as recent history has shown, in devastatingly large numbers. At this stage I had no answers, but I felt that there was something wrong with a system based almost entirely on large-scale handouts.

At a function in the City in the summer of 1994, I had the honour to meet Prince Charles and I spoke to him about the emerging new media and the increasing use of the telephone in all sorts of businesses, like First Direct (for telephone banking) and Direct Line (for insurance). He asked me if I thought the telephone would take over our lives, and, to prove my earlier point about future gazers, I answered that predictions for home usage of the Internet (five per cent by the end of the century) were wildly optimistic. As I write we have already reached the five per cent figure!

On 6 January, I promoted David Abraham to Deputy Managing Director. Not only had he been a stalwart executive who had held together the Midland Bank account during the agency's wildest ups and downs, but he was a sound thinker, the main contributor in the Chrysalis project and a passionate, vocal believer in the agency. We complemented each other's skills sets perfectly. Andy the dream-creator, David the idea processor. We worked closely together, as did Dave and Naresh, each of us focused on our tasks, all of us believing in innovation and creative risk-taking.

I felt we could go further than ever before and unite the whole agency around the concept of Human Capital – one of the major pieces of thinking to have emerged from Chrysalis.

The idea was very simple. All businesses have one thing in common. They are made up of people. If you treat your people correctly, the business should operate more smoothly. This is true of all businesses, manufacturing and service alike, but it is particularly true of service industries, for human beings are the most critical element.

Humans, however, are very complex and are subject to a wide-ranging set of rational and emotional principles. They need to be truly understood if you are to maximise their potential. The more they are understood the greater your human asset.

I decided to take the whole company of 30 people away for a weekend during which we would really understand each other and take the first step in working more harmoniously. We would learn how to respect each other.

Remembering the value that Rhoda Pitcher brought to The Chrysalis Group, I sought a moderator who was trained in this kind of 'company group therapy'. Isabel Bird pointed me in the right direction. I found Ruth Lederman. I explained to Ruth that I wanted to harness the full potential of everyone in the agency, from junior account clerks like Lyn Ellis, to seasoned experts like David Abraham. I told her that we felt more together than ever before, but I wondered how much everyone trusted each other, given the incredible number of management changes and hirings and firings of the past three years.

We assembled on a Thursday evening in a fairly nondescript hotel near Gravesend in Kent, the kind travelling salesmen would stay at, rather than holidaymakers. Ruth began by reminding everyone of the value of Keeping Agreements. The more you make and stick to an agreement with your fellow worker, the more efficient your company will be. It all sounded too simple, but that night, as we talked in the bar, we realised that the first thing humans needed to do was to connect to each other better and failing to keep an agreement was like a circuit breakdown.

The next day we worked hard doing all sorts of uncomfortable things that challenged the boundaries of our comfort zones. People like Sally Kelso and Lyn Ellis, unused to public speaking, spoke in front of everyone. They were so nervous they almost fainted, but we willed them to succeed and realised that if you have the support of your colleagues you can take enormous personal risks. To make himself uncomfortable, as he was used to speaking publicly, David Abraham stripped off. Almost naked, literally, he exposed to us all the deep feelings he had about the company.

We learned that The Truth is totally compelling, refreshing and fascinating and that it was the theatre of business that made us behave as if we were not being truly ourselves. It was the theatre of business that caused us to lie on behalf of the company, that caused us to bully our colleagues and that created great distances between the people in the business, their families, their suppliers and their customers.

By the end of the first day we were all high on a rich cocktail of brilliant thinking and new respect for each other. We agreed to meet up at 9.00 the next morning and spend a couple of hours summarising what we'd do next.

Almost a quarter of the company broke that agreement. I was devastated. The boozing the night before had taken its toll and it was almost 9.45 when the final stragglers made it into the meeting.

The effect on the whole agency was very destabilising. Caught between reprimanding the stragglers for not keeping the agreement and understanding that a 'night on the piss' was all part-and-parcel of awaydays such as this, the room fell into an uncomfortable silence.

I decided to risk it all. I told a hushed room about my early childhood in a children's home, so antiquated that even in 1956 it was called a home for 'Waifs and Strays'. I told everyone that my father was Indian and my mother English, and that they were teen lovers whose mixed association was an affront to both the middle-England Christian community and the Sikh community of my natural father. I told them how painfully embarrassed I had been all my life about mentioning this, and how I had often feigned an Italian background, which, by dint of dark Italian looks and a smattering of the language, was perfectly feasible. I told them how I was adopted at three by my parents (my father, now retired, was then the Vicar of Battersea) and grew up in a series of vicarages and rectories, in town (London), country (Northamptonshire) and by the sea (Portsmouth). I told them that this honest assessment of myself would make me more honest with them and that the title of Managing Director was not going to be some screen for me to hide behind and manipulate events to my own satisfaction.

You could have heard a pin drop.

In the archaeology of my background is something about people working better with each other. I was bound, I guess, to see this group of people as a family unit that had to be protected and had to get on. I really wanted everyone to realise that unless you give something up and strip yourself down you will never develop, you will never change. The baggage of your past will always emerge as the strongest decision-making voice. I also felt that for this assembled group of Human Capital to work properly, it must know that you are not a different person when you come to work. You are the same person, with the same values, emotions and ethics. It's just that you can be easily persuaded to drop those values, emotions and ethics as you become 'Businessman', the person who stalks corridors, climbs the greasy pole, tramples on weaker colleagues, stabs people in the back and exploits situations to his own benefit in a secret boardroom life that champions fear and greed as the essential ingredients for success.

All my past experiences caught up with me in that awayday.

And from that day I began to emerge as a Managing Director people could trust, in a company of people who would work hard to understand each other's strengths and weaknesses.

We returned to work the following Monday absolutely pulsating with energy. We wanted to put in place a hundred and one ideas about how to redefine existing relationships with ourselves and our clients. We believed we could create anything we imagined.

We began to reposition ourselves as an ideas-driven company with a much broader view of what advertising meant. We sat for hours in 'The Edge' (a glass conference room hanging over the side of the office, ten floors up, that looked and felt precipitious) talking about how we might make a move into TV and film production, or whether we could invent totally new forms of communication.

And business flowed in.

Positioned as a risky outsider in the pitch for Boots cosmetics, we came through to win against well-established competition. Then Coca-Cola appointed Chiat/Day New York to handle their new-age fruit drink, Fruitopia, and the London office was asked to launch it throughout Europe. Talking Pages came to us and even Cable & Wireless re-emerged with a brief for global advertising and an advertising budget to do the job!

Dave and Naresh produced a wonderfully simple and evocative commercial that ran simultaneously around the world on CNN. The first time it was to be seen was slap bang in the middle of the televised coverage of Nelson Mandela's inaugural speech on being voted President of South Africa. Nice of Nelson to lend our advertising campaign some status we thought!

In the spring, John Crowley was working hard to keep us in the forefront of developments in new technology and soon we had formed a venture with Videotron, the Cable TV service, to produce interactive commercials. The truth is we were way ahead of our time, but, remember, we had convinced ourselves we could do anything. We coined what we did 'New Media' and we brazenly borrowed from the work of Marshall McLuhan, who in the late 50s wrote what is still to my mind the most valuable book about communication and technology – *Understanding Media*.

One of the first companies to express an interest in our New Media thinking was The Body Shop. John Crowley and I were invited to meet with Anita Roddick and talk to her about interactive advertising and how we saw the future of communications. Anita was fascinating and fascinated. Sitting cross-legged on the floor of her office in Little-hampton, she absorbed the whole presentation with such enthusiasm that when we were asked to think even more broadly about The Body Shop and its communication requirements we knew we had a potential client who would not only push us, but who would also teach us something too.

The Body Shop was such an exemplary company for us, one we constantly referred to, that being in discussion with them about how they should communicate was almost too good to be true.

Anita was spellbound by the possibilities of what new technology could do for her business and her mission. She saw the emerging Internet as a tool for communities to stay in touch. She saw interactive television as a way of being more honest with her customers. She saw creativity as a business tool that might focus and rally her workforce to the overall vision she set. We fully briefed her on what technologies were likely to appear and how she could use them, and we signed her up to our Interactive Test, along with First Direct and Lever brothers.

Meanwhile, Jay was increasingly full of optimism. All the offices in the network were doing well and producing some excellent work. He even revisited the Chrysalis Project and that June asked me to introduce the concept of Total Role In Society (TRS) at a magnificent launch conference in downtown Los Angeles. In the audience was Jilly Foster, Worldwide Marketing Director for The Body Shop, who told me she was keen to take their relationship with Chiat/Day further. She felt our connections with the USA (an important market for The Body Shop) as well as our Chrysalis thinking would make us the ideal creative communications partner.

In August, I, Steve Alburty (Head of IT in our New York office) and Marty Cooke joined Anita and Jilly at Anita's Scottish retreat in a secluded and beautiful part of Scotland. There Steve introduced Anita to the Internet and we spent long hours debating the virtues of The Body

Shop and how communications could help enhance the company's reputation.

In September the news broke. Anita Roddick, who had publicly slated advertising agencies and the false dreams they sold, appointed Chiat/Day as their agency for new media and internal communications.

It was a coup. But more than that, it was a signal to the advertising world that after just a year, the new boys were alive and kicking.

In the wake of the new creative force and my increasing sense of self-confidence and belief, The Oxford Cabal broke apart. It had been an important but temporary steel girder in the crumbling edifice of the previous year, but now its value had been exhausted. Richard Warren left to work in the USA; Tom Knox landed a plum management role in another company; and Mike Skagerlind joined his favourite client, Nickelodeon, where he was soon promoted and posted to Australia.

To fill Mike's role as Planning Director we hired John Grant. I interviewed John over breakfast in the stuffy and austere surroundings of the RAC club in London. He was wearing a grey suit that he must have wheeled out for interviews and funerals and his haircut looked like the sort your mother would give you before you went back to school. He looked unbelievably ordinary, but it was clear that his thinking was far from ordinary.

John came with a brain the size of a planet. At Cambridge he had read Physics, Applied Physics and Astrophysics, and he continually supplemented his formal education by effortlessly assimilating writers such as Sartre and Wittgenstein as well as more contemporary thinkers like Francis Fukuyama.

John joined with a mission to innovate advertising, starting with the strategic, up-front component – the brief. He transformed the brief from an internal memo with a market analysis and consumer proposition to a piece of creative work in its own right. John's brief triggered the creative process and at times melded and merged with it so that it became difficult to know where the brief stopped and the TV script started. His influence over the company's output stretches from Boots, to IKEA, to Midland Bank and Eurostar. In fact there is almost no part of the company devoid of John's influence. John saw the opportunities at Chiat/Day and later would mould what became St. Lukes. He summarised the journey we were on as one of Personal Transformation and, through professional input and personal risk, transformed himself beyond where even he could have imagined.

In the summer we decided on a rather odd form of corporate entertainment. We wanted to say thank you to the clients who had stuck with us and those who had more recently awarded us their business. There were also others we had met with whom we had been debating issues raised by the Chrysalis thinking. People like Charles Handy, a constant inspiration to us, Geoff Mulgan of the independent think tank Demos ('I would not be surprised if one day Geoff became Prime Minister,' David had said when we first met him a couple of months earlier), John Drummond of Integrity Works, the business ethics consultants, and the wonderfully charismatic Reverend Crispin White of EECR, an ecumenical group which advises companies on ethical decision-making.

To accommodate this disparate group and their wives we took a tent at the Chelsea Flower Show and provided a day-long retreat with drinks and refreshments. It was a wonderful day. The sun shone and all our guests showed up. As I passed amongst them I began to realise something very important. The failure of the Chrysalis Project was to try to simplistically replace one workable but broken system with another untried one as if a new mantra was the answer.

No, the answer was to start behaving differently, to start talking differently. That way you begin to meet other people who have been thinking along the same lines, possibly for longer and with greater application than you have yourself. You meet people who share your beliefs and it changes and develops you. You change from within, because as you change you begin to believe in different things.

I really began to believe in the potential for people to change and improve themselves. I began to realise that people are wonderful assets. They are possibly the only business assets that truly appreciate in value if you look after them. People, I realised, were going to be the key to our success.

David and I had met with Dr Elaine Sternberg who talked about the application of ethics in business. She talked to us about Common Decency and Distributive Justice as mechanisms for ensuring that decision-making was done ethically, and was due to publish a book, *Just Business*, on this very subject. David and I began to write our own code of ethics and started to think about what business mechanic was truly the most honest and liberating for everyone in the company.

That summer we also hired our first Graduate Trainee, George Porteous, who, with an excellent degree from Oxford, was so adamant that he wanted to join Chiat/Day that he overlooked the fact that we didn't have a Graduate Trainee Programme and came as a secretary/PA instead. We promised George that he would get the best training he could as a secretary, because he'd learn the importance of respecting other people. (George's career never looked back. He may have put 'secretary' down as his profession in 1994, but two years later he was to be voted a Trustee of St. Luke's and is now in charge of some prestigious business.)

Jerry Wales was promoted to run the Finance Department of both the London and New York offices; his departure meant that I was the last surviving member of Jay's original team in London and confirmed the fact that Chiat/Day London was now completely reborn, with a whole new act.

By my own admission I became Jay's favoured son. He started to love coming to London, meet with Charles Saatchi, have lunch and compare art collections. Then he would take the opportunity to drop into his agency which was now so obviously focused and highly productive. He never asked how much money we were making (as it happened we were making record profits); all he wanted to know was that the work was up to scratch. He promoted me to the Partners Board of Chiat/Day Inc. and each month I was in either LA or New York, often attending full Board meetings in an advisory capacity, rather than as a Director.

David Abraham and I flew to New York in September for the official opening of their brand-new office. It was designed by Gaetano Pesce, a Venetian, who fell out of love with the ageing city of gondolas and devoted himself to designing absurdly over the top interiors with recycled materials. He's a 'love him or loathe him' designer, who took Jay's brief of the 21st-century cyber office to heart. You have to see it to believe it, but the floor is a red-painted resin and there are rooms made out of recycled videotapes.

It was a great party, Jay was in his element. His office was the toast of New York and had already been featured in half a dozen books and documentaries the world over.

But Jay also looked old and on the plane coming back David and I scoped out what might happen were he to 'fall under a bus' or succumb to some debilitating illness that might result in his early retirement. There had also been increasing gossip, for over a year now, that we were to be associated somehow with TBWA, another advertising agency who handled the Nissan account in Europe. Jay point blank refuted the suggestion that we were to be merging with TBWA.

We developed what we called 'Plan B' and it was essentially a kind of Doomsday Scenario involving an idea to stave off those remaining US executives who still thought the London office was a bad idea. We thought we would recommend, sooner rather than later, that we turn the London office into a franchise, with Chiat/Day and the staff in London all having a stake.

I was back in New York the following month, attending a Board meeting. Jay seemed eager to have me there. After discussing the financial results of the four key offices, the topic of selling the company appeared on the agenda. I couldn't believe my ears. It was as if David and I had willed this meeting to happen when discussing its likelihood on the plane only three weeks earlier. Jay remarked that he was in his 60s, feeling old and in need of a retirement plan. As I sat and listened to Jay, Bob Kuperman and others like Tom Patty, who ran the Nissan account in Los Angeles, I realised that although this was being discussed in general, conversational terms, this was something that they had all been discussing for some time. All the rumours were true.

We were asked to comment on how we felt about a sale (at this stage no buyer was proposed). Everyone agreed with it except Jay, who having started the discussion abstained from holding a view, and me. I was asked why.

'All the offices are doing well,' I said. 'We've been tumbling down a mountain for the past four years and now I really think we're on our way back up. New York is a fabulous office now; two years ago it was on its knees. London is doing really well, Toronto had been recently voted Agency Of The Year and LA have just moved into their state-of-the-art Frank Gehry offices. It'd be crazy to sell now, just when we're about to turn the whole company around. It would make no sense.'

There, I'd said it. I was angry at the way it had just 'suddenly' appeared on the agenda. But that's what happens, you see, in corporate life. If my view had really mattered I'd have been involved in earlier discussions.

Needless to say, I wasn't invited to any more Board meetings, although I knew, from friends I had in New York and LA, that there were regular weekly Board meetings taking place. Once I was invited by mistake by an over-zealous secretary who naturally assumed my presence would be required. I was very quickly uninvited, and told it was a mistake.

Although I knew something was happening it didn't over-concern me that I was being excluded. I guessed that there would be a working party put together, in time-honoured Chiat/Day fashion, and that I would only make a negative contribution so my services were not needed. I had also had a bellyful of travelling. In the past two years I had been round the world and over the water to the USA over 20 times. I had growing responsibilities to my team in London and a young family at home who soaked up any spare time I had.

That Christmas we had a spectacular party at the London Dungeon. The buoyant mood of the company was palpable and the working relationships we had formed with each other and with our clients were way ahead of any other advertising agency in London.

I felt I had pulled together the whole agency and I had taken the extraordinary step of reissuing everyone with new contracts that talked about the importance of Common Decency and fairness and which included a code of ethics.

We felt successful and we felt different. We felt creative and we felt we were breaking new ground with our thinking. We felt we had all been through something together and the shared experience of steering a company from failure through to success was a sublime feeling. People like Tessa Wire and Andy 'Smudger' Smith, Rachael Plant and Paul Johnson, who, though given many opportunities to do so, had not left the sinking ship, felt they had been part of a process of transformation.

Next year was going to be a fantastic year, we all knew it.

⑦　Mutiny!

There I am, in my pyjamas at 7.00 in the morning, when Jay calls me from Vancouver to say he had sold the company.

My shock at receiving the call was more to do with the speed of events than the nature of them. David Abraham and I had been anticipating this call, but we were sure that negotiations with a prospective partner would take a long time and that we would be given some warning. I was faced with a *fait accompli* and under strict instructions not to mention a thing to anyone. At ten past seven I phoned David.

'It's Plan B, then,' he said, referring to the doomsday-scenario conversation we'd had on the plane back from New York only three months earlier.

'Looks like it,' I said. 'Let's meet at ten in The Edge with the others and work out what to do next.'

I rang Naresh at 7.15, who in turn rang Bono.

The four of us met at ten. It was one of those meetings that everyone in the company knew was important. With faces set for the task, we strode into the all-glass meeting room and talked about what Jay had asked me to do.

I explained that he saw me very much as a senior officer of the company and that it was expected of me to comply with all instructions. I was to meet the senior managers from TBWA in London and talk about how we would merge. The key to this being a successful merger was to make sure Midland Bank was happy.

It was a sad meeting. All four of us felt that the company that had been so vibrant and full of potential was now fading fast.

We asked John Grant to join us at eleven along with Charlotte Zamboni, an experienced manager who had joined us in the week before Christmas to relieve David of his day-to-day handling of Midland Bank. We were nervous about our next actions and even more nervous of implicating others who might not want to debate the instructions we had been given. The six of us was about as small a group as we could trust ourselves with, at that stage. We agreed that I would meet the TBWA executives, since they might have an interesting view on the announcement. I called them to arrange when and where.

Jay called again at lunchtime. Again he reminded me of the secrecy of the news. The deal had not yet been ratified by The Securities and Exchange Commission (SEC) in the USA. If the news got out, there would be a breach of the code which set out the rules for a stock-market company (Omnicom) to buy the shares of a private company (Chiat/Day). The news was to be issued by Reuters the next day, the 31 January 1995 at 5.00 p.m. our time, which was lunchtime in New York, which was breakfast in LA. Jay would address all the offices sim-ultaneously by satellite video conference. I was to make sure everyone important in the office got there to hear it.

At seven that evening I made my way to the Four Seasons Hotel in Marylebone, the biggest, most corporate, most *American* hotel you could possibly imagine. I walked through a sea of large ferns and aspidistras and found the TBWA guys sipping Kir Royales in the cute hotel lounge. They wore double-breasted suits, club ties and shiny black brogues. I was in T-shirt and jeans.

'Hello, old thing,' the more senior one beamed, as I joined their table. 'Great news, eh? I think we're going to get along famously.'

In an instant I flashed back to a world of advertising that I had long forgotten. Here in front of me was advertising as pure business; advertising as corporate wheeling and dealing. I hadn't realised that all of us at Chiat/Day had moved so far away from this, so fast. They were nice enough guys, it was just that we viewed business from two totally different perspectives.

I felt as if I was from another planet.

There was nothing inherently wrong about what they said. The meeting was about finance and staffing. They had some well thought out plans for how the merger could go smoothly. The words all made sense but the whole thing just didn't work for me.

You see, this was a 'big wigs' meeting. We had all the cards, so that meant the others in the office were insignificant.

The deal was talked of in terms of a 'merger', but that wasn't actually what was going on. These people were buying us. And what a shiny, new jewel we'd be in their crown.

They had to offer me a job that would secure my services. Jay had hinted that something would be in the pipeline. As these early negotiations were played out, it transpired that I was the only one in the company whose contract was actually secure.

I was offered the post of Deputy Managing Director of the combined operation.

I returned to meet the rest of the 'six', who were holed up in the splendour of the mahogany and brass comforts of The Mountbatten, where I'd first met Dave and Naresh almost 18 months earlier. We chatted late into the night. No one wanted to go with the deal, that was obvious. It meant loss of jobs, integrity and trust. We had all made an agreement as a company – to work with each other in as innovative a way as possible – and this was a deal in the polar opposite direction.

But then again, we didn't have a leg to stand on. My contract was with Chiat/Day Inc. in Los Angeles – just having this discussion was putting me on shaky ground. And none of us had any money. So we would be borrowing if we wanted to set up a new company and then we would just have the hassle of being owned by banks. We didn't want to be owned by anyone.

We had a blank sheet of paper and a question: 'Do we want to form a company together?' We went around the table and tried to work out what we were personally able to commit. Yes, we wanted to stick together but, no we didn't want someone else in control of our destinies. Naresh's wife was about to have a baby and they were moving into a new house, David was in the process of adopting a child from India and I had just moved into a near-derelict house in the country and all my finances were tied up in making it habitable.

I left that evening feeling exhilarated but worried and didn't sleep a wink that night. I knew, I had known all day, that we weren't going to go into the TBWA deal, but at the same time, I knew we didn't have the right cards in our hands to set up a new venture.

We seemed to be stuck.

On the station platform at Waterloo, waiting for my train home, I did something rash. I phoned Stefano Hatfield, the Editor of *Campaign*.

'I've been told to merge Chiat/Day with TBWA. I don't know what we're going to do, but it's not going to be that. I'm going to keep you right on the inside track and tell you blow by blow what's going on. This isn't right. Its just not right.'

Why did I make that call? It was to goad me, and to set myself a task that had to be completed. In three days the world would know we were not playing ball.

After a perfunctory birthday party at breakfast for Olivia, my two-year-old, for which the family had to be up an hour earlier, I arrived in the office just before nine. It took me a minute to work out that something strange was going on. Then it clicked.

Almost the entire office were in and had been since at least 8.30 that morning.

Everyone just *knew* that something was up. All around me people were searching for clues in my manner and tone. It was unbearable. I really wanted to say something, but Jay had been so heavy about the SEC that I felt I really could not say a word.

Smudger pestered me hourly right up to the live satellite broadcast. He was a touchstone in the agency. When he asked a question he was asking it for everyone.

'What's up? Something's up? You can tell us all, you know that. We don't let our secrets out.'

'Something's up, you're right,' I kept telling him. 'But I just can't say. Just be at the Intercontinental Hyde Park at five, with the rest of us, and you'll find out.'

I had invited the whole office to the live broadcast. One by one we all filed into a tiny room in the Intercontinental Hotel and sat poised to watch Jay's speech from New York.

For at least ten minutes there were the usual hiccups in putting together this kind of show. First, the screen flickered and we saw friends from the New York office sitting cross-legged on the wild red-resin floor. Then the camera lurched and we stared blankly at just the floor itself. We heard someone say 'Are we hooked up yet? Where's Jay. Are LA on?'

The normally boisterous London crowd sat quietly.

Then the screen burst into life and Jay Chiat's head appeared. It was monstrously distorted by a weird camera angle and a bad satellite feed and there was a small time delay when he spoke, so that he looked like Max Headroom, the futuristic android.

'Hi everyone. I am here to announce that as of this afternoon Chiat/Day is merging with TBWA around the world. This is a great new future for all of us. It will give us the global presence we always wanted.'

Someone in London murmured: 'Sounds like he's made himself very rich and us very redundant.'

Jay went round all the offices in his speech to explain what would be happening to them and their clients. Everything seemed sorted and very logical. Then he paused and stood back from the camera.

'What?' he asked. He had been irritated by a heckle from the New York crowd.

'What about London?' the heckler persisted. 'You haven't mentioned London.'

By this stage all of us in London were dumbfounded. We didn't even feature in Jay's speech.

'Oh yeah, London,' Jay spluttered back onto the screen.

'They're merging with Holmes Knight Ritchie.'

Who?

Jay had mentioned the name of an agency that TBWA had bought two years earlier. It didn't exist now.

'Andy Law has met the guys there and they got along fine. Its going to be great.'

I felt 30 eyes beaming into the back of my neck.

There were a couple of questions. Someone in LA popped open a bottle of champagne and the screen died.

I turned round to everyone.

'Don't say anything now. Just go back to the agency. We're all going to meet up back at the agency.'

'So something was up, then?' smiled Smudger.

'Just a bit,' I said.

'He didn't have a clue what he was saying, or what was going on,' said David Abraham, summing up everyone's mood. 'His script had been written for him by Wall Street. We've spent a year talking about how to turn Chiat/Day into a different sort of company and then this.'

In the cab to the agency I reflected on the day. Last week it was going to be the day I embarrassed my family by dressing up as 'The Great Waldo' – magician *extraordinaire* – for my daughter's second birthday. I had inflicted this on my son for the previous seven years and persisted against a rising tide of ridicule from adults and children alike. As it was I was to miss all her birthday celebrations. The days following would be full to the brim. Family was pushed to the side. That's what big business can do.

Back at the agency everyone was present. We broke open two cases of beer – Tuborg – we had just won the account.

And then the phones went berserk. The news had gone onto Reuters as we made our way back from the hotel. As we started answering the phones we realised it was the headhunters, one after the other. It was incredibly fast. They were commiserating and offering new jobs in the same breath. Ah! Advertising. Its so wonderful.

After the headhunters came the press. It was too late for any of the UK trade journals to run a story on Wednesday, but I knew *Campaign* magazine would run a story on Thursday...

I turned to the assembled crowd.

'I'm not permitted to speak to you about the details of this deal. You see, I have a contract, a copy of which is in Los Angeles, with the company's lawyers. I'm absolutely forbidden to suggest to you that you might not want to go ahead with this deal. In fact I'd be grateful if some of you would step forward to be fired. Because that's what's got to happen next.'

No one moved, or spoke. I spoke very slowly and very carefully.

'But you know, I'm inclined to stand over here and just look at the view from this window. It's a great view. It offers all sorts of ideas for the future. Some of you, and I understand why, might not be as interested in this view as me. If you're not, don't be afraid and don't do anything that might compromise yourself. Just walk out now. We are about to enter uncharted territory and I can make absolutely no promises for a safe journey.'

Again no one moved, or spoke. I waited for a couple of minutes and looked at David, Tessa, Smudger, Johnners, Planty, Sally Kelso, Dave, Naresh. Brilliant, loyal and unfireable in anyone's book. The whole company stood silently still. Rock solid.

'Well, it looks like we're all in it. Now its action stations!'

We were mutinying. *En masse.* And the strangest thing was that all we cared about was each other and sticking together. Exactly how we were going to succeed as a standalone company seemed a distant hurdle to cross. We started divvying up the tasks that needed to be done.

Johnners, like the rough gruff Regimental Sergeant-Major everyone loves bellowed 'Or-der!' (and has done ever since to silence a throng prior to a talk).

'Right, this is what we're going to do,' and I outlined a plan to start the ball rolling.

One by one we phoned all our clients. And one by one they all said what we wanted to hear. As long as we could promise the same high level of service, they would stick with us. Anita Roddick, the supreme entrepreneur, asked if we needed financial help. Cable & Wireless said they would support us however they could. As the evening went on the adrenalin flowed and the list of clients who were to back us grew. It was like election night. And all the votes were going our way.

But there was one big vote left to come in.

We had had difficulty contacting Midland Bank. Their strict security measures made it hard to contact key people out of hours. Eventually David Mills, our senior contact, called in, alerted by his security people.

'I hope this is important, Andy, I was just about to settle down for some supper.'

Breathlessly I told him what we were doing.

'Andy,' he said calmly, 'don't worry about a thing. Go home and have a beer.'

The cheer from the agency must have been heard halfway across London.

We were a going concern.

No one could go home. By now it was 10.30 p.m.

A distant, lone phone rang. It was Bill Tragos, Worldwide Chairman of TBWA and as big a wig as you're ever likely to come across in the advertising world. He monopolised the conversation entirely, with an unremitting heavy New York drawl.

'Andy, this is great. Particularly for you. You're going to do great. Did Jay talk to you about the stock options. TBWA is one big happy family, you're joining a great firm. The London guys like you. I hear great things about what you're doin' in London, maybe we can incorporate some of your ideas. I just wanted to ring and say Hi.'

I was speechless. I had not fed this call into any plan. 'Oh. Hi!' I replied. 'I think there's a lot of sorting out to do.'

'Sure there is. Don't worry, this is a perfect marriage. There's always a lot to sort out. But hey, it must be late in London, get some sleep. See you soon, in New York maybe.'

I phoned Jay: 'We have a problem.'

⑧　What A Wonderful World

J ay went ballistic.

Of course he did. He hadn't for a moment thought his pet manager in London would contradict him in such a specific way.

'You're just upset,' he advised me.

'We covered that already, yesterday. Of course I'm upset.'

'Don't do anything rash. Don't talk to anyone. Don't talk to the media,' Jay further advised.

Whoops.

'Look Jay, we just don't think it's right. You didn't do this deal for us in London, you did it for you guys in the US and for Nissan. In fact we've got all sorts of business conflicts over here. TBWA have Direct Line Insurance and we have First Direct. Did anyone stop to think about that?'

Jay persisted: 'I'm coming over. ASAP. Just calm down and think about things. What are you going to do? You gonna raise money? You gonna steal the business? I mean, what are you gonna do? I'm coming over. Soon as I can.'

I joined the rest of the agency; everyone was still there. The mood was exhilarating. I thought, 'Mad. This is mad. This is a group of people that was fired *en masse* a few hours ago, now look at them.'

Bob Kuperman called. He spoke to David Abraham. 'Hi. I hear you're unhappy. Chill out. Don't panic, give it time. You're all great guys. I know Jay fluffed the London bit, but don't take it personally.' David explained the situation to Bob in detail.

'Oh,' said Bob, 'you're right. There is a problem. I think Jay's coming over.'

By midnight people started drifting home. It seemed like the phone calls had died down. Drunk on the atmosphere and, OK, on not a little Tuborg, we were exhausted.

The fax machine whirred just as the last man was about to put out the lights. It was a fax from TBWA Sweden: 'Welcome to the wonderful world of TBWA. We look forward to meeting you soon.'

The next day, the agency warmed up quickly after a somewhat drowsy-headed start. We met at lunchtime at The Iceberg.

'We'll meet every day, here, at lunchtime or in the evening,' I said. 'As this plays out I'm going to tell you all everything. As it happens. We're all in this together, so we must all know what lies ahead and what decisions are being made. If there looks to be a tough call on anything we'll all take a vote.'

We agreed that David Abraham and I would deal with the Americans, while everyone else serviced their clients above and beyond the call of duty. Our clients had put life back into our company. Our clients were our life blood. None of us will ever forget the cold reality that we experienced first hand of what a service business is. It's about the relationships you build up with your customers and the trust they place in you to deliver what you promise. Sounds simple enough, I know, but when you could lose all your business you wonder if you have lived up to those sort of implicit agreements.

The agency went on to work harder and better than ever before. The Creative Directors, Dave and Naresh, formed a day-to-day operational team with John Grant and Charlotte and ensured that the highest possible standards were maintained.

David and I focused on Madison Avenue and the wrath of Jay, and Bill Tragos and Bob Kuperman and Tom Patty and you name it.

The CEO of TBWA London called me in the early afternoon. He'd had an early morning call from his superiors in New York.

'Hi, Andy. I hear the troops are restless. I thought I'd pop over this

evening and address them. Thought I might be able to calm things
down.'

'Um, not a good idea,' I responded. (To be honest, I thought he'd be
lynched.)

Before I left the office that evening I called Stefano at *Campaign* and
updated him.

'Got everything you need?' I enquired.

'Yep,' he said, 'got everything I need.'

The next day David and I honoured a meeting we had arranged with
Peter Simpson, who had now moved from Midland Bank to First Direct.
We wanted to make sure it was business as usual. The meeting was in
the north of England and we left too early to receive our Thursday
morning copy of *Campaign*.

Rachael Plant called me on my mobile and read out the headline on
the front page:

TBWA Deal with Chiat/Day Triggers London Revolt

'TBWA, the Omnicom-owned network, merged with Chiat/Day this week
to create a $2-billion global operation – but the deal instantly ran into
trouble in London.' Our mutiny was made public.

The article went on to explain that Jay was stepping down from active
management in the merged operations and that the deal was done to
cement the two agencies' relationship with Nissan. It also referred to a
'clash of cultures' in London.

Tragos, however, called it a 'perfect marriage' and Alasdair Ritchie,
Chairman and CEO of TBWA London, was quoted as saying: 'If there is a
culture that is most like ours, it's theirs – open, creative and challenging.'

For my part, I wanted it recorded that we were opposed to the deal.
My main argument at that time was that there were too many client
clashes – they had Nivea, for example, and we had Boots Cosmetics. But
the truth was that there was a culture clash. We had all worked hard to
reconfigure how we would interrelate and contribute to a more contemporary service proposition. In the process we had created a company
in which each human was an integral part, a discrete cog with a specific
role. To break us up, or merge us with anyone else, it didn't matter that
it was TBWA, would have been as cataclysmic as breaking up a watch
into small pieces and fitting the parts back into a large clock.

TBWA and Chiat/Day were right to be angry with us and were right to assert the importance of due diligence and company governance. Having put the deal together they obviously relished its benefits. We were a small, annoying grit in the ointment.

On the way back from the meeting, later that afternoon, Isabel Bird called me.

'You'll need a lawyer,' she said.

'Good point.'

'Go to Roger Alexander at Lewis Silken, he's the best.'

⑨ Fred

I arranged to meet Roger the following morning.

Roger Alexander was a softly spoken polite man with the looks of a Greek philosopher and the wisdom to go with it. Not only a first-class lawyer, but also highly competent in accountancy, he was to prove to be one of our major assets in a fight that would go all 15 rounds and which would take a staggering ten months to complete.

'Ten months?' Roger said to me recently. 'That was fast.'

Roger began to plan all our next moves. We discussed the fact that Jay was coming over and we talked about the possible routes to independence that we could take. He asked me what my ultimate goal was and I replied that at this stage I didn't have an ultimate goal, but I had something better. Something the ancient Romans called a *casus belli*. It was a reason for falling into a fight. A purpose. A mission.

Our mission was to continue the work we had started which sought to create a more harmonious, effective and profitable working environment. Nothing should get in the way of that. And to be treated so casually by the Americans only added fuel to our fire.

'Right,' said Roger. 'By the way, I'd better meet up with your Financial Director.'

'Our Financial Director?' I asked, somewhat surprised.

'Yes, you do have one, don't you?'

'Er, no, we don't.' (Jerry, remember was now in New York. He was probably *one of them*, who knows.)

'It would be a rather good idea if you had one, don't you think?'

'Good point.'

When I returned to the office, there was much commotion. Before I could walk into the reception area I was hijacked by David Abraham. 'There's a guy in reception. He says he's from Omnicom. He wants to know if you've got a minute.'

'Who is he?' I asked.

'Don't really know,' David replied. 'Says his name is Fred Meyer. I think he's American, but he's got an accent that sounds German. He's been here for half an hour.' (Fred Meyer was Swiss born, in fact, but had lived most of his life in Manhattan. Like so many émigrés, he never let Americanese intrude on his native voice.)

And what a half an hour it had been. It was Friday lunchtime. All the key meetings of the week had come to a close. The energy in the agency was transparent. Since yesterday morning the phones had never stopped ringing as friends and family called in to find out what was happening first-hand.

The Receptionists were laughing and giggling, there were games every-where, donated by our client Nickelodeon, the kid's TV channel, which included slime throwing and fart-noise machines. Two people were playing on a Sega Mega Drive rigged up in open view. It felt like a kids' Christmas party. And someone had put a whoopee cushion on the guest seats in reception.

'Mr Meyer?' I enquired.

'Hello, yes, pleezed to meet you. Lively company you haf hier.'

He sounded like a German spy who was trying to infiltrate the English, but with an unconvincing accent. And he was big. Huge actually. Well over six foot and a touch portly. He had grey thinning hair and sharp eyes. He must have been 60.

I took him to The Wedge, our largest and smartest conference room, fitted out with an enormous wedge-shaped steel table. Dutifully, the agency calmed down somewhat as the meeting went under way.

'Allow me to introduce myself. I am Fred Meyer. I am zee Chief Financial Officer of Omnicom, Worldwide, owners of TBWA.'

I gulped. I hoped he didn't notice. We had just kept this Worldwide top financial honcho and Number Two of Omnicom waiting in a children's playground for half an hour.

He went on: 'I just happened to be in London reviewing zum of our concerns over here. I heard there vas some trouble and wondered if I could help?' This man was a class act and I felt he needed to be treated with some respect.

Which doesn't explain why I rattled out fast and furiously a 12-point list of fundamental reasons why we were unable to join in the merger, like a soapbox agitator trying to stir a crowd.

When I finished he looked at me and David very closely.

'I see. Yes. Zer is a problem here. But I'm sure I can be of help.'

With that he flourished a business card and swept out.

Roger was right; we were going to be in need of a Financial Director. And quick.

There are people around the world who have worked for Fred Meyer for many years and never met him. Some of them would tremble if they knew he was coming to review their performance.

The fact that we had met him and that he was to become our main point of contact throughout all the negotiations was testament to the fact that little Chiat/Day in London was a much more fundamental part of the deal than we had envisaged at the beginning. Our refusal to join in was not so much a grit in the ointment as a real pain in the arse for Omnicom.

It was fortunate that he and I, from that day on, struck up a wonderful relationship. It transpired that he was honest to a fault, amiable and supportive. 'If you're going to be taken over by someone,' I thought, thinking of my pals in Chiat/Day America, 'you could do worse than Fred Meyer.'

Calls came in thick and fast from the USA. Tom Patty, who was in charge of the Nissan account, tried to persuade me to change my mind. I stuck to my resolve. At the end of our conversation he said, 'I guess you just don't want to go in the direction I want to go.'

Bill Tragos rang. He rang a few times. He was palpably upset that we had rejected his company. He was the 'T' in TBWA and I know he took it personally that we rejected his London office. He was a very different man from Jay. I left conversations with Jay feeling exhilarated. I left conversations with Tragos feeling, well, almost threatened. He was a tough Greek success story in New York who had worked hard to build his successful network. Worms like me didn't compute with his growth plan. I told him: 'With the best will in the world I don't think you have anything over here. None of the clients and none of the staff want to do your deal. Therefore, you have nothing to negotiate with over here. Nothing.'

'You don't think they're so mad they'd do anything dangerous, do you?' Amanda my wife asked me at this time, semi in jest. There had been long phone calls to my house from New York and LA late at night and into the early morning. They were tough calls, hard, anguished, with people I knew and sometimes with people I had only ever spoken to over the phone whose faces and demeanour I would vividly imagine as they pressed their case for me and the office to 'stay within the system'.

I knew what she meant. The events of the past few days and the ones that were to follow could have come straight from a John Grisham novel. I dreamt one night that a large black Mercedes had pulled up outside my son's school and whisked him off. 'We have Tom,' a Slavic voice said. 'Sign the deal and merge, or else!'

The following week, as the news of our revolt settled into the London and New York markets, we were inundated with calls from all sorts of people offering financial help and advice.

Someone would telephone David: 'Do you want a White Knight?'

Someone else would call and say, 'Merge your agency with ours. Lock, stock and barrel. We'll take you all.'

'Even our Creative Directors?' I would say.

'Er, no, we've got our own; but I'm sure they could work well enough under them.'

'No thanks.'

Midweek Jay flew in. He had booked into Claridges, where he always stays, but he had flown in such a hurry from LA that he packed only jeans and T-shirts.

Claridges welcomed him as usual, but were compelled to confine him to his room because, driven by their quaint English penchant for custom and routine, they demanded a high standard of dress etiquette – certainly jacket and tie; certainly not jeans and a T-shirt. Jay was only staying a few hours, so it seemed crazy to buy a whole new wardrobe. When I arrived I found him holed up in his bedroom.

Jay's position became clear from the outset. He did not want to be cast as the villain. He was avuncular, in good humour and thinking positively (although downright annoyed at being cooped up in his room). Jay had always supported me personally and had been a strong sponsor of the London office despite fierce criticism from some of his senior US executives.

We ordered lunch and two solitary *croque-monsieurs* appeared in under ten minutes. He raided his mini-bar and found two export beers.

'What do you want to do?' he asked.

'Well, look, Jay. Think of it this way. Imagine you're 38 years old and this happens to you. You've got a whole gang of people with you, everyone's focused and the clients are totally supportive. What would you do?'

'I'd break away,' he said.

From that moment Jay had given us his moral approval. It was critical to have him on side, not least because we wanted him to know that we had always been loyal to him. I was also acutely aware that we had to behave decently from now on. In the papers every day was another break-away story. It involved Maurice and Charles Saatchi being ejected from the company they founded by disgruntled shareholders and it was messy, bitter and fraught with High Court writs.

If we were going to construct something akin to the kind of company we had envisioned in the Chrysalis project the Saatchi model was not the way to behave. Everyone we were to ultimately deal with would be a stakeholder. They had to be treated with respect and honesty.

With Jay supporting us and Fred Meyer prepared to do business with us, we knew a deal was possible. Although we still had no idea what kind of a deal.

A week later, on Wednesday 15 February, David and I were in New York. We were due to meet Fred Meyer the next day at 10.00 a.m. and wanted a night's rest and composure. We met up with Jerry Wales who was in the unenviable position of emotionally supporting us but professionally obliged to back the deal. He joined us for dinner that night with Richard Warren, who had heard about our revolt. Richard was working in an up and coming New York ad agency. Both of them told us that the mood in New York was not favourable to the deal. The Chiat/Day employees, so recently installed in Gaetano Pesce's extra-ordinary offices, felt unable to raise any enthusiasm for the deal. Jerry asked us about the plan of attack.

'Good cop, bad cop,' I said. Jerry looked confused. 'I'm going to play the nice guy and David's going to appear unhappy throughout. He'll try to destabilise them by typing into his portable computer every time anyone says something that sounds significant.' Jerry looked unconvinced.

'Yeah, but what's the plan?'

'We haven't got a plan yet.'

The next morning David and I took a cab to 437 Madison Avenue, the worldwide headquarters of Omnicom. It was a skyscraper like any other skyscraper, but positioned charmingly close to New York's impressive Roman Catholic cathedral. It looked remarkably like the one in the *Godfather* that witnessed the massacres on that infamous christening day. Ominous I thought.

Corporate modesty was not at all present. The skyscraper had about a hundred floors. All were listed and named. All were Omnicom offices.

As we entered the car-park-sized entrance hall three lifts faced us. Each went to different floors.

Scanning the information board we discovered we were due on Floor 9. The second lift would take us there. We emerged on Floor 9 to find ourselves in a battle-grey reception. A lone receptionist sat in an odd space that resembled a pulpit. There were no magazines and no flowers. There were a row of identical chairs. We started to laugh quietly.

'What are we doing here?' giggled David.

'I've no idea,' I replied.

'May I help you, gen'lemen?' asked the receptionist, barely looking up from her desk.

'We're here to meet with Fred Meyer.' That made her jump.

Within minutes a big beaming Fred appeared. 'Come gentlemen, vee are going to zee boardroom.'

Fred led us into the lift we had arrived in. He pressed 'G' for ground.

'We're going to another building?' I enquired.

'No. We are going to another floor.'

At the ground level we got out of the lift and immediately got into the one next to it. It took us all the way to the top.

We got out and walked into the largest meeting room I have ever seen. In it was the largest boardroom table I had ever seen. A flock of men in dark suits emerged from nowhere; who they were I'll never know, because Fred realised our negotiating team consisted only of me and David. They were waved silently away, although Fred had two other people with him.

One was Adelaide Horton. Adelaide was Chief of Operations at Chiat/Day and always became involved when complex legal or financial issues were at stake. She was a middle-aged lady, bespectacled and with a conservative hairstyle. She had a slight southern states drawl. She was a serious player in Chiat/Day and her presence in meetings always meant the agenda was meaty and potentially explosive. The other was David Weiner. He was close to Jay and had advised Chiat/Day on its various share distributions and share buy-backs. He was not employed by the agency directly, but his impact was very direct indeed. All three of them were seasoned experts in the art of buying and selling companies.

David and I stared across the giant boardroom table at them. Fred spoke. And David started typing.

Had Fred looked over David's shoulder he would have realised something significant.

David couldn't type.

The three corporate executives began by asking what we wanted. We said we wanted to take over the company and that we had been offered funds to buy it (not quite true, but hey, this was gamesmanship). Fred thought about it and said he wondered if an earn-out wasn't a better way.

'It might be,' we said. (We didn't know what an earn-out was.)

Fred sketched out an idea whereby we would buy the company for one dollar (so far so good, I thought) and then pay Omnicom a royalty on our income for seven years. At any stage we could buy the company outright for £2 million. He suggested how the figures would all work out and we studiously wrote everything down.

'What do you think?' he asked.

'We will have to consult with our advisers before we can agree anything.'

They were aghast. They had fully expected us to agree things there and then. This was the deal. What was there to discuss. 'You can't do this, you've got to agree now.' Adelaide took me aside: 'You don't talk to Omnicom like that.'

'The way I look at it,' said David, 'you either have something or nothing.'

They looked at us. They understood what we meant. If we wanted, we could all go and work from my living room and service the clients from there. We had income, we had access to all kinds of help.

Jay knew we wouldn't do this. The big question was, had he told them we were keen to leave with a deal?

Evidently not.

Fred was not flustered. 'Fair enough. How long do you need?'

'We'll get back to you at four this afternoon.'

'Good. I'll meet you in the Chiat/Day offices at four, after you've consulted with your advisers. Bruce Crawford will be there; he's giving his inaugural speech to the agency. By the way, Bruce would like to meet you.'

Tragos was big. Myers was bigger. But Crawford was the biggest. He was a legendary figure in the advertising world.

Even Adelaide got nervous.

We left the giant boardroom and went to the lift. Fred pressed 'G' and we raced to the ground in seconds. Out we hopped and in we went to the adjacent lift. Up to 9 again. We were ushered into Bruce Crawford's inner sanctum. The shag-pile carpet was so thick my trouser bottoms brushed the surface.

After a minute, Bruce walked in. He walked very slowly. He was a small man, impeccably dressed and in his mid-60s. He sported an uncomfortably large head of white hair above his petite face, which also bore extra-large glasses. His feet seemed too small for him to stand up in, but his shoes looked hand-made. In fact he looked like the kind of guy who would put on a new pair of thousand-dollar shoes every day.

'Hello, Bruce,' I said, as soon as I saw him. 'I expect you'd like to know why we're being such a pain in the arse.'

I thought Adelaide was going to faint. No one speaks to Bruce that brusquely, let alone use such a common profanity.

He smiled. 'That would be nice.'

I proceeded to explain what we had been doing in London. He nodded throughout. David explained the work he had been doing for Chiat/Day and the huge benefits of employing some of the thinking from the Chrysalis project.

'I think you guys know what you're doing. At Omnicom, though, remember that we like to keep tabs on exciting companies. That's why Fred's deal at least means you'll talk to us once a year.'

Keep tabs?

He was about to leave, when David interjected with a question. 'What's your five-year plan for Omnicom, Bruce?' he asked.

Bruce looked startled. 'What do you mean?' he replied.

The room fell silent and everyone but me and David stiffened in corporate salute.

'I mean, what is the strategic purpose of Omnicom – what is its purpose in the world?'

Silence still reigned. He sat down and sank into his generous armchair. 'The strategic intent of Omnicom is to increase shareholder value. We buy agencies and merge them with existing ones.'

'Is that it?' David replied.

Crawford looked nonplussed. Fred and his team looked alarmed.

'I wish you luck with your new venture,' said Crawford and a secretary appeared like magic to whisk us away.

⑩ Sale Of The Century

David and I went off to consult our advisers.

What advisers? There was none, of course.

We wandered down to the harbour at Battery Park and bought a beer and a hot dog. It was 11.30 a.m. and the bars and restaurants were bracing themselves for the Wall Street lunchers who would come pouring in an hour from now.

We wondered what our 'advisers' would be telling us and decided we still had nothing to lose by pushing the deal much further in our direction. We agreed we were going to halve the £2 million figure that Fred had offered. In addition we would refuse to take the ten-year lease on the very expensive designer offices in Shaftesbury Avenue. It would be good to move, to start afresh. And anyway, rents in London had tumbled to a fraction of what they were when Jay took out the lease in 1990.

Then we burst into hysterical laughter. Who did we think we were?

We arrived at the Chiat/Day offices at 4.00 p.m. There was a sense of anticipation in the air. The great Bruce Crawford was coming at six to talk to everyone. People behaved like you do at home in the minutes before your parents come to visit. There was too much tidying and too ordered a row of glasses ready to take the champagne toast.

Fred, Adelaide and David Weiner arrived and we resumed our negotiations. We had just started when Jay walked in. The mood of the meeting changed instantly. Jay had that effect. Everybody, including us, felt slightly uncomfortable. It seemed odd to have him there. His protégés were dealing with his paymasters, what was his role? Jay sensed the awkwardness.

'Relax. Thought I'd just make sure everything was going smoothly for everyone.'

I told Fred that after much consultation and deliberation we felt £1 million to be nearer the mark. His jaw dropped.

'Don't push it,' Adelaide warned.

Before anyone else could speak, David said, 'And we don't want the building.'

There was silence.

No one looked at Jay. Least of all me. The money was one thing, but wishing to vacate his designer palace was another. It seemed like a direct snub, although it wasn't meant that way.

Meyer broke the silence, and spoke slowly and deliberately. 'Gentlemen. I can bend, but if you push me any further I vill snap. I'm going uptown for a drink with some nice people and I don't vant zis meeting to cast a shadow over my evening. Vy don't vee settle on £1.2 million and, OK, zee lease is fine.'

'Agreed,' I said. 'It's a pleasure doing business with you.'

'Likewise,' said Meyer.

'Is that right?' I asked half jokingly. 'Can we both have got a good deal?'

'Sure,' said Meyer, 'that's how all good negotiations end. By zee vay, the Securities and Exchange Commission are going through their regular checks on this deal. You can't do anything until vee have their permission to proceed vith the purchase. That could take up to six months. So calm down, don't speak negatively to the press. As of now you are still to be purchased by us and you can break from us some time at zee end of zee summer. In zee meantime you retain an independent status in London.'

I shook Fred's hand. There was nothing in writing. A handshake seemed appropriate for Fred. I knew he was not someone who would renege on a deal.

The room began to empty. As I left Adelaide grabbed my elbow. 'You two are lucky to have survived with your manhood intact,' she drawled.

We milled around the office waiting for Bruce's Big Announcement and caught up on the gossip with Marty Cooke. 'I don't know where I stand yet,' he confided in us. 'The TBWA guys are backing their Creative

Director; he's a different sort of person from me. Very different. So I'm all up in the air. Hey, you guys, are you really breaking away? That's great.' We told him everything we had been up to and took time to point out that he should be proud of the legacy he left in London.

Tragos saw me chatting and called me over. He beckoned me into a room. Ira Matathia, the CEO of the New York office was near by.

'Ira, you join us,' he barked.

He turned to me. 'OK, so you've got a deal. But I don't want you badmouthing our office. Understood?'

I didn't have time to reply. He swept out of the room as fast as he swept in. Ira looked at me as if to say, 'What was I needed for?' We smiled at each other and joined the people gathering for Bruce's announcement.

When it came, it wasn't what he said that made the biggest impact. It was the theatre of the event.

Jay introduced Bruce and then stood back. As Bruce spoke about his delight at having Chiat/Day 'in the family of Omnicom', it dawned on everybody that from this moment on it was no longer Jay's company. In that single moment the spirit of Chiat/Day emptied out of the hearts of every employee as if it was disappearing down a plug hole.

The pirates had been captured and were going to have to toe the line.

'Any questions?' Bruce asked.

There were a couple. They were procedural: when will the TBWA guys be moving in? Will they need more space? But there was such an overwhelming mood of disappointment that few could be bothered to ask anything.

Then Tragos piped up: 'I just want to say that from my point of view selling TBWA out to Omnicom a few years ago was the best thing we ever did. I don't regret it for an instant.'

I thought to myself, that seems like rather over-egging the pudding and I glanced at Jay. He murmured something inaudible under his breath.

David and I were booked on the 10.00 p.m. flight out of JFK back to London and would have left straight after the talk if Jay hadn't collared us.

'Fancy a quick bite?'

In the Cuban restaurant, the three of us chatted about how the negotiations had gone. Jay was in a strange mood. Throughout the dinner he seemed like someone who had just said goodbye to a girlfriend. He wasn't his usual sparky self.

We couldn't stay long and soon we were hailing a cab to the airport. Jay stood on pavement. 'Looks like you guys got the sale of the century. Go home. Good luck.'

On the 'red-eye' going home we were too excited to sleep. We drew up a prototype plan that would allow us to create an extraordinary company and were meticulous in our efforts to ensure that it was based on the central ethical platform we had talked about in the Chrysalis meetings.

We went into fine detail and costed out as much as we could. We even started to think about the layout of the offices.

'One day we'll frame this piece of paper,' said David, as the plane flew in to land at Heathrow. It wasn't until we had cleared customs that we had realised we had left it on the plane, tucked in neatly behind the sick bag in the compartment of the seat in front.

For the second time that day we burst into uncontrollable laughter.

⑪ We Go To A Desert Island

We arrived back in the agency in London victorious. We had a deal. We did not have to go to bankers and put ourselves in debt; we did not need to mortgage our houses; we did not need to do anything ugly and spoil our bond of trust with Jay. It was almost too perfect to believe.

While David and I concentrated on Omnicom, the rest of the agency was fulfilling its obligation to service existing clients. We were hiring the right sort of talent to ensure the agency could deliver in the way we had always imagined. Clare Nash joined in January to oversee The Body Shop and income was strong enough for Tessa to hire a much needed assistant, James Wood. Everything felt more professional than ever, although we knew we had a long way to go to make sure we would always win against the best.

The work we were doing for The Body Shop, Midland Bank, First Direct, Boots and Radio One (won in January) stood out. It was all truly inventive and we seemed to have found clients every bit as risky as we were.

They say the candle flickers brightest at its moment of extinction. Well, the creative output was prolific and all of an extraordinary high standard in the year we very nearly got snuffed out.

David and I went over and over the deal with Roger Alexander. What were the traps? What had we missed? 'There's nothing in writing you know,' Roger would say. 'Fred won't renege,' I would respond.

Not to say we weren't nervous. Fred probably did deals like this every week, every day, who knows? We were novices. Had we been lambs to the slaughter? Were they laughing their heads off on Madison Avenue?

So it was with some relief that Fred's secretary called towards the end of March. 'Fred's in Paris next week. He wondered if you'd like to meet up for breakfast, to tie up any loose ends, or ask any questions?'

We spent hours rehearsing what we were going to say. We met with Roger and agreed that we would shave down some of the finer, more detailed aspects of the deal and we would reassert that we would be moving out of the premises. We thought Fred had been too casual about the premises and we felt they were too expensive, too glitzy and too much of the past for our liking.

We took the Eurostar to Paris and booked into the Hôtel Crillon where Fred was staying. Neither of us had ever stayed in a hotel that expensive before. It was ridiculous. Positioned centrally on the Place de Concord, it was the sort of place that royalty or billionaire rock stars would stay at. We only wanted bed and breakfast (with Fred). For that we were charged nearly £300.00 each.

'See,' said David, who can compute cost versus value instantly, 'this is where our hard-earned profits would go if we'd stuck with Omnicom.' He was right. What's the point in working your guts out as a manager in one of Fred's company's if all he did was give it to the Crillon?

Not that Fred would ask that question. It was a case of two worlds. The old world versus the new world. We weren't making a political statement. We're not communists trying to boot the Czar out of the splendour of his Winter Palace. No, it was about fairness and respect to those who worked for you.

Over breakfast we bargained like buyers and sellers in a Mediterranean market. Fred accepted some things and declined others. On the property he agreed a bonus payment for us if we left the place in an orderly fashion. For a bonus payment we'd have left the place any way he wished!

'How did it go?' Roger asked. We told him.

'You're quids in,' he said, 'but Fred's toughening up. Now, about your Finance Director...'

We had failed to find ourselves a Finance Director who we thought could work the way we wanted. It was a tricky brief. We wanted someone who could run a tight ship – we wanted utter professionalism, but also someone who could see the advantages of a business that was going to operate in a different paradigm. Money to us was like health. We needed it, but it was not going to be what we lived for.

We had met ten candidates, all of whom were too conventional. We had broached the subject with Jerry; maybe he would consider returning from New York? But he was following a different path, and with all the new faces in London, he was unsure of the credibility he would have.

Thankfully we had on board Denise Webber, who Jerry had hired to run things and report to him in New York. She was an excellent administrator, but we all knew we had to find someone highly qualified to deal with Omnicom and help forge a new financial model for a new type of company.

We kept searching.

By early April things started to drag. We had, possibly, six months to kill. Six weeks ago we would have stuck two fingers up to anyone, gone to my house and ran the company from there. All that energy and drive seemed to be seeping away. We were all dressed up with nowhere to go. Was this Fred's master stroke? Attrition. Was he wearing us down?

The three months since The Phone Call had been totally absorbing. Family life had been pushed into a corner by the sheer volume of meetings that occurred, by the avalanche of phone calls at home in the evenings, by the burdensome mental preoccupation with dealing with a giant like Omnicom, by the ruthless detailed dedication to our clients whose support was critical and to whom our first duty lay, and by the rush of excitement that accompanied all of these that brought with it energy, persuasion, inventiveness and a nagging guilt that Ordinary Life was being brutally passed over.

Everyone in work has to deal with times like these. When things at work are just simply too exciting to permit home life to rudely intrude. They are vibrant, passionate times that render Daily Life humdrum and drab by comparison. They are times filled with discovery and the banter and merry-making of people other than your family.

For David Abraham and his wife Maria, it was a particularly fraught time. To provide a sister for their son Saul (who was born within days of my son Tom), they had decided to adopt a baby girl. The process was a long one which had required in-depth interviews and regular visits to their home by authorities who were clamping down on ill-thought-out adoptions. Since the Ruth Lederman sessions David knew he could regularly confer with me about my adoption and would ask questions which I had never asked myself and to which I was not sure I always knew the answer. David and Maria had chosen to adopt from India and on top of the necessary UK bureaucracy there lay a mountain of laborious hard work as negotiations between London and the small hilltop town of Pune in the State of Maharastra, some miles East of Bombay, got under way.

Throughout the entire dealings with Omnicom, David would make phone calls from the larger-than-life, multicoloured steel, glass and vinyl advertising palace in Berkshire House, to the dusty, down-at-heel orphanage in Pune. Eventually in the last week of April, David set off, utilising the full value of his four-week sabbatical to secure the arrival of Vaishali, the two-year-old he and Maria adopted. Later I told him that whilst Maria had laboured for their first child, in many respects he had done the same for their second.

I had decided to start dreaming again. I wanted to go as far as I could. I wanted to dream up the ideal company. We were under no financial pressure. We had no investors to satisfy. No one was forcing us to adopt one approach or another.

We wrote to all our clients and suppliers and told them that on Friday, 21 April we were shutting the agency.

And off we went to the Marlborough Crest Hotel in Bloomsbury, into a room with no windows and invented the perfect company.

You would not have wanted to be Verity Johnson, who joined the accounts department that day, or Colin Lamberton and Seyoan Vela, an exciting young creative team who joined us from Lowe Howard-Spink. Or Libby Cuthbert or Phil Teer who joined the agency on that day too

They joined us as we all bared our souls to each other, under the experienced tutelage of Ruth Lederman again. We would stand in huddles of six or so and in turn tell someone why we thought he or she was so wonderful. We were pushing the limits of reserved British sensibility as far as we could go. We were on a Desert Island, there were no lawyers, accountants, politicians or edicts from Companies House. We could do whatever we wanted. We were going to invent a company that worked for us.

It was OK for those of us who had done a similar thing a year ago, but the new faces were stunned. What had they joined? A weird Moonie sect? Was all this hugging and loving and Primal Screaming and 'Est'-like honesty and crazy inventing really necessary?

I thought so, because the type of company we were going to invent would have total involvement and empowerment. We had seen the immediate beneficial effects of us humans interrelating and we knew we could unlock in all of us some deep-seated honest values that would join us together as an irrepressible force.

We talked of going back to the idea of a craftsmen's guild. A community that was creatively driven. A collective whereby people felt they had real ownership to direct themselves and find time and respect for personal exploration.

The ideas we generated were fabulous. We would all buy houses in the same street and live together like an artists' commune. The office would be a laboratory for experiments funded by just a handful of select clients. We would only have a client for a year to demonstrate that we could truly affect their business very quickly.

We wanted to be proud of our company, because so much of ourselves was going to be in it. Therefore we wanted to produce work we would be proud of. So much of advertising is thoughtless junk. We didn't want 'Produced Thoughtless Junk' on our headstones. We were determined there and then to produce work that meant something, something that had real effect and something that people would enjoy and talk about.

We also wanted to right the wrongs of business. We wanted everyone to be able to enjoy work without fear of coercion or the threat of being fired for speaking out of turn.

We agreed that we would audit future clients to make sure they were not needlessly careless in the environmental field, or flagrantly flaunting human rights.

We wanted to take forward the idea of the 'Virtual Office', which Jay had started in the USA last year. But we knew we could go further. Not only would there would be no personal offices, there would be no personal computers even. We would share everything. We saw the office as an amazing location. A place you would want to go and visit. It would be a fabulous resource for creative people to create in and have fun.

During the breaks, Bono started drawing his impressions of the perfect office layout, with big round tables and special rooms for clients set in a woodland glade and a sparkling Elysian stream of fresh water running throughout.

Almost everyone summed up in a word, what we were really trying to achieve. We wanted to be a *movement*. A movement for change. Here we were at the tail end of the 20th century and almost everything about our lives at work resembled 19th-century attitudes.

Yes, St. Luke's would be a movement. It made sense to us. We knew it would be seen as laughable by others. That just made us want to do it even more.

From that moment St. Luke's was being created and I was very aware that whatever we invented it would be at its most fragile when we started to introduce conventional ideas. Everybody had been given the opportunity to move to a very different type of company and no one would tolerate any idea that looked as if it came from the past.

This was going to be a company that truly belonged to Lyn Ellis, the accounts clerk, George Porteous the graduate trainee, Clare Nash the Body Shop Account Director, Smudger, Tessa, Rachael and everyone who put a piece of themselves into it that day.

On his return from Pune, a week later, David was charged with the responsibility to 'wire together' all the ideas and make sense of everyone's wish list, however crazy they might be. He knew that everyone wanted an open, inclusive, creative company, but all the models on offer from our lawyers and accountants were conventional, hierarchical and uninspiring. David produced a plan that made sense from a business perspective and was true to many of the ideals of the individuals, but it failed to address the risk-taking spirit and real personal values of the company.

Everyone hated it and threw it out.

David gathered everyone together and voiced the issue. 'I've learned a very early lesson in consensus management,' he confessed. 'I realise that you'll get personally very, very upset if something you want has been sidelined, for whatever reason. My big mistake was trying to sort out in a small group how the company should be organised when everyone should have been involved. It was obvious, but it's taken me some time to realise it.'

What had happened was that everyone had become truly empowered. Everyone had been given a say. And unless it was just some management trick, or gizmo, everyone's say had to be made important.

Now there were 35 Managing Directors. At this stage, I was unsure of what had been created.

The following Wednesday I interviewed someone who was billed to me as 'the best Financial Director in ad land'. It may have been just me, but I found him singularly uninspiring. The more we all moved together to create something very special, the more I worried about not finding a suitable person.

'Got your finance man yet?' Roger would ask, each time I met him.

'Not yet,' I would reply.

'Better hurry up.'

⑫ From Lucky Pigs To St. Luke's

We began to search in earnest for a property to move into. We thought about trying to buy somewhere. We thought about the row of terrace houses (seriously). We covered every option and looked in almost every part of London.

It was, in theory, a good time to be looking. Rents had plummeted since we had moved into Jay's spectacular office in 1990. But all we found were conventional squared-off glass and brick rectangles. It seemed hopeless.

I was beginning to worry, when I was taken to visit some offices above Hennes on Oxford Circus. From a financial perspective, the deal on the premises looked wonderful, almost too good to be true, and while it wasn't exactly what we were looking for (it was on two floors and we really wanted one big space), I liked the way it overlooked the busy commercial centre of London with its huge advertising hoardings and throngs of shoppers every day of the week.

Rachael Plant, promoted from secretary to Office Manager, gave it a good looking over.

'It's OK,' she said.

Tessa Wire, whose passion for the company extended into every facet of our daily lives, from internal systems to office parties, gave it the once over.

'It's all right,' she said.

Smudger went for a recce. He took Johnners.

'Location's great,' Johnners said.

'You're sure about a ten-year lease?' asked Smudger.

I took that as a mandate to start negotiations and booked a meeting with the agent for early June. It was a relief to have found somewhere.

In mid-May I flew to New York to meet with our Nickelodeon client, Geraldine (Gerry) Laybourne, and to take the opportunity to meet with Fred again. Gerry was a great person to meet at this time. Actually she's a great person to meet at any time. She is one of the few people at the top of corporate America who knows how to take risks and, commendably now, has a seat right at top of the Disney empire.

'When you say the scary things,' she said, 'I get excited. When you descend into all that legal guff I get bored. What are you going to do, call it The Law Firm?' She had Jay's urgency for innovation but with the playfulness of a naughty child. I thought she was just what I needed before a meeting with Fred.

But Fred was in a fabulous mood. Many of the minor concessions that he had mowed down earlier, he gave in to. He listened as I talked about our awayday. He was genuinely fascinated.

'This company you guys vant to create. It sounds fabulous. It sounds like Utopia.'

On the plane back I thought about Gerry's question. What are we going to call it? It had a pet name – ONC (Our New Company) – and everyone was getting too comfortably used to that. The issue became increasingly more important.

We couldn't call it after ourselves, in time-honoured advertising fashion; there were simply too many of us. Names started to get thrown into the ring. United Advertising Artists was favourite for a while, then it was dropped – it was too much like United Artists. Other names at the time were The Federation of Creative Minds, Now, House, Panoptican, and Chapter 2.

We were getting nowhere with names, we had hundreds. None seemed right. In a fit of desperation one hot afternoon in June, in a claustrophic editing studio in Soho, I said, 'Right, the first name I see as I open this magazine is what we'll call the company.'

A headline at the top of the page ran:

Lucky Pigs Survive Transit To France

Perfect. Lucky Pigs we were.

Well, until August.

The headhunters trying to find us The Financial Director of The Decade despaired and insisted there was no one left to interview. 'Well, there is someone. But we don't think he's right really. He hasn't got an advertising background.' My ears pricked up. Bearing in mind that everyone they thought was good was bad, maybe someone they thought was wrong might be right.

Neil Thomson was everything you would expect an accountant to be. Greying hair, bespectacled, nervy with an unbelievably boring suit. And Scottish. As he walked with me through the agency I could feel people eyeing him up. And I knew what they were thinking: 'He's not like us at all!'

As the interview progressed Neil revealed more of himself, slowly and surely. He had an MBA, he had been involved in a buyout, he believed in honesty and fairness. David and I fired questions at him relentlessly for over an hour. He took each one as it came and calmly answered, adding just the right amount of financial detail to dazzle us, but not enough to make us look stupid. He was an unexpected find – highly qualified, experienced in boardroom battles, and wholly trustworthy. He was just what we were looking for.

Neil joined us in mid-June, and although we didn't realise it at the time, we had hired the most significant weapon in our armoury. As the six-month purdah drew to a close, Fred opened his doors to serried ranks of Omnicom lawyers and accountants, schooled in the art of finessing the finest detail to their advantage.

Neil was to outwit them all.

June, July and August were not fun. Having to keep quiet about our deal with Omnicom for so long sent out confusing messages into the marketplace. Our friends and allies began to doubt we had a deal and the press were getting bored with 'wait and see' every time they asked what we were doing. There was even time for a holiday, such was the annoyingly relaxed mood that summer. I called Fred whenever I had the tiniest reason to do so. I asked him whether things were going according to plan his end. 'Don't vorry,' he would laugh back. 'I promise, zee minute zee SEC gives us zee go ahead you can do the deal vith us.' 'Yes, but when?'

'Soon, soon. Go on vacation.'

'I've been on vacation!'

The summer months gave Neil and Roger time to make sure that every single element of the deal went smoothly, that we would benefit wherever and whenever we could. We rehearsed the final stages of the deal time and time again until we were word perfect. It was also a good time to plan out the new office. Rachael, Tessa and Smudger had been there many times since they first saw it. Something was telling them it wasn't right, and I seemed to be in constant negotiation with the agent over a deal that was getting more complicated than the one we were doing with Omnicom.

Sally was working out her IT requirements and Clare Nash was sizing it up for aesthetics. She walked about for weeks with rolled-up floor plans and costings for various project rooms for our clients. These would be special rooms for our clients, which would house all the creative thinking and work we were doing for them in an environment designed to stimulate and focus on that client's business. It turned the tables on conventional office space, because we wouldn't have any offices ourselves at all. We liked this idea; it was a step in the right direction for a service company to take. It showed we cared for their business and revolved our working routine around them, and not us.

Sadly we parted company with First Direct that summer, which caused us to make one of our earliest group decisions about how we would be affected by the peaks and troughs of business. The financial picture was much gloomier without First Direct and any normal company would have made some instant dismissals. This just wasn't an option for us. You see, we felt we were all in this together. Our attitude was that it would have to be a much greater calamity than a drop in income to start losing people. We were like sailors on a voyage of discovery. We had nearly been completely killed off only months earlier; the First Direct decision was a mere squall. We were determined to carry on with our quest for the perfect company regardless. If necessary, we said, we would all take a pay cut to keep everyone together.

The realities of business and the desire to be accountable with a high standard of creativity led Naresh and John Grant to develop a position for the agency as 'experts in brand turnaround'. They believed that we should only attract those clients that were in real trouble and, like a hospital, we would repair them, and put them back on the road.

It was a risky strategy. So we liked it, of course.

By early August the thrill of calling ourselves Lucky Pigs had worn off.

We liked it, but we realised we weren't being nearly as strategic as we could. We had a wonderful opportunity to create a brand from scratch and were just toying with an essential ingredient – the name. We wrote a brief for a name and logo device and handed it to Dave and Naresh.

Two weeks later, Bono nonchalantly called me over. 'Cracked it. Mediaeval trades and guilds called themselves after Saints. They found a Saint that fitted the task. I think we should be called St. Luke's.'

I panicked. Had we gone from the sublime to the ridiculous. An advertising agency named after a Saint? But I'll be honest. By that stage we had taken so many risks that the last thing I wanted to do was make an unadventurous decision about the name.

'Its brilliant,' I said.

St. Luke turned out to be an inspired choice. He was the patron Saint of creative people and doctors, and since we used our creativity commercially to cure sales or image problems, there was a logic that struck dumb even the most cynical observers. He is also credited with bringing in iconography as a means of communication and is often represented in Renaissance paintings holding a pen in his hand.

There is no religious connotation to the name beyond the fact that St. Luke was a disciple. Many have looked for one, not least because my father is a (now retired) vicar and our ethos has a spiritual side. St. Luke is, like St. Michael, or even St. Ivel, a suitable brand name and we associated ourselves with him as freely as those schools and hospitals who have long since lost their religious links.

Julian Vizard (who had designed the Conservative Party torch logo many years earlier) was charged with designing a logo and he worked furiously with Robbie Sparks to get a typestyle and feel all of our own.

Fortunately, St. Luke came with a ready-made logo. In Dante's *Divine Comedy*, he is to be found in the underworld represented as an ox with wings. (If you visit St. Mark's Square in Venice, you'll see that St. Mark too is depicted as a winged animal – in his case a lion with wings.)

Julian set about creating a winged ox logo. It was fabulous. Dante aside, we saw in it a substantial image and if you wanted you could diagnose it as emblematic of what we felt we stood for – a strong, honest animal with the ability to soar to great heights.

And so the company was christened. Our hesitancy over the name diminished fast as one by one we revealed the new-look company to our clients.

I learned two big lessons as we developed the name and logo. I now know that the braver you are with your creative statement, the more energy and resonance it will have in the marketplace. I also know that we applied to ourselves the medicine that we so often dish out to our clients. 'Go on,' we say, 'it's a risk, but trust us.' In so doing, we began to understand what it really is like to create a brand from scratch and launch, rather than just talk about it, or read about it in books. It's made dealing with our clients a little more honest.

Stefano blushed when I told him the name. 'You're joking,' he said. 'St. Luke's. You're joking.'

'St. Luke's?' said Fred. 'Different. Catchy.'

The name wasn't to be the only thing that astounded the market.

As the summer drew to a close Fred confirmed that the SEC was going to pass the deal on 31 August. 'What time?' I asked. I was joking. 'Ten o'clock in the morning,' said Fred. He wasn't. We had almost everything in place, except, possibly, the hardest thing of all.

We had agreed to buy this company for £1. Fine. Then we would pay a percentage of our income as a royalty payment to Omnicom. The royalty scheme would last seven years, or until we paid them a stop-dead sum – £1.2 million, less what we'd paid in royalties. So far, so good.

But who was going to own this company? After all, someone had to.

David and I had talked in the past of placing the whole thing in trust, so that no one would own it, thus removing what we felt was a potentially evil force in business – the master/servant relationship. We had also talked about creating a business that would live beyond us. It was an essentially uncreative act to grow a company only to demolish it by merger or acquisition. And anyway, wouldn't we be just like Chiat/Day or Omnicom if we had at the back of our minds the potential sale of the company?

Lewis Silken and our accountants, Willott Kingston Smith, were urging us to create a standard Limited Company, with a conventional board and shares distributed judiciously to those who 'mattered'. They had a strong case. It was a model that had been tried and tested for generations. There was no point, they would say, just discarding things because they were conventional. Their model was the most obvious and the most sensible. It was also the most reasonable, they felt. It was fair, for example, that those who had been there the longest and worked the hardest (me, David, Naresh, Bono, for example) should have a larger stake in the company. If a Limited Company wasn't right, then, they suggested, the only other route was a Partnership.

But we were all uncomfortable with these options. And all for slightly different reasons. Dave and Naresh were keen to create the perfect creative collective that was not overburdened with management and which had a democratic share scheme which gave the maximum flexibility internally. David was searching for an even more radical solution which gave ownership to no one and turned the company into, for example, a charity.

I was searching for something that gave fair shares to all, maximised personal responsibility and engendered a real sense of ownership. No other subject stretched the relationships we had all formed as far as this one did. There were tortuous discussions which went round and round in circles, often taking us deep into the night. Exhausted and infuriated by the debate and worn out by Omnicom's insistence on silence until the deal would officially get done, things got fractious and I know that it was now, in the last few yards of the race, that some were ready to jump ship, if only to find themselves some quiet from the storm. (John Crowley left at this stage, convinced, against strenuous arguments to the opposite, that his New Media department would be deemed a luxury in the new company. And a senior planner, alarmed at the pace of the rate of change, the hundreds of new ideas we were throwing into the ring and the prospect of working in a virtual office with no set desk, started to search for a more secure job in a less experimental environment.)

When things went badly, and this still holds true today, it was because we were not thinking positively and creatively. I believe every problem can be solved by forcing yourself out of the negative, defensive cycle we all find ourselves in, and getting into a positive creative cycle where every obstacle becomes a signpost to a better way of doing something.

But we were dog tired, and the negative cycle prevailed.

We formed a small group to devise a way to distribute the shares to everyone in proportion to their worth. But we found it very difficult to sort out why one person should be worth more than another. There were fierce arguments about this issue of worth. Did, for example, the lucky chance of being in a senior position at this moment in time make you worth more than someone who had not yet proven themselves?

The lawyers and accountants were getting nervous. We were all getting fractious. It looked as if the unimaginable was about to happen. Six months after our glorious revolt, and with 100 meetings with lawyers, Omnicom and accountants under our belts, God knows how many air miles chewed up in trips to Madison Avenue, and on the eve of being handed over the company we had given blood, sweat and tears for, we were going to be unable to accept it, because we had no idea how we were going to own it.

It felt like we were all about to commit mass suicide together.

Neil, new to the team and new to the spirit of open debate, took himself off to research every kind of unusual company that this and other countries had thrown up over the years. Day after day, deep in the heart of the London Business School, he pored over cases of novel entrepreneurial set-ups. He felt obliged to find a solution and was concerned over the deepening rifts that began to appear.

After a few days a quirky employee scheme began to appear over and over again. It was called an ESOT. It was rarely used. Neil could find only six that had ever been established in the UK and it had been passed over by successive governments in the various reviews that took place of companies and ownership. It was considered too insignificant. The ESOT was an Employee Share Ownership Trust, and the reason it was rarely used was that it required every *single employee to be a shareholder.*

He began to research it in more detail, but it was difficult to find any real information. It seemed to give Directors less power over the allocation of shares and certainly allowed for a much wider participation and governance in the company than any normal self-respecting business leader would contemplate.

Although Neil did not understand its full ramifications, he knew he was onto something, because, from what little he could discover, it seemed to answer everyone's brief. It truly empowered the employees by making them owners and it truly negated the need for owner/bosses. It seemed to suggest the creation of a trust which had the right kind of ring to it. And most importantly, although it was on the statute books, no one, bar the odd bus company in the north of England and private coalmine in Wales, seemed to utilise it. It was highly unconventional.

Neil phoned Lewis Silken from the LBS to ask them to find out more, then raced back to the agency and immediately convened a group of people.

Around the table were myself and David, Dave and Naresh, Charlotte, John Grant, Sarah Sanderson, Tessa, Smudger and a handful of others.

'I think I've found what we've been looking for.' We were transfixed. Slowly Neil unveiled this rare entity, the ESOT, and the more he spoke the more we all got excited.

It was early evening, and the overwhelming sense of relief ran like a contagion through the company. Good old Neil. He had saved the day.

At six that evening Andrew Johnson, Roger Alexander's number two, rang Neil. 'Oh dear, Neil. You're not going to like this.'

'What?'

'ESOTs don't exist.'

Neil was silent.

Johnson persisted. 'They must have weeded it out of the books ages ago. I'm sorry. We've treble-checked. You've discovered a redundant idea.'

How do you think we felt?

We all limped home. It was late August. Omnicom was going to sell to us in a matter of days and no one had the stamina to fight their personal corners any more. We were back to square one. And all of us had the same attitude. Unless this company was going to be extraordinary, it was not worth doing at all.

Andrew Johnson, upset at being the bearer of bad news, delved back into the books himself. Every hour now seemed to count.

As the days to the SEC decision rolled by, more lawyers from the USA began to emerge. Neil and Roger were ready for them. They were going to debate the small print every hour of every day. We debated it. The battle may have been won back in February, but it was in these last final days that we won the war. If Omnicom raised two queries, we raised three. It became clear that we were winning every minor point.

Then Andrew Johnson phoned again. 'Found it,' he said. 'ESOTs aren't ESOTs any more. They're QUESTS. The name has changed. They are now Qualifying Employee Share Ownership Trusts. And they're perfect for you.'

It was downhill all the way. Well almost.

It was agreed that the shares would be handed out equally to everyone, but that because I was ten years older and had put in so much I was to take a ten per cent stake, which I would only be able to realise in ten years' time. It was both a commitment to a new and fragile company and it was a recognition of the role I had played.

It was announced to the company and to my utter amazement there was no cheering. Hang on. Wasn't this the most extraordinary thing we had done? Created a company of co-owners, each with an equal stake? Had we forgotten how amazing we were? Were we getting blasé?

'None of that,' Smudger told me later. 'You've forgotten that we've all been through this together. It's what we expected. We were all wondering what took you so long.'

For the second time that year, the power of an emancipated, empowered, envisioned group had been temporarily forgotten. It was another harsh lesson. We were not about to create Utopia, we were just changing yesterday's known management problems for tomorrow's unknown ones. We were like blind people carefully feeling the way, and often tripping over.

A year later, I changed my arrangement and gave up the ten per cent deal, but not without much heart searching and personal reflection with Amanda, my wife. It was wrong of me to be seen as an exception. 'All for one and one for all' meant total fairness and equality. But equally I learned something else – in fact, The New Rules kept hitting me hard in the face – that unless you are prepared to give up something valuable you will never be able to truly change at all, because you'll be forever in the control of the things you can't give up.

The fact that the senior managers of an advertising agency held the same share as the receptionist caused most raised eyebrows. And I cannot say that at times I did not descend into self-doubt. In fact, I thought about it a lot. Everyone, Omnicom, Jay, our lawyers, accountants, my friends in the industry, friends outside the industry and family, were to challenge me on my motives. Many still do. At the end of the day I just knew that if you created something different it would have to feel very different, otherwise it would be just cosmetic. And that kind of dishonesty is the dishonesty that we had set out to destroy.

I never owned the company in the first place, neither did David, nor Naresh, nor Bono. Taking a disproportionate share would have been theft of the sweat equity of everyone else. And this sweat equity was the very thing I was keen to unite because it was the honest contribution of the Human Capital in the workplace. It was the key to our specialness and our difference.

I would go further. When you are exhorting people to co-operate with each other and to trust each other, to impose an unequal system (as is most commonly done) is completely contradictory.

But I'm no angel. I would love to be rich. Who wouldn't? As David Abraham said to me once, 'I can't find a way of making myself rich without using other people, which I am not prepared to do.' A sentiment that lies at the heart of the St. Luke's ideal.

I'm not poor though. No one at St. Luke's is. The salaries we pay ourselves are way over what most people would earn. In fact our lowest salary is higher than the *average* national wage.

We have forced ourselves to take a different outlook on entrepreneurial ownership and constitutionally removed greed from the business. That, I can tell you, is our most liberating force.

⑬ We Are Sailing In A Strange Ship

At 10.00 a.m. on 31 August Omnicom bought Chiat/Day. At 10.01 we triggered the buy out. We were back in business and the adrenalin surged back into every corner of the company. All the hard work of the last seven months was now going to mean something. All our detractors would have to eat their words. This wasn't just going to be a new type of advertising agency, this was going to be a different sort of company altogether.

We didn't rush into things. Although the deal was assured, it wasn't signed and there were still a few hurdles to get over before we were 100 per cent satisfied with the paperwork. We gave ourselves September to brief all our clients, suppliers and stakeholders (lawyers, accountants, close advisers, headhunters, *Campaign* magazine) and to finalise what we needed in the new office to deliver the working lifestyle we wanted.

Rachael spent weeks reviewing various phone systems that would give us the flexibility to move from location to location in the office. She struck a deal with Erickson who promised delivery of their latest internal mobile which was incredibly light and had all the features of the fixed phones we were used to.

David presented to the agency a strategic plan of how we would be positioned and what we would need to do to achieve our goals. The presentation was called 'The World Does Not Need Another Advertising Agency' and it passionately made the point that unless we strove for fundamental difference, we would be eaten up by bigger, more established agencies and – down the line – by newer, more interesting ones. By the end of the month he was able to begin communicating to the outside world that we were a new name, with a new structure.

Sally and Smudger pored over layouts and spent hours working out in fine detail how the client rooms would work and how it would affect the computers we had.

When we were totally ready, we went live.

Campaign released the news first as was fitting for the magazine which had been so close to us throughout the eight-month ordeal:

Chiat/Day Rechristened as St. Luke's

The article faithfully recorded our new positioning and began to hint at some of the new ideas we wanted to deploy.

The national press picked up on it positively and enthusiastically. The *Guardian* was first off the mark:

Staff Buy Advertising Agency and Plan to Replace Red-Rimmed Glasses with Beatific Vision of Future

The *Sunday Times*, The *Independent* and others followed suit.

The trade press picked up on our desire to be seen as a 'brand turn-around company.'

Saint's Alive! Luke's Becomes a Business Saviour

wrote *Marketing*, the trade paper for our clients in the marketing community.

The following week *Campaign* followed up with an in-depth article. 'Is the co-operative structure right for agencies?' Industry observers were intrigued and a little wary. 'Democracy is laudable,' commented Rupert Howell of Howell Henry Chaldecott Lury, 'but I'm not sure that communism is.'

On 18 October, St. Luke's Day (yes, it just fell that way), we held an official launch party for all the employees/shareholders and family. It was to be the first and certainly the most modest of an annual ritual. It was a fitting occasion for a speech. We had fought, thought, designed, desired and cried our way to an extraordinary moment. Seven months earlier, in the same spot, I had been looking at a sea of faces doomed to redundancy. That evening, I stared at revolutionaries in the world's first advertising agency, possibly company, *actually* owned by all its employees and all the employees who were yet to come.

It was a magnificent achievement by everybody. We lost only a couple on the way – John Crowley and John Robson (the latter left in December to join Frank Lowe's agency). Apart from them, as I write, nearly three years later, no one has left St. Luke's since to join another advertising agency. Two have become mothers (Sally has two children and lives in Hong Kong), two have travelled the world and three have pursued new careers as a teacher, deep-sea diver and music-shop manager.

We had stuck together with a common purpose and were in a position to challenge every business convention and scale any new creative heights we wished.

Towards the end of September Rachael had cornered me.

'Right,' she said, 'practically everyone's seen the Oxford Street offices.'

'Great,' I said, 'I think we're close to signing up.'

'Don't. We hate them.'

I called this episode 'The Silent Protest'. I should have got the message earlier, but I was so wrapped up in launching the concept of the company and finalising everything with Omnicom.

The shareholders did not like the office, mainly because it had that kind of 'instant office' feel you see everywhere in new developments. OK, Oxford Street was great for shopping, but at the end of the day it was all cream walls and cable conduiting. It was soulless. It would have sentenced us to Office Life. We wanted Human Life to flourish.

We were back to square one again and it wasn't until the beginning of October that we found something interesting, not a stone's throw from the hotel where we dreamt our vision, seven months earlier. It was a quirky red-brick building just south of Euston railway station, in Bloomsbury. It had been occupied over the years by all sorts of concerns. Originally a toffee factory, it was used by the SAS in the War and by London's top design company, Wolff Olins, in the 80s. It had been empty for months and its present owners were desperate to get someone in to pay the rent.

Neil, fuelled by his combat training in Omnicom deal-making, pounced.

This time I made no mistake. I went immediately with Rachael, Tessa, Smudger and Clare.

'Lousy for shopping,' said Clare.

'Dangerous at night. I can see King's Cross,' said Rachael.

'Hardly Covent Garden,' said Smudger.

Perfect they concluded.

Neil secured a rent a third of what we were paying in our current place and a spectacular rent-free period. The landlords really were desperate to get a tenant in. We had a matter of only weeks to move in and took the rather unusual decision to recycle most of our existing office. Computer by computer, cupboard by cupboard, table by table we dismantled Jay's amazing office and reassembled it in our new space, with a new purpose and to a totally different specification.

Paul Johnson, the last man operational in the old building was reduced to working on a packing crate.

We had ripped up the past, and were building the future.

I am interrupting the story to tell you about the business thinking behind St. Luke's. When you pick up the story again (on page 187) you'll see what happened to us as we put this thinking into practice.

PART TWO

Change The Way You Work

⑭ 21st-Century Business

believe work today could be much more liberating and fun.

But for many it isn't. (In fact, of all the EC countries, the UK has the highest rate of dissatisfied workers.) Why?

Well, we might ask ourselves whether it was ever *meant* to be liberating and fun. If you consider what it has been like for everyone but the super-rich, it looks like a litany of hard labour.

I split the development of work into four phases. I'm not an historian, but from a general human perspective these splits make sense to me.

Agrarian:	**pre-1700**
Industrial:	**1700–1939**
Communication:	**1940–2000**
Creative:	**now (and possibly for ever)**

Whilst hard labour and rigid regimes might typify the first three ages, the fourth, Creative, benefits from free-thinking, flexibility, imagination and enjoyment.

Let me explain.

Agrarian Age

For the ordinary person, life before the invention of the steam engine in 1750 may have been simpler (no rush hours, no ticking wrist watches, no GATT trade agreements, no giant agro-chemical corporations offering worrisome genetically engineered food) but then life itself was harder (rampant disease, few human rights, no equal opportunities, poor sanitation and conspicuous heinous crime). Work and life were one and the same thing and you probably lived very near, if not above, the place where you toiled every day for as long as it was light. You were governed by daylight hours and you ate what you grew or what you could easily barter.

Today, very few of us anywhere in the world work in this way, yet the agrarian life evocatively holds an image of a more sublime existence. When Rachel Carson published *Silent Spring* in 1962 and told a 'fable of tomorrow' about how our environment was being secretly, subtly and irrevocably poisoned, she kick-started a whole generation into understanding that we had a responsibility to nature. She invented the modern concept of Environmentalism and in the process caused many to weigh up the material benefits of 'The Rat Race' versus the modest benefits of living simply and honestly from the land.

The incredibly successful 70s BBC TV series, *The Good Life*, touched the right nerve as it portrayed a businessman, Tom, who with his wife, Barbara, jacks it all in and creates a sustainable economy out of what their plot in Suburbia could provide. Tom and Barbara's neighbours, Margo and Jerry, are the perfect dramatic counterpart – materially driven, image conscious, schooled in oneupmanship, fearful of change and nestled comfortably in the 'gin and Jaguar set'.

This desire 'to get away from it all' visits all cultures which raise business to a high and intense art form. Even in ancient Rome, which in its heyday was a dense, noisy, smelly, dangerous cosmopolitan city, where business and politics went hand in hand, and factions and political shenanigans decided your fate, the poet Horace yearned for a simpler life in the countryside.

But Horace noted something many of us feel today. Either/ors are not satisfactory. Running away to the peace and quiet of the countryside to avoid the stress of urban life creates a yearning for the buzz of the town. The congestion and frenetic pace of the city makes us crave the bucolic charms of the rural life. His perfect solution was to have all the benefits of the countryside at hand in the city – *rus in urbe*. To have that luxury today, you would need about £10 million to buy that fabulous residence off Cheyne Walk in Chelsea, in the heart of London, which has an acre of gardens.

Harking back to life in the pre-Industrial Age is a process of cherry-picking some customs and rituals that add value to what we do today. It's a permanent opportunity to say, 'This is crazy, life was so much simpler then.'

I agree. Everyone at St. Luke's agrees that much of modern work is crazy. We would also agree that we can learn a great deal from the way things were done in the past. We talk about the Mediaeval Hall as a model for an office layout. We refer to old Trades and Guilds as examples of craftsmen working together co-operatively and looking after each other. But, importantly, you will see that these notions come about from a hankering for a better future rather than a desire to wallow in the past.

Industrial Age

In 1709 Abraham Darby introduced coke smelting to his ironworks at Coalbrooke in Shropshire and unwittingly launched the Industrial Revolution. Innovation followed thick and fast: the first workable steam-powered engine was developed by Thomas Newcomen in 1712; the seed drill by Jethro Tull in 1730 (which freed hard dirty labour from the fields); and the Spinning Jenny was invented by James Hargreaves in 1763. With the development of the canal system, all these inventions and more created a fundamental change in the nature of work. In 1771 Richard Arkwright established the first cotton-spinning factory and concepts like 'division of labour', 'mechanisation' and 'mass production' were born.

Moreover, as a consequence of the wars England was fighting against Louis XV, the Bank of England and the National Debt were established. These innovations were bitterly contested at the time, but they were the main reasons why the UK was able to evolve from being a comparatively poor agricultural country to the world leader in industry and to being the principal loan market of the world.

Very simply, it was the introduction of bank credit that enabled the steam engine and the Spinning Jenny to become the extraordinarily successful new products they were.

So much of office life still owes its derivation to these days. Small businesses became business empires in the Industrial Age and the vocabulary of business today, with its militaristic, strategy and supply connotations, was born and bred in this age. Strategy, rank, takeover, campaign planning, command and control, divisions, operations, are all used in a modern business context.

City life as we know it developed from this era, as banking and trade concentrated the nation's skill sets and propelled industry onto an international stage.

In 1821, London's population reached a million people. A generation later, in 1888, it was a staggering five million. At the same time, across the water, New York was to become the first American city of over a million people.

Commuting, traffic jams, traffic systems, rates, offices have all been with us for over a hundred years.

You've got to challenge that, haven't you? So much of the infrastructure we live with is from the past, but so much of what we can actually do would be totally alien to the likes of, say, Cornelius Vanderbilt and John Jacob Astor, who became amongst the first and certainly the most prominent millionaire businessmen of the Industrial Age, back in the 1840s.

The Industrial Revolution is not a model blueprint for the way businesses today can be organised and run. Just to write that comment is ludicrous, but that's the way so much commercial interaction is done.

Communication Age

Uncomfortably, life in the post-Industrial Age has been bedevilled by a number of names. The problem is, we know we have progressed, it's just that we are not sure what we have progressed to. For some it's the Technological Revolution, for others the Information Age. I opt for the Communication Age, because the direct forerunners of present-day analogue and digital technology began to appear around 1940 and, as a term, it can encompass the plethora of developments from television, telephony and computer that have so characterised the last 60 years. Post-War life can be clearly differentiated from the decades that preceded it. We changed morally, culturally, militarily, socially and technologically. It's a good starting point to demonstrate the differences between life prior to the Second World War and life in the 50s, 60s, 70s and 80s.

If I'm honest, the term 'communications' does not satisfactorily explain the scientific advances since the War (military, medical and man on the moon, for example), but it does explain the cultural effect all these developments have had, which I believe have become more significant than the advances themselves.

Millions saw the bomb dropped on Hiroshima and baby boomers like me dreamt of the ghastly vision of a mushroom cloud throughout most of the 60s, 70s and 80s. The SALT accord in Vienna, signed by Carter and Brezhnev, certainly caused a sigh of relief, but it was the televised START negotiations between Reagan and Gorbachev in 1986 and 1987 that finally stopped the apocalyptic nightmares.

Hearing of the first heart transplant by Dr Christiaan Barnard in 1967 caused amazement, but seeing the 54-year-old patient live for 18 whole days seemed, curiously, more amazing still.

If I were to list the enduring memories of my life, being allowed by my father to stay up into the early hours of the morning to watch Neil Armstrong land on the moon will rank amongst the highest. It was so exciting. We were literally watching a man-walk-on-the-moon. How he did it, or even why, were secondary issues.

Although telephones have been around since 1876 and televisions since 1928, it was this era which has been most clearly defined by them. Marshall McLuhan's prognosis that electronic media would become 'media extensions of man' has come totally true.

Today we have seen that the major event of 1997 was not so much the sad fact of the death of Diana, Princess of Wales, but the mass, global mourning that immediately followed it that revealed a homogeneity in the reason why, and manner in which everyone grieved so much. The world went to Diana's funeral and even had a hand in its organisation.

We have never been more connected to each other. Computers don't compute, they commune. Televisions talk to us and now can respond to our requests via interactive digital technology.

You'll find all three of these technologies – telephone, television and computer – in the workplace. But how much have they actually changed work life? Isn't it true that telephones, through the development of mobile technology, are just with us more (every businessman on my train seems to have one)? That televisions – if you have one in the workplace at all – just tell us more (CNN, CNBC, Ceefax, Teletext, Bloomberg TV, SKY News *et al.*)? That computers have just taken the drudgery out of work (laborious typing, complex financial modelling, lengthy trading procedures). These developments have fundamentally changed the way we communicate, but have they fundamentally changed the way we work? I think not.

Most working routines remain belligerently unmoved by these amazing technological resources, so that this era is different from the previous two in that it sees us as people changing, but the same as the previous two in that we as workers still remain rooted in the past.

The hunters, fishers and farmers of neolithic times became, via the invention of agriculture, an agrarian civilisation. The agrarian world was heaved forward into the Industrial Age by inventions of less than a century ago. Televisions, telephones and computers have not, to the same extent, substantially changed the way we work, although they have completely changed the way we see and interact with the world.

Big international firms have recourse to expensive, stage-managed video link-ups, and there are occasional examples of teleworking. But they are the exception rather than the rule.

In fact almost every facet of modern work echoes the past.

Most offices that are built resemble Industrial Age headquarters. They house Industrial Age hierarchies (a nice suite of offices for the boss, corner offices for the directors and who cares for the rest). Look at Canary Wharf in London's Docklands or the towering commercial blocks in Hong Kong: why build something in our times that emulates a 1920s New York skyscraper? There is hope to be found in the Pudong New Area in Shanghai, China, and in the Putrajaya development in Malaysia, both of which take on and incorporate the exciting possibilities of technology from an *a priori* basis (although I reserve judgement until they are completed since I saw a poster for the Pudong New Area featuring (wait for it) a skyscraper that looked remarkably like the Chrysler building in New York!).

Office hierarchies and careers resemble that of H. G. Wells's Port Burdock Drapery Bazaar, where Mr Polly, the 40-something with a mid-life crisis, worked for six years. Mr Polly 'spent most of the time inattentive to business, in a sort of uncomfortable happiness'. Besieged by office politics and tedious routine, and saddened by seeing friends dismissed, I can't help read it and think that little has changed for middle management in the last 100 years.

Our story of St. Luke's ended at the point we moved office. When we opened our new office, we opened much more than a simple redesign or clever computer networking system. We had spent months, years in some cases, looking at what was important and influential in our lives today and constructed a working environment every bit as unique as the ownership structure we had put in place.

We borrowed learning from agrarian societal structures and at the same time from any and every new organisational model we could find, from Japan to Silicon Valley, Russia, China and bourgeois Paris. We reviewed customer relationships throwing out the militaristic conventions of Industrial Age businesses, which insist on territorial rights and confrontation. We embraced the technology of today to change the very routines and patterns of working life.

Creative Age

Whilst for many, understanding the demands of the Communication Age is complex (and expensive) enough, I believe our changes have delivered us into a different, newer age. It's an age The Nomura Institute in Japan and contemporary writers such as John Kao would classify as the Creative Age, not because it defines the business we, as advertising practitioners specifically, are in, but because it defines the way we can, should, all work.

The Creative Age started neatly in mid-1992 when Microsoft's market value outstripped that of General Motors. From that moment, the world's markets would begin to be less manufacturing-led and more service-led.

Not service as defined by those businesses that do not make anything (lawyers, accountants, doctors, for example), although that's obviously part of it. But service as in British Airways' motto, *'volare servare'* – 'to fly to serve'. That is to say, the concept of service which now dominates every aspect of business, whatever business you are in, and which has introduced benchmarking, a wide range of auditing and government quality standards. Even if you make rivets and ball bearings, you will be judged by service standards which include quality of manufacture, of course, but also, delivery times and flexibility of supply.

We are in a Service Economy and the most important component part of that economy is the human being, because it is humans that make or break the vital elements in the service-agreement chain.

I expect my car to be built properly – most are nowadays by law if not by competitive pressure – but if the guy who services it leaves grease on my seat, I will be furious enough and enabled enough to re-evaluate everything from the model of the car to the quality of the dealership to the overall brand.

Almost anything that is made today can be emulated. Even a brand-new car design can be stripped down, analysed, copied and mass-produced in under a year. The strength of the Industrial Age and the facilitation afforded by instant connectivity and communication can be undermined by only one thing. Human failure.

As it happens, we humans are incredible machines. Tony Buzan, a world-renowned and respected author on the brain, creativity and learning, assessed that we humans use less than one per cent of the one trillion (as in 'one million million') cells in our brains. Pyotr Anokhin, a Russian neuroanatomist, calculates that the inter-connections between these cells is 1, followed by 10.5 million kilometres of standard, 11-point, typewritten noughts. We are an untapped resource. Clearly.

When trained we can change and adapt and, as we get older, we can use experience and judgement and include it instantly into calculations which involve the very latest theories. In one second, your brain can grasp a concept that would take a mainframe Cray computer operating at 400 million calculations per second, one hundred years to complete. In fact, no other machine on earth can do this.

In *The Age Heresy*, Buzan and co-author Raymond Keene make the case that the human brain itself does not become more inefficient as we get older. In fact the brain is every bit as vital at 80 as 18 – assuming disease has not wrecked it. In this way humans can appreciate in value whilst the majority of machinery (and certainly computers) depreciate in value fast and become redundant. In the case of computers, this obsolescence occurs after only four years of life.

Humans in a service economy are our most valuable asset. Our human capital is more valuable than property, fixed assets or agreeable contracts. It is valuable not just because it affects the quality of the service prop-osition but because it can adapt, develop and enhance the service prop-osition, through inventiveness, initiative and enterprise.

For the Industrial Age magnates of the 18th, 19th and early 20th century, looking after the machinery was a priority. It had to be regularly maintained, it would not be overworked, it would be well insured and it would be given the longest possible life. Do today's business magnates do the same to their human resource? Do managers, at any level, come to that?

Across a wide spectrum humans are treated with a casualness that defies belief. I'm not just talking about the poultry producer from the Midlands who makes workers who want to go to the toilet put their name on a list and wait up to two hours to get permission to do so. These cases are rampant (as highlighted by the Trades Union Congress 'bad boss' confidential helpline which on day one received 1,771 calls from people reporting cases of exploitation and mistreatment), but there are more general cases, every day, in every workplace. Subtle sexual harassment, lack of regard for personal difficulty, poor training, deliberate suppression of good performance lest it lead to an increased wage bill, and so it goes on.

When one day I heard my friend Jeff, a car mechanic with 11 years, six-days-a-week loyal service, was made redundant (the registered letter of dismissal went to his house for his wife to read, while Jeff was at work!) and that he received the legal minimum payment (currently £220 for each year of service) for his loyalty, my anger echoed around the country as hundreds of thousands of honest workers are treated shabbily, but legally, by managers whose own poor performance has taken the company down. We've all got a story like this to tell, haven't we?

Business has failed to learn how to treat human capital properly. Yet with a little time and thought managers throughout the world can untap a creative, flexible resource that can add real value to their business.

To do this businesses must stop seeing themselves in the old industrial model, as pyramidical, bureaucratic concerns, where 'The Boss Is Always Right'. Unleashing the power of the imagination of your employees, will force you to accept that brilliance can come from any quarter, that geniuses might be of any age (I guess Mozart proved that to all musicians beyond debate!).

Creativity can provide all the solutions to the complex problems of the workplace. Creative thinking is a positive, generative force that uses imagination to power business.

At St. Luke's we decided to audit all those occasions where creativity might be finessed out of the working day.

Strangulating senior control, repetitive habit-forming routines, cynicism, greed, fear, ego – all these contrived to force out creativity onto the outer margins of business. And for us, in the creative imaginative business, that was illogical, unconstructive and unproductive.

To put it simply, and at the risk of sounding naive, I think that if Tony Buzan is right, and we do use barely one per cent of the one trillion cells in our brains, we would want to increase that to two per cent. We would also want to get the individual's cells to work together more and in so doing gain competitive advantage.

It is incredible what happens when you connect one thing to another. Kevin Kelly calls this the 'Law of Plenitude' (in his 'New Rules for a New Economy', outlined in *Wired* magazine, September 1997). He observed that 'mathematicians have proven that the sum of a network increases as the square of the number of members. In other words, as the number of nodes in a network increases arithmetically, the value of the network increases exponentially. Adding a few more members can dramatically increase the value for all members'.

This part of the book is a peek inside St. Luke's. It explains how we work. I don't want you to think I'm espousing a 'General Universal Theory Of Work', which ordains that this way of working is 'The Only Way'. All businesses are different. But what I do want to show you is what shape a business takes when you really do put humans first.

This 'peek' lets you look at our ownership structure, our organisational model, our office life, our culture, our use of technology and our output.

⑮ Ownership

You may remember in our story that whilst we were highly focused on securing our independence from Omnicom, we were almost in danger of scuppering the entire venture by not addressing the important aspect of ownership early enough.

We didn't know how to own the company, all we knew was that we didn't want to create a conventional business oligarchy, whereby the 'names on the door' or the company directors owned the majority of the shares and therefore created 'their' business. We didn't want to do this for a number of reasons:

1. It would have created an 'us and them' – bosses and employed – that ran counter to our ideas of true co-operative working. It would have simply and slavishly followed the conventions of business in the organised Industrial Age, which unnecessarily seemed retrogressive for a company established to take advantage of the 21st century.

   Bosses have acquired a non-too favourable reputation over the years, but never so bad as today. Businesses do not command public trust and the good business leaders are cast into the same barrel as those who are mercilessly exploitative, or even criminal. Seventy-five per cent of all Hollywood movies that portray business leaders portray them as evil! Being the boss has its personal rewards, but so often at the expense of others.

2. It would have been theft of the work of the entire company whose spirited and imaginative servicing of the clients caused every single client to come with us. After all, neither I nor David Abrahams, nor any of the London management owned the company in the first place, so by what law could we seize control? This notion of theft of the sweat equity of others made common sense to us, although it was at the heart of our disagreements with lawyers and accountants.

We debated whether people had the right to own something that they didn't maybe care about, or didn't maybe contribute much to. But it's a Catch 22. Employees who aren't owners don't act like owners. And people who don't act like owners shouldn't be owners.

Recognising the sweat equity of everyone forced those of us who were, conventionally, going to lose out of owning a company to realise something very important. If you can't lose something, you won't change. And the bigger or more personally important a thing you lose, the bigger the change you'll make. It was a particularly long and hard lesson for me to learn. I was adamant that we had to have a co-operative structure with everyone a shareholder. Yet, through age and, I guess, nervousness at losing control (I was 'In Charge' don't forget with a mandate and contract from Los Angeles) I took the most convincing that equal ownership was the true recognition of sweat equity because it recognised that everyone's contribution, regardless of where they were in their lives, was equally important in a company that valued humans and human imagination.

3. It would have forced us to live out our working lives with a small number enjoying increasing wealth and it would have left us in the position in a few years' time of having to work out a sale strategy. But we wanted to create a company that lived beyond us. It was decidedly uncreative, we felt, to create something and then destroy it for nothing other than personal gain.

A study by the Royal Dutch/Shell Group (not available to the public but referred to in Arie de Geus's thoughtful and gently inspiring book *The Living Company*) suggests that the average lifespan of a company is 40 years – almost half that of the expected length of human life. Others like Ellen de Rooij assess it as more like 12.5 years. Examples of companies living to extraordinary ages are very rare. There is the famous example of the Swedish paper, pulp and chemical manufacturer, Stora, which is on record as having been around for over 700 years. Or The Sumitomo Group which has been trading since 1590.

Companies seemed to be dying all around us. Companies that make the *Fortune* 500 in one year disappear the next. Or they are merged, sold off or wound down and made bankrupt, so they literally vaporise. The dying of companies makes life miserable, at some time, for all employees. If you have a lifeboat (a large amount of cash stashed quietly away would do the trick) you always know that you can escape. Here's another Catch 22. Managers manage to create a short-term (30 years?) exit plan, because they don't expect the company to stay true to them (or be around) for long; consequently companies die and prove these managers right. Companies can live a long time and be rewarding and fun and fulfilling for many generations of people; but only if you go in deep and re-jig the DNA of business. Ownership was, for us, a major part of that re-jig.

Ownership should be endemic

Every employee at St. Luke's, after they have successfully completed a six-month apprenticeship, owns the company.

The shares are distributed every year in equal proportion to everyone who has been in the company for the previous year. Ownership of the company is real ownership – you get a share certificate which tells you how many shares you have and your legal rights to ownership are registered at Companies House. All the owners are listed for all to see in the St. Luke's Annual Report. The owners are also listed on our stationery.

Ownership is at the core of St. Luke's.

We remind ourselves constantly that we own the company and talk about what owners of companies can do. Owners employ people. Well, we employ each other and we take great care to ensure that we employ the right people. After all, if we are going to give a part of the company away to someone, we must be absolutely sure that we are not diluting the company's power of creativity as we dilute the share ownership.

Everyone, whether they be a receptionist, accounts clerk or senior manager, must demonstrate that they can add value to the company beyond 'just doing their job'. The principle quality we want new people to have is 'risk-taking'. The majority of businesses are not like St. Luke's so we need the pioneering risk-takers who will keep experimenting with the idea. We believe that everyone can benefit from being an owner and that everyone will develop in the changed environment of St. Luke's. We're not recruiting the same kind of people. On the contrary, different people are more likely to stimulate different points of view. But until there are more businesses offering everyone, from Receptionist to Chairman, a slice of the pie, we are keen to employ people who are demonstrably not afraid to exercise their rights to ownership without fear of reprisal.

The rights of ownership are considerable.

Think about it. If you own a bicycle factory and you are what UK law would describe as a 'sole trader' (i.e., the business is entirely down to you) you can decide exactly how you would like your business to run and how your life can benefit.

You might decide that you would like to work seven days a week for 11 months, then take a whole month off to rest. I know a film director who does just that. Apart from the obvious exceptions (Christmas Day, Easter, etc.), he works flat out all year, weekends as well, and then takes August off. He rents a house in the South of France and de-camps there with his family. He remains resolutely uncontactable and will turn down even the biggest offers from Hollywood.

You might decide to buy another bicycle factory and create a bigger company.

You might decide to get some components made abroad, in China say, where you discover labour is cheaper but of comparable quality.

You might decide to trade internationally.

You can do whatever you want. Within the law. (I suppose you can break the law as well if you want. Who would know? Your company is entirely owned by you, you have no directors to monitor what you do, although the Trading Standards Officer might catch you out.)

Ownership is the central dynamic of business. Owners drive companies (some owners like Richard Branson drive them very dynamically). If your company is quoted on the Stock Exchange, you are responsible to your owners, your shareholders, even if you have never met them. Delivering value to shareholders is the primary responsibility of businesses floated on the Stock Exchange.

When you own something you tend to look after it. But actually few people ever own anything of significant market value until, maybe, very late in life. But we all own something of importance to us individually.

You might own your car (40 per cent of cars in the UK are not owned by their drivers but by their companies or lease-hire firms). If you do, you will probably look after it. You will check the oil and make sure there is antifreeze in the radiator. You will hold back your kids from drawing over the seats with a felt-tip pen and you will try not to get the smallest dent in your bumper. If you own your own car, you will care for your own car.

You might own a nice dinner service your parents gave you as a wedding gift. If you're like me, you won't use it all the time in case it gets damaged. You will bring it out for Christmas or birthdays or smart meal occasions when maybe the boss and his wife (or your parents) are coming round for dinner. Special, expensive items like these will be well insured by you. If you own items like these you will treat them with considerable respect.

You might own a toy. It could be a child's toy (a *Jurrassic Park*-branded roaring dinosaur) or an adult's toy (a video recorder or camera). When you play with that toy it will give you hours of delight and captivate you.

You may own something less tangible but just as valuable. Like a GCSE, a diploma or a degree. Or a driving licence, or a voting slip that recognises your age and your responsibilities. If you have something like this you will own it with pride.

Owning a company gives you all these qualities. If successful, you will own something of considerable value. You will care for it and you will respect it. It will delight and captivate you and you will speak with pride of your possession. This is an intensely high level of association with a company and it is one which brings terrific rewards.

Ownership increases loyalty

As an employer you really pay the price for a workplace that is not truly committed. Constant change in the workplace and growing competition to find suitable and stimulating work have meant that the cost of labour turnover to employers is on the increase. A December 1997 survey by The Institute of Personnel and Development (IPD) estimates that the cost of replacing staff has risen by 17 per cent from £4,140 per person in 1996 to £4,861 in 1997. The highest labour turnover rate of all occupations was sales staff. Nearly 25 per cent left their jobs in 1997 and it takes employers an average of ten weeks to fill a sales vacancy.

Sales staff. There is a prime example of people in the service sector. It demonstrates that there is a significant percentage of humans at the coalface of the service economy who have little loyalty to their companies. This lack of loyalty weakens the service proposition and makes the company itself less profitable.

Since we moved into our new premises in the toffee factory, just south of Euston and King's Cross Stations, no one has left St. Luke's to join another advertising agency. Those departures that did occur were the result of personal life changes rather than job swaps. None of them moved simply to transport and trade their skills for more money. There are tangible and significant benefits to an ownership structure that increases loyalty.

Firstly, recruitment costs are reduced. Our staff turnover percentage has fallen from 20 per cent in 1993 to less than five per cent today. That represents a one per cent increase in our income figures.

Secondly, we have reduced the number of write-offs (costs down to us for bad management of a project) from a dozen to just one a year. (In 1996 there were none.) This is because loyalty evolves a more experienced group of employees, at all levels. Experience is the ideal form of training and is a prime example of how humans can appreciate in value. This represents a two per cent increase in our income figures.

Thirdly, loyalty allows for greater retention of business. Most clients cite poor and inconsistent service as the principal reason for leaving their current advertising agency (they cite 'creativity' as the main reason why they go to their new advertising agency). Our annual client turnover rate was almost 50 per cent in 1993. Since we started as St. Luke's in 1995, we have lost only one client. The hidden cost of constantly replacing business is twofold: you are permanently pitching for new business and your human capital is almost permanently operating beyond their capacity and with low morale. If you lose a piece of business you have to win two to regain your pride. Pitching less often, costs you less. We spent over ten per cent of income in 1993 pitching for new business. We now commit less than five per cent on income streams which are over 100 per cent bigger.

We only pitch when we are fresh and only then if the business excites us. It's a decision we all took as owners and it's the kind of decision that finds its roots in our desire to treat ourselves properly at work. Pitching less often and with greater discrimination has meant we have a very high conversion rate (i.e., we win many more pitches than we lose).

Finally, loyalty strengthens the brand. There is currently no one moving amongst our competitors either providing demonstrable benefits from using any of our ideas, or speaking ill of the company. Poor word of mouth about a company can affect morale and slow down new business enquiries. New business enquiries are at an all-time high. In 1993 we received 18 unsolicited new business enquiries. In 1997 the figure trebled to 55.

Ownership increases productivity

Most jobs today require teamwork. No matter whether your firm is grouped into tight departments or works on an interdisciplinary project basis, if you can't work together cohesively, you will be inefficient. Modern work requires humans to communicate with each other. Gone are the days when cars were built in a linear fashion with the same component being introduced onto the car by the same person day in, day out. Teams of people are responsible for the build quality and jobs are changed and shared. This avoids the mistakes that come from repetition.

Computer networks assume a high degree of cross-fertilisation from one job to another, and it is felt that the successful manager is one who has assembled a good team around him.

Politicians work in teams nowadays. A Prime Minister or President will have a team of advisers. These advisers help to construct a single focus, but they also allow for wide-ranging debate and a sharing of ideas.

You might say that the essence of work is teamwork. But if you think about it, when was the last time you really worked together with others in a team? By 'really worked together', I mean worked naturally with others with an open mind and in a way that didn't seem forced, or riddled with protocol? A boss saying, 'You three, work together on this', isn't the same as three people coming together with a shared ambition to achieve something. Teamworking doesn't come naturally, I believe. You train until you drop in a team sport. You train on the job in a marriage.

You probably worked best in a team when you were a child, lost in the joys of play. In a shared make-believe world, you invented and imagined scenarios that only the two or three of you could possibly understand. Time went fast and you covered more ground than you could possibly have imagined at the outset.

The fact is, the notion of 'working together' is difficult to define. If you are told to work together, does that mean you are genuinely working together? If you don't benefit together, are you really working together?

The barriers to teamworking are subtle and innately human. They are self-perceptions like ego (should I be working with that person, I'm much more senior?), power (I need to be seen to be leading this, my review is next month), and fear (I'd better not say too much, I'm out of my depth).

But what if you own something together? What if each year you are handed out the same share as the person sitting next to you at lunch? What if you voted for the actions of the company and so had a hand in what projects you might be working on.

A team that works together for mutual benefit works the best. 'Two heads are better than one' is an adage we coyly quote from time to time. When you sit round a table of equal partners, whose *potential input* is equalised, you become hungry to hear everyone make their point. You will benefit if someone, anyone, makes a contribution that will add value to your company. At St. Luke's, we have a process called 'Get Inventive Early'. It's a brainstorming session that happens right at the beginning of a project and which involves a large number of people, many of whom will not be directly involved in the project.

Why do people not involved get involved? Because they care about any event happening in the company that might add value to their company. It's that simple.

Wired magazine coined a term I rather like. It's the opposite of what I'm talking about – it's 'Blamestorming'. Blamestorming is when half a dozen people sit around the table and spend hours analysing why a deadline was missed or a project failed, and who is to blame. Every business Blamestorms on a regular basis. They resemble kangaroo courts and are charged with a gang mentality and negative thinking.

Blamestorming is the opposite of Brainstorming. Teams of people Brainstorming new ideas is a highly effective way of getting a business to move fast and they add zest to the life of a business. It is, in fact, a major tool in increasing productivity. Yet I warrant there are more Blamestorms than Brainstorms in most businesses. Blamestorms have a drag effect on business. They are the worst example of teamwork. They rarely add value to a company (they consume too much time and therefore become a cost) and at best they reconfirm an existing protocol that has been forgotten or abused for reasons other than malicious disobedience (usually lack of care).

Ownership increases responsibility

If you own a company you can behave as you like. You can behave like Mike Johnson and Phil Redding who set up Pret À Manger, the chain of sandwich shops that takes pride in delivering a fresh quality product every day. They hire good people, they pay well, they are a success.

Or you could behave like Julian Richer. He opened his first HiFi shop, Richer Sounds, at the age of 19, and now features in the *Guiness Book of Records* as having the highest sales per square foot of any retail outlet worldwide. He achieved this by treating his staff with considerable respect and by recognising that his people made the difference.

Or you could behave like Gerald Ratner who publicly criticised his own business, a national chain of jewellers, calling the product 'crap'. Or like Douglas Hall and Freddie Shepherd, the Newcastle United Directors who, the papers reported, had insulted the football team's fans and called the female supporters 'dogs'. Gerald Ratner and the Newcastle United Directors provide a chilling example of what happens to irresponsible executives. Ratner was ousted from his business, Hall and Shepherd left the board.

Irresponsibility can cost a business dearly. But it can cost an individual even more. If a director acts irresponsibly, for example, there might be just cause for legal action.

Irresponsibility costs a business because it breaks down the hundreds of transactions that occur daily between humans. If you turn up for a meeting late you are not being responsible and you slow down the progress of that meeting. If you don't give yourself time to discover the typing error on a letter because you want to catch your mates in the pub, you weaken the quality perception of your company. If you lean back on a chair in a way that you know will damage it, but which in the short term makes you feel comfortable, you add to the cost of fixtures and fittings.

In business you are either adding value or you are adding cost. Irresponsibility does not, clearly, add value, and extended meetings, misspelt letters and broken furniture are all needless costs.

Everyone at St. Luke's is responsible for their own demeanour, behaviour, appearance and attitude. But as multiple owners, everyone is responsible to themselves and everyone else for the smooth running of the projects within the company. There is an inherent under-standing that you will not let yourself, your colleagues or the company down.

Ownership reinforces this point. If you act irresponsibly you are deemed not to be living up to your fair share and this would be high-lighted at one of your six-monthly reviews.

This relationship, between the gift of ownership (remember, at St. Luke's ownership is free, a guaranteed right, if you like) and the reci-procated personal responsibility, is witnessed every day in the company. If someone at our office party acts disgracefully, the response is more likely to be, 'I don't want to own a company with someone like that', rather than, 'He's a jerk, why do they employ him?' If someone is letting their teammates down, the view of the team will be, 'That's unfair', rather than, 'Well blow him, there's more opportunity for the rest of us to shine'.

In an organisation with as few direct rules as St. Luke's, personal responsibility becomes an exacting and high moral specification for how we behave. The Trustees, voted in each year, take their decision-making mandate from the near-Stalinesque adherence to personal re-sponsibility.

A high degree of responsibility for one's company quickly turns to passion. Passion for what you do adds value because it provides energy and determination. Often, people in business take the source of their passion from their inspirational leader (as in the case of Richard Branson, Julian Richer or Anita Roddick). In the case of St. Luke's, when you have almost 100 owners, you have a passion that at times becomes almost religious. Passion raises your game, it knocks down your problems and it protects you from cynics and general detractors. There's nothing like a passionate workforce to make your business hum.

In a survey of our staff conducted in the autumn of 1997, 81 per cent felt ownership for the organisation's values and vision and 95 per cent said they had made an effort to contribute to the decisions that affect them. When asked whether their own values chime with those of St. Luke's, 86 per cent of staffers said yes.

Ownership breeds 'High Trust'

In the jargon of current academic books, we are a 'High Trust company'. The truth is that in every aspect of how we work, trust is the binding force. At St. Luke's you are trusted to do your work, with your teammates, on time and to the standard required. You are not forced to do it between nine o'clock in the morning and six o'clock at night.

You are trusted, for example, to take the right amount of holiday. In one early experiment we asked everyone to take the holiday they felt they needed. The result was that in many notable cases people were not taking enough holiday. It wasn't 'presenteeism' (a syndrome whereby people don't leave their posts in case they find their employment circumstances have drastically changed on their return), it was just that some simply could not find the time and didn't feel they needed the break. We had to intervene and positively send people away!

To be trusted in the workplace brings considerable rewards.

You negate the need to have lengthy approval procedures designed to check on breaks in the system. You can dispense with the need to build in systems that ensure everyone is doing their job. You can positively promote people into doing things they thought previously impossible, thereby improving the value of your human capital. This happens because you trust them to succeed, rather than expect them to fail. In fact, you redefine failure as a learning experience designed to improve your performance.

If you take away trust, you immediately operate in the old paternalistic model of our forefathers who believed in a carrot and stick approach to personal development. You controlled people's growth because they could not be trusted to enhance their careers by themselves.

As owners we afford ourselves the freedom to treat each other as if we are all going to succeed.

Ownership is better than empowerment

Empowerment. To empower someone. It's a curious notion. Empower is a transitive verb; empowerment is a modern concoction suggesting the state or action of being empowered.

Someone gives you the power of empowerment. Who? Your boss, of course. It's handed out either as a token of your success in the company or dispensed generally as a management guru's liberating idea.

Empowerment offers you the opportunity to take the reins of the bit of the business that you handle and control your own destiny. It liberates you to think entrepreneurially. It treats you like an adult. It encourages you to put every ounce of energy into thinking imaginatively. It buys you into an exciting company vision.

But does it offer job security? No. Even empowered people can unfairly get the sack or be made redundant. Does it make you more valuable? Only if you can handle the responsibility. Does it make you better off? Only if your boss thinks you've been succesful and gives you a fat bonus. Salary scales don't change automatically simply because empowerment lies at the heart of your company's management ethos.

The principle effect of empowerment is to create an artificial circumstance whereby you think, when you go home at night, when you talk to friends over the weekend, when you tell your partner or parents what you are doing, that you own your business agenda as truly as any owner owns their business.

Why should you pretend that your bit of the business is really yours? So many businesses are already an alternative reality, with their parochial codes, rituals, dress codes, etc. Why dupe people into thinking that they own something which they don't? And probably never will.

I suggest empowerment is a cynical management tool designed to maximise the output of your human resources without there being an honest quid pro quo (real ownership of the company and/or participation in the company's direction).

Why should someone who labours for someone else in a business put in more thought and time than he or she is fairly contracted to do? (My plumber doesn't; he contracts to do the job and will do it well, but to the minimum.)

Because you'll get left behind if you don't? You might even be considered less effective for 'working to rule'. Because it might be more fulfilling, more enjoyable to feel as if you are your own boss and not have someone breathing down your neck?

Come on. It doesn't work like that. Empowered people are more likely to be *more* monitored, because empowerment can get, should get, out of control if it is to succeed properly. For empowerment to work, managers have to let go. Completely. Then their jobs have to change. From bosses/leaders, to sages and trainers.

Next, bosses have to condone the fact that mistakes will be inevitable. Because the newly liberated will trip up. That means bosses must lose the 'The Buck Stops Here' mentality that you hear when things don't go according to plan. 'My Board/shareholders aren't interested in fancy management ideas, they are only interested in the bottom line.'

Then you have to spend more on training. (At St. Luke's we spend the same on training as we do on IT – 15 per cent of net profit.) If you don't, you will have liberated your human machine, trained to do one job, to suddenly take on a whole new remit. It would be like upgrading your software but not your hardware.

And one more thing. Empowerment flourishes in an organisation with no secrets. The empowering boss will have to open up all lines of information to the empowered troupes, otherwise rumour and gossip will come flying in through the window to destabilise you. 'Is he getting more responsibility than me?' 'Why did she get invited to that meeting and not me?' 'He's done well, a true entrepreneur, but only because he plays golf with the boss.'

Empowerment is a paradox. It liberates openly and ties secretly in equal measure. Ownership is much more honest.

Ownership releases a trapped spirit

No one has ever been truly enslaved. Physically people have been, still are, bound in chains and tortured; regularly they are made to write things they don't believe. Chemical alteration of the mind might be forced upon someone, but the human spirit cannot be owned by anyone other than itself. It lies somewhere deep inside us.

When people are employed, they mete out just enough of that spirit to enable them to make the right contribution, but, at the drop of a hat, they will clam up, hold it in reserve, or transfer it to a new owner.

You cannot own someone's maximum contribution. Even by fear or greed. Although in business, there are many attempts to do so. Control freaks will say, 'Grab someone by the balls and their hearts and minds will follow.' Not true. They will pretend very artfully that their hearts and minds are following.

But if you say to someone, 'Hey, this is your company, you own it', you are not making any false demands on the human spirit. And then something extraordinary happens, which none of us, when we envisioned the company, thought would happen.

Real people start to emerge from behind the suits.

John Grant, be-suited when I first met him in the Old Boy clubby surroundings of the RAC Club, and with a schoolboy haircut his mum must have given him, now has cropped hair (with Japanese symbols shaved into the back) and wears regulation 'clubbing gear' (in 1997 it was pseudo-military, boots and fatigues).

Neil Thomson has swapped his accountant's suit for a more sporty, relaxed outfit (he chooses to go jogging most lunchtimes and feels he is more 'himself' in loose clothing). These are not superficial changes. These are real signs that the theatre of business, with its uniform suits and unambitious haircuts, don't gel with real life.

Real people make a better, more real contribution. Everyone is who they really are and visitors are amazed at the 'fabulous collection of individuals' we have. It's true that ownership has created teams of individuals, bringing to the workplace their wonderfully rich personal stories. But, curiously, this has bound us together more, because, I guess, we trust each other more to see who we really are.

Ownership: a final thought

The ownership structure of St. Luke's is so radical that, sadly, I fear few will emulate it. If you are already in a successful business, moving to a scheme like ours might be impossible. And, anyway, the rewards of the owners and senior managers will be too big to part with. You might be in a large quoted company with owners you, and maybe many of your bosses, will never meet. Owners who, in fact, have no day-to-day contact with the company at all, but who just want to see your profits going in the right direction. How can you affect a structure like that?

Well, you probably can't, from within. But if you were ever to break out of that domain, could you ask yourself the right, stiff questions?

Like, is it possible that salaries alone can define the differences between age, experience and marketability. A salary can be reviewed fairly each year. Or must unequal ownership be the only way to reward differences in employees' contribution to the value of the company?

If you are going to set up a business, you will have to ask yourself the question: 'If this business is my idea, why should I hand equity to others?' Well, my response would be, 'Fine, then make it successful by yourself and yourself alone.'

You see, in the Creative Age, your competitors will be seeking ways to maximise their human capital. Different, no doubt cleverer, schemes will abound which will recognise in an honest and motivating way what every individual can achieve for the company.

You simply cannot deny the contribution everyone in the workplace will make. If you are honest, you can't be successful without other people. Admit it.

⑯ Organisation And Exploring

'It sounds like anarchy.' That's what I usually hear when I first begin to outline how the whole idea hangs together. 'Good,' I respond. I know that anarchy lies deep in the heart of the creative process. I know that chaos is so valuable that ideas produced without it sound hollow and dull. We believe we open minds, ours, those of our clients and those of our stakeholders and competitors. When we are not opening minds we fall short of our avowed intent and reduce the value of our company.

If you can open minds, you can create fascination, and fascination is a great prize. It is rare that successful companies are not fascinating and the opposite is also true. There are too many similar companies in the service sector. And it is particularly true in the advertising industry. The processes and output, the physical layout, and the strategies and presentations of advertising agencies are strikingly similar. There appears to be no sense of wanting to differentiate each company beyond bald assertions that one is more 'creative' than another. Even the names sound the same – BMP, BDDP, BBH, BDDH. Lawyers and accountancy firms are guilty of this blurred homogeneity, too. It suggests that companies in themselves have no character, no life beyond the tram lines of the service they offer and the personal desires of the people who own them. As such, these companies are no more than simply unremarkable vessels filled with employees. No wonder so many jobs are so dull.

We see fascination as a specific and distinctive facet of our image and output that creates value for us and our clients. Whilst for many of our competitors our organisational structure and its cultural ramifications are an irritating sideshow, a marketing ploy or, worse, a closed Moonie cult, for us they are evidence of a group of people hard at work creating a company that *means* something and which provides a valuable framework for the production of commercial creativity that is distinct and hardworking.

Whilst the crazy creative conduct of the company is unforgiving, we also know we're being paid as professionals who need to deliver a product on time and to a high standard by people who do not want to be cowed by the conventional pressures of work.

I often say to visitors that St. Luke's is like an upside-down swan.

You see, most companies want to be seen like the graceful swan which glides effortlessly and serenely about its business, whilst underneath, hidden, its feet are going crazy, working as hard they can to deliver the swan to its destination.

Companies often favour this analogy because it represents an image to the outside world and to its employees of an organisation that is finely tuned, honed to perfection. An efficient, elegant entity, every bit as precise and well oiled as the tiny mechanisms of an intricate and ornate carriage clock.

We are an upside-down swan, because the tiny interactions between humans explode daily, the detritus of creative interrogation lies around everywhere and overspills wastepaper baskets; routine discussions and decisions are debated and discarded openly. Our feet flap wildly and energetically in people's faces every minute of every day and provide a charged, noisy, vibrant and fun atmosphere from which there is little escape.

But underneath, the body of the company glides purposely forward. We are driven by our ideals, not by the theatre of business. And, deep down, we gain satisfaction that our *modus operandi*, confusing (particularly to new people) though it might be, is making us increasingly more successful.

So our organisational model is predicated on three requirements, each managed separately but wholly interconnected:

1. We need to keep exploring. This is my responsibility, along with the Chief Operating Officer David Abrahams and the Finance Director

Neil Thomson. The company stands behind a vision – 'To Open Minds' – which gives purpose and meaning to the exploration.

2. We need to meet client deadlines with fascinating product. This increases the value of the company, creatively and financially. Operational managers with total authority handle this part.

3. We need to be happy and true to ourselves and our personal value systems. The Trustees of the Qualifying Share Ownership Trust (QUEST) oversee this. There are six and they are voted in each year. Normally we expect at least 15 people to stand for these six posts. We strive to remain fascinating ourselves in everything we do.

Figure 1: Three Pillars of our Organisational Structure

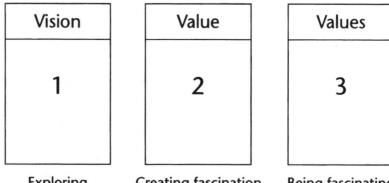

Vision	Value	Values
1	2	3
Exploring	Creating fascination	Being fascinating

St. Luke's changes each year, because its owners change. Each year, new owners take over if you like. These owners come into St. Luke's on an understanding that we keep exploring. If we ever stop exploring, we will be as guilty as everyone else of finding a formula and blindly sticking to it. Formulas work in the short term, like prescriptions work in the short term. But if you stick to them, you become increasingly immune to the effects of the changing outside world. You allow your company to age slowly in comparison to the changes outside. You allow yourself to attract like-minded customers or clients who are stuck in the same gear as you, so you are duped into thinking that the world is at one with you. You know your company is ageing when the proportion of people who want to inflict change is smaller than those who want to rely on the practices of the 'good old days'.

If you stick to a formula, you might even allow your company to die eventually.

Our vision – 'To Open Minds' – is there before us to remind us what will happen when we stop exploring. We will close down our potential imagination rather than open it up. That would lead to competitive disadvantage. And the company will fail. In the course of a long, slow death it will have to shed people and that is almost too painful to even write about.

Many companies don't have or don't like visions. It's all too much tree-hugging and not enough 'common sense'. For example, it's common sense simply to produce good work that your client will buy and which (ideally) will win plaudits and awards from your peers in the industry.

But that's not enough. The blind pursuit of product quality and sales belongs to an older business paradigm. One of over a hundred years ago. It places humans below products and sends humanity down lower than revenue streams.

I am not against product quality and good sales (we have both), but I am against any institution that worships them alone. A vision provides a greater purpose and requires bosses to think further than shareholder or personal (monetary) value. It can create an opportunity for people to develop as they aspire to the vision. It can keep morale high.

To keep exploring, we must remain inquisitive and each year we build in a process of self-examination. It's time consuming and expensive and its output has to be properly managed to make sure that expectations are made real.

Everyone in the company is involved in this process which usually, but not always, happens on St. Luke's Day (18 October). It is my job as Chairman to stimulate and provoke any debate about the future. The Finance Director has to budget and plan for its outcome. The Chief Operating Officer has to know he can make it physically happen – and in a fascinating way.

We are servants to the idea or ideas that the company creates.

I described to you one of these sessions in April of 1995 facilitated by Ruth Lederman at which we began to talk about a co-operative. They are hard work and they are uncomfortable. Hard work because we are thinking, working, writing and drawing for up to 12 hours a day almost non-stop; and uncomfortable because they set out to challenge our preconceptions.

Having done a few, I believe I know how they work best for us. They should be used to create a shared experience and deliver one definable objective. If you try to do any more, you get into a process that perpetually runs at odds with your daily routine. Agree one thing and one thing only. And agree it will change the way you work and change the way you think.

It could be to change your daily routine by starting the day at ten in the morning no matter what the consequences. But don't let sessions like these give you a process, such as 'Form a series of task forces to examine ways of starting the day differently'. You will never achieve it. I promise.

At the 1996 St. Luke's Day awayday, the issue of the company's growth came up. For many in the company the fact that we had shot up in numbers, from the 35 originals at the breakaway to almost 70 in just one year, was too fast. They feared that the culture would disappear and that we would become too bureaucratic.

This was fair comment. Certainly there is a kind of kitchen-table wisdom I hear that says 25 is the right number for an entrepreneurial group (some would even say four or five is as big as you should get). You might or might not hold things together beyond that, but certainly at 50 the company culture would change (for the worse).

When we got to 50 people, the same wisdom decreed that 75 would be our break point and all manner of empirical evidence would be marshalled to prove it.

There was also fear that growth for growth's sake was more to do with the pursuit of money than the pursuit of an 'Alternative Way'. 'What's the purpose of growing,' people would ask, 'if all we do is just get bigger?' Being big wasn't our primary objective. Creating a company that meant something to us as individuals was what we wanted to do. Creating a movement for change was high on our agenda.

There were counter-arguments to this.

Growing was in itself an act of creativity. Staying the same size was stagnation or at best treading water. As a creative company we should enjoy watching ourselves grow up.

Growing increased our creative possibilities – provided a wider creative canvas. It would reinvigorate our creative thinking and output and add value to existing clients and make us more attractive to new ones.

Growth would provide financial security as we became less and less dependent on any one client to provide the income that would keep all the shareholders in employment.

Growth meant our idea was not simply a funky little small company thing. It could provide a growing platform of people and influence to espouse our missionary zeal, to let everyone know that we were challenging work itself, not just glitzy London ad agencies.

Growth meant a business success; being taken seriously commercially was and is important to us. You can run a business on these wacky ideas. Big Business might even sit up and take notice if we made a real success of it. Hey, we might even *affect* Big Business.

David Abraham and I were responsible for solving the growth issue. We canvassed widely, and in the end, we returned to a version of a model that Naresh and Dave had proposed in January 1996 and which was rejected out of hand at the time by the owners, probably because it came too early in our development.

The Naresh and Dave proposal was to split the company into two teams (reds and blues, or Celtic and United) and enjoy friendly rivalry. Our modified idea was to form a potentially infinite number of self-managed groups, in a system I called 'Citizen Cell Structure'.

Citizen Cell Structure

We have come to learn that 35 people is about as big as you can get before you cease to care about the people with whom you directly work.

When you're a small number you want to know why Mary on reception is unhappy, or you send flowers when she's ill or had a personal misfortune. You do these things because Mary is in your mind and her absence somehow destablises your daily routine. Her absence could be filled by a temp, but you'd prefer to muck in and make do until Mary returns.

Everyone chips in when you're a small company. You'll sit on reception for an hour so that Mary can visit her Mum in hospital one afternoon. No job is too small or too menial. If you run out of toilet paper, you will not feel downtrodden or put upon if you have to nip around the corner and buy some more.

You will work late and passionately and collaboratively when you are small. You have instant, unprogrammed fun when you are small.

As you get bigger, your attitude to people who do not directly affect you changes dramatically. It's as if you have an alter ego which switches in.

'I've noticed Mary isn't on reception this afternoon, where is she?'

'At the hospital, visiting her Mum.'

'Who gave her permission, and anyway, why don't we get in a temp? This is all so . . . so unprofessional.'

When you are small you live on your wits. Money is tight. You take the Tube to meetings instead of a taxi. You always travel in the cheapest seats, rather than Business Class.

Small, entrepreneurial companies are fun and lively and infinitely more human than large bureaucratic institutions. Yet they are sadly very vulnerable, too. Unexpected loss of income, lack of new opportunities, key individuals leaving (innocently to have a baby maybe) and multi-service (cheaper) competitors can knock small companies for six.

We desperately needed a system whereby we could be small and big at the same time! The Citizen Cell Structure does two things:

1. It establishes groups of not more than 35 people who are connected together by a bond of trust that comes from an operational require-ment to work cohesively and co-operatively together.
2. It allows the groups to grow as micro-cultures under one larger, overall culture – St. Luke's.

They are bonded to St. Luke's via the share scheme and via a series of weekly, monthly and annual events. There are other bonds, too. They are bonded to other groups by departmental affinity. The Trustees of the company (The QUEST) are from different groups.

The citizen cells join with shared recreation, like yoga on Tuesdays and aerobics on Thursdays. And there are inter-group friendship bonds, too.

The cells meet, bond and break in a variety of ways. But the essential thing is that each affinity must form a strong relationship centred on trust.

The operational heads run their groups and have complete authority over their *modus operandi*, budgets and income streams. Some resources are shared, such as IT, marketing, catering, cleaning, me, David, Neil. We are grouped together and nicknamed 'Euston'. Euston is a supplier of services to the groups which are the generators of income.

Figure 2: Different Facets of the Citizen Cell

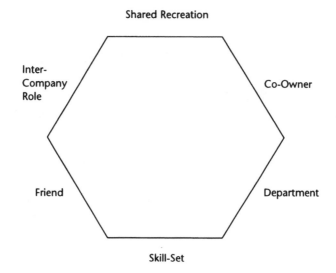

Amoeba Growth System

When a group exceeds 35 it must split and form two groups, each as self-contained as the one they left. It could be two groups of 18 or so or one small group and one larger group. Each can then grow and form a new micro-culture. This puts focus onto the recruitment of people in the groups. Too many juniors and you won't affect the split. Too many seniors and one split group will have an imbalance.

We call this the 'Amoeba Growth System'. Currently, we have split into four groups with Euston supplying a service to each. We have no idea how many we will end up with, or whether they will all be in the same building, or, indeed, the same country. The possibilities for growth in this way are endless.

Real amoeba are recognised by their ability to form temporary cyto-plasmic extensions (pseudopodia) which are like feet that enable them to get about. This amoeboid movement is considered to be the most primitive form of animal movement. They also feed and lose food from any point of its cell surface.

Like these amoeba, the groups can stray in any direction they wish. They can experiment and they can change the systemic rules that they first started with. Moreover, just like real amoebae, they are encouraged to take in and reject food (for thought, in their case) at any level and at any time.

The Citizen Cell Structure preserves the cultural and operational requirements of worker groups; the Amoeba Growth System allows for cultural growth, more opportunity and personal transformation.

Personal transformation

Our premise is that work can be liberating and fun. Being co-owners, we afford ourselves the opportunity to behave like owners whenever we can. We plan for the company to enrich and fulfil us. In many senses we see the company having an obligation to fulfil and enrich us.

Personal transformation is a gift that the company can bestow at no cost (in fact it benefits itself!). You see, we talk about jobs for life – within the same company. This cuts rudely across a well thought out current view that as companies downsize, and expertise is outsourced, work will fall into a series of finely dissected individual skills which we will carry with us and take from company to company as portfolio managers. Companies will pay directly for what we do rather than for how much time it takes to do it.

Portfolio managers is the term given to a new breed of workers ejected from the world and left to fend for themselves. Our model cannot properly contain portfolio managers because we reject the notion that companies shrink and grow by market forces alone. Instead, we accept a situation where companies can reorganise, retrain and reuse its human capital before it considers discharging it.

Personal transformation is the on-going process whereby through training, experience and personal desire, the human asset value of a company can be profitably expanded. Organisationally, we manage this with a 'pull and push' system. The 'push' comes at the operational level with two reviews a year that are designed to bring out the best in you. The 'pull' comes from the long-term potential of the company which is managed by me, the Chairman, David, the COO and Neil, the Finance Director.

Biorhythms

Overall the company runs to practical metre.

Every Monday morning, everyone gathers in the Ristorante San Luca (our internal dining area) for a 15-minute 'Start The Week' session. They remind me of the opening scenes in *Hill Street Blues*, when the duty sergeant bangs out the orders for the day. If anyone has something particular to say (for example, announce a new IT system, explain a new division, introduce a new person), then this is a good time to do it.

Every last Friday of the month we have a 'Flag Meeting'. Held, literally, under a flag of a winged ox (the company's logo, taken from Dante's *Divine Comedy*, where St. Luke enters the underworld as a winged ox), this is a raucous, lively get together with a packed agenda. We review all our product, congratulate ourselves in general and individuals in particular for good work, and focus on the demands of the month ahead. It's a time when we are reminded of what the vision of the company require us to do, in terms of innovation and experimentation.

Since we don't enter the creative award ceremonies, it's a good time to contemplate on the standard of our work and to discuss how daring the teams have been.

At this meeting we have 'Five Favourite Things', a now legendary moment when someone tells us their five favourite things. It might be the Beatles, shepherd's pie or clay modelling; clubbing, a family photo or the Toronto Blue Jays. What they are doesn't really matter. Hearing the person talk and, in the process, introducing himself, is what really matters.

I love these sessions for a particular reason. They are totally devoid of cynicism. Everyone listens closely to what their co-owner is revealing and everyone learns something valuable about our human capital.

A wilder moment is 'Man Of Month'. It's an opportunity for some of the girls in Finance who keep an eye on the work in progress to pick and honour their favourite guy. Flag meetings are long sessions, often taking over two hours. We let them lapse briefly, when we convinced ourselves pressure of work meant they were easily sidelined. We missed them immensely and The Quest reinstated them at the earliest opportunity.

In March/April we have Shareholder Day, when our accountants officially declare our financial results and the share price is fixed. New shareholders are announced on this day and there is a certain 'coming of age' for those whose names duly appear the following day on our letterhead.

On Shareholder Day, we also audit our creative output and review our environmental and social standing. The meeting one year was held during a special lunch; another was held at the Guggenheim Museum in Bilbao.

Every St. Luke's Day (18 October) we go away *en masse* to a crazy venue (one year it was the bleak surroundings of the Trade Unions Congress in north London) and work together to reinvent ourselves. One didn't go well (the one in north London). We worked too hard, tried to solve too much, got exhausted and achieved next to nothing. The following year was fabulous. It was lighter and had a less strict agenda. We all trooped off to the Anugraha Hotel in Esher and the groups briefly presented their plans to each other. The real work was done in the evening over drinks, dinner and the dance floor!

These four calendar items (Monday Mornings, Flag Meetings, Shareholder Day and St. Luke's Day) provide a rhythm and pace to the company. They are a kind of biorhythm, if you like, that metres a living, human, changing organisation.

Creating fascination

In business you are either adding value or adding cost.

You are adding value if, for example, you are thinking of ways of enhancing your product. You are adding cost if, say, you are bickering about how to make the product.

A long time ago, in the late 70s/early 80s, I worked at an advertising agency called Foote, Cone & Belding. It was riding high on a breathtaking number of concurrent new business wins and with accounts like British Airways, Rover Cars, Cadbury's Dairy Milk and Gordon's Gin, was the envy of many in London.

The ad agency was putting on staff like there was no tomorrow and fat bonuses were paid every year. The Directors decided to open a staff bar in the mews behind the offices and asked for names.

'Bearing in mind it's where everyone will go after work to slag everyone else off, I think we should call it The Whine Bar,' said a wisecrack.

The Directors were not amused. No matter how successful or how fat the bonuses, people were still moaning and groaning.

'It's part and parcel of work life,' a careers counsellor told me once when I talked about that subject. And I guess it's true.

Do you moan about your company?

Do you start passing round gossip: 'Who's she? Why's she here when we're laying people off at Head Office?'

People moan all the time and in the process they sort and share their particular, personal issues. Sadly, it's a very negative procedure. And moaning and gossiping almost always never solves any problem.

This negativity is a slow death in the workplace. It eats up your time; it leaves no room for imaginative thinking; and it permeates an increasingly bad atmosphere.

Now, if you're expecting me to say that there is no gossiping or bad-mouthing at St. Luke's, then you're wrong. Human nature belligerently ensures they are always around. In fact you need some discontent to recognise contentment. (When people join, their contracts impress on them the need to work harmoniously together. To be courteous. To never use threats, fear or coercion.)

The truth is that the operational running leaves little room for this kind of negativity to thrive, charged, as it is, to create fascinating product.

Our clients are managed tightly by dedicated operational teams who have their own rules about how to be organised for success. They are not soft on issues of product delivery standards. The thinking must always be of high calibre and the creative output must be regularly striking and challenging.

In this environment it is easy to get confused about something like courteousness. It doesn't mean you shouldn't say anything when you don't like something; it doesn't mean you should be nice all the time. It means you should say thank you and recognise the different ways people contribute to the teamwork.

In fact at the operational level is a strong requirement to be robust. Challenge and counter-challenge exist every day in almost every decision. And the implicit requirement to contribute to the heated debates can be onerous for many.

The individual operational groups have their own clients, communication philosophies and income streams. They, and only they, decide on their required resources. They recruit into their groups themselves and have their own status meetings. They can opt to invite anyone else from outside the group to add value to the group at any time.

These are self-managed, entrepreneurial teams who know and care about each other well, work hand in glove and never promote themselves away from the real value of the company – the creation of a fascinating product that produces the company's income streams and the value of the co-operatively owned shares.

Being fascinating

'I've heard that every Monday morning you all sit around cross-legged in a circle and chant, whilst a Shiatsu masseur relaxes you.'

If only. That sounds wonderful.

But actually, we're not that far away.

At a meeting in the Cabinet rooms off 10 Downing Street to present our final recommendations on the Labour Government's Welfare To Work advertising campaign, the other finalists from the large and conventional DMB&B noticed the entire St. Luke's team waving their hands in the air and laughing out aloud. It wasn't a tactic to destabilise the enemy (although I'm sure it did), it was just one of the ways we loosen up in team or company gatherings.

At one of our 'Five Favourite Things' sessions, John Grant stood on the table and danced by himself in front of everyone to demonstrate his love for dancing and clubbing.

We have a 'Chill Out Room' full of aromatherapy oils. Massages do take place in there, although you are just as likely to find someone asleep.

We are not afraid to experiment. And we will go to extraordinary lengths to think laterally about our working lives. We want to be happy, but we also want to know that we are challenging ourselves. So we concentrate on our own internal values as much as we concentrate on adding value to our client's business.

We see a very clear correlation between creating a fascinating culture and creating fascinating work.

Our culture is run and maintained by the QUEST (Qualifying Share Ownership Trust). The QUEST is the financial system that permits the equal shareholding scheme to happen once a year. By law, the Trustees have to be voted on each year. Many people stand for nomination to the QUEST, which has greatly expanded powers beyond its legal and financial obligation to oversee the share issues.

The QUEST is the barometer of the company. When things get hot it can cool matters down and when the company is too cool (for example, lackadaisical, conventional) it can turn the temperature up.

Although as a Limited Company we have Directors of the company, they never meet apart from once a year to fulfil their legal requirements. The very idea of Directors in a flat, non-hierarchical co-operative is ludicrous. One day we will do away with them altogether. The QUEST is the nearest thing we have to a regular governing force, although there are two specific areas over which it has no jurisdiction. Personnel and operational systems, both of which are within the remit of the operating groups.

Despite the influence of the QUEST, it is often made up of people with little or no management skill. But that's fine, because they are not voted in for those skills. They are voted in because they are trusted. It's as simple as that.

They are trusted to ensure the shareholders are properly represented. They exist to remind everyone that the company has a wide and widening franchise of employee owners who are keen to exercise their right to contribute to the democratic running of the company.

They maintain the values of the company which are an aggregation of the personal values of everyone – freedom of expression and thought, lack of coercion and fear, and a determination to make work fun.

One year, after talking to the operational heads, the QUEST introduced 'The Summer Of Love'. Everyone was getting too busy to enjoy themselves. We were pitching for and winning business like mad. And we were recruiting non-stop. It was a classic situation. We were concentrating on everything but ourselves. It was becoming a sweat shop, and the bigger we got, the more people we recruited to sweat with us.

The Summer Of Love stopped all pitching (in fact we withdrew from one of the biggest ever pitches in recent years, the £50-million Cable & Wireless account). But the QUEST's view was that far from making good, sound business sense, an account that size would make no sense at all to a company like ours. It would have changed our status. It would have doubled our profitability and the value of the company would have risen considerably.

Yes, from a profitability perspective, we would have coined it. But as Tom Peters once said, 'Profit is like health, you need it, but it's not what you live for.' Such a colossal amount of money (were we to have won it, of course!) would have increased the financial value but decreased the other values of St. Luke's. There is no better way to explain how the QUEST can intervene.

There is a saying that 'good values drive bad values out of business'. And vice versa I would say. Policing the behaviour and mood of a constantly changing company, subdivided into a series of entre-preneurially run groups, with an overall mandate to innovate, should be one of the toughest management jobs on the block. But the girl from finance and the young copywriter do it brilliantly.

Which proves to me that it may look and sound weird, but organisationally it hangs together just fine, thank you.

Me. 'Whose idea was it to have no desks?'

David Abraham. 'Is that Madison Avenue?'

Jay Chiat. The Great Innovator.

In the café, where you can work and play.

Phil Teer hard at work planning IKEA.

Andy Palmer, Kate Stanners and Tim Hearn in Bilbao for 'Shareholder Day'.

Sarah Naughten. Also known as Naughty!

Tessa Wire – 'ultra-cool'.

Andy 'I've got it sorted' Smith, a.k.a. Smudger.

Robbie Sparks – 'the father of the house'.

Paul 'Johnners' Johnson. 'Order Please'.

John Grant. Not with the haircut his Mum gave him.

Julian Vizard. Created the St. Luke's ox logo.

oung. Invented girl power 3 years before Spice Girls.

Neil Thomson. Omnicon didn't expect to deal with the likes of him...!

Naresh Ramchandam (r) and James Gillham at work in 'The Womb'.

Dave Buonoguidi. 'Bono'. 'I'd like to change everything.'

Clare Nash – instrumental in designing the Project Rooms.

Rachel Plant 'Planty' was office manager when we moved. (That's why she got herself into another department asap...)

Natasha
Rampley, our
official 'Artist
in Residence'.

Working in 'The Womb'.

'Ah, how sweet it was to win the Eurostar account.'

Winning the Government's New Deal campaign was a dream come true for a company dedicated to improving the world of work.

⑰ Daily Life At St. Luke's

Have you ever stopped for a moment to think about your work-place?

Who designed it and why? Who laid out the corridors? Who planned the number of desks there would be, or the siting of the amenities? Was it always a factory? Is it a purpose-built office block? Has it been used for thousands of different things over time?

These are not questions that plague us every day, are they?

Actually, we probably never even think about the place we work in, beyond making sure that no one has messed with your desk or redesigned your machinery without telling you.

You see, there is no real science of the workplace.

There are designers and architects. There are various time and motion studies. You will hear estate agents talk about the optimum number of people being one person per 100 square feet.

The decision on where the workplace should be will be a financial one, so the Finance Director will be involved. He will hire an estate agent and in turn they will assign someone to 'fit out' the space and make sure IT is fully briefed.

Then the office manager will tell you all where to go.

The process of moving office and the allocation of space is a functional and financial one. It requires, and invites, little imagination or real understanding of the flexible role humans can play.

I know. There are exceptions. But not very many. And those exceptions, like the New York and Los Angeles offices of Chiat/Day or the 'Arc' building in Hammersmith, London, are by and large design statements rather than a reflection of the potential of 21st-century working.

The truth is that the architects who design factories and offices slavishly follow designs from the past. For evidence look no further than Canary Wharf in the Docklands of London, with its imposing skyscraper looking every bit as if it had been designed by William Le Baron Jenny, the American architect who was working in the 1880s rather than the 1980s.

'Factory' and 'office'. Such old words to describe our 21st-century workplaces.

Factories (or 'manufactories') have been around since the 17th century. As a description for a building of the manufacture of goods, it can be traced to at least 1618, although obviously it rose into general and common use with the Industrial Revolution. It is an old word, but it is honest, in that it describes exactly what happens. But it's persistent and lazy use is a hurdle to lateral thinking about how product assembly can really be achieved, especially when the requirement of humans is the predominant factor. From a product manufacturing perspective, 'factory' is a good honest word; from a human perspective, it lacks humanity.

Some manufacturers have looked closely at making the assembly process less tedious. Teamworking has been successful, for example, and Just-In-Time inventory systems have reduced the 'industrialness' of assembly plants. Changing the way you work, will change the way you think. If humans feel greater pride and take greater care in what they do, then I feel it should be reflected in the physicality and routine of the workplace to a much greater extent.

'Office' is an even more contentious word for me.

It started off well enough. In late mediaeval times an office was some kindness, service or attention paid to someone. Half a century later, it was found to describe a place where a service is done, as in post office. It is closely associated with words such as 'official', 'officer' and even 'officious', and it lends an authority, a set of expectations and a certain faux-dignity to a place where humans gather for the simple purpose of the transaction of business.

All offices are the same. They are brick and glass edifices, either purpose-built or redeveloped, full of conduits for cables, and neatly squared-off working zones. They are full of doors and desks and phones.

Inside, many are painted the same off-white and have the same oatmeal-coloured carpet. There are vending machines for drinks and low maintenance greenery.

They are stratified with the most important people on the top and the least important (postboy) on the bottom, or even the basement. They have receptionists you meet every day and switchboard operators who only meet you at the Christmas party and who greet you with your extension number.

They are command and control centres, full of secrets and memos and rules of engagement. They are 'Them and Us' places. 'They' live on the Directors' floor, 'Us' don't.

There are some experiments in different ways of working. There are open-plan offices, virtual offices, offices with teleworkers and offices based upon flexitime.

Open-plan offices represent the most extensive divergence from 'normal' office life. There is hierarchical open-plan and non-hierarchical open-plan. The stupendous First Direct site in Leeds is a good example of non-hierarchical open-plan. Everyone, from Directors down, share the space. They work in teams, each of which gives some thought on how to personalise their areas visually. Hierarchical open-plan places the more important people on the outside, with the windows and nice views. Everyone else is placed in the middle in what Douglas Coupland in *Generation X* called 'veal fattening pens'. You know – those easy-to-assemble, fabric-covered MDF desks and low-level walls that are more preoccupied with how your computer sits than how you like to interact. In 'veal fattening pens', you are invisible when you sit down and noticed when you stand up (to talk, go to the bathroom, have lunch or go home).

Virtual offices are those where workers can achieve the fulfilment of their assignments without physically being at the office. Technology facilitates this by linking everyone to a central file server that graphically represents the office environment. Thoughts and ideas are worked on together by teams who might never have met each other. Most are usually semi-virtual, in that there is still physically a building to go to where some functions permanently reside. There are hardly any fully virtual offices (such as the computer sales company in California where the employees only meet up once a week for an hour), for obvious reasons.

'Virtual Office' has a marvellous 21st-century cyber-age ring to it, but my view is that the idea is manifestly a further drive down the path of alienation in the workplace. Working permanently from home (not fun if you are single, not easy if you have young children), from your car (uncomfortable and cramped) or from anywhere only goes part of the way towards reinventing work. From the point of view of value, you might argue that virtual working saves on rent, but I am not convinced it is more liberating and fun. If the business itself is not transformed into one where human capital works co-operatively together in a trusting environment, then virtual working serves to hot-house the conventional paranoia of everyday working life – Is the boss noticing me? Am I getting the right projects? What are they saying about me?

Offices and factories are not designed for humans, they are designed for no reason other than production. They are not designed with the Communication Age in mind and they are certainly not designed for the Creative Age.

So who do they belong to? Well no one actually. Whereas currently in the UK 67 per cent of houses are owned by the people who live in them, less than 15 per cent of offices are owned by those who work in them. The office is not associated with the workforce, its product, its culture or its values; it is associated with the Finance Department. It is a cost. It adds little value.

It is a high cost, too. In the advertising business, we reckon that your rent, rates and heating should account for no more than 15 per cent of your income. But why can't you at least try to turn that 15 per cent cost into some kind of value? Let's look at the workplace from a different perspective.

Businesses, I feel, are very simple things. They are just collections of humans gathered together for commerce. I don't know of a business that doesn't employ humans. Even robot manufacturers employ humans.

Human activity in the workplace is substantially displaced and endangered by boring offices with repetitive regimes, unimaginative surroundings and a tedious adherence to Industrial Age convention. Yet there are ways of enhancing human activity (and hence your bottom line) through the physicality of the building.

Actually, it's obvious. The psychology of home improvement through paint, wallpaper and well-designed furniture is a concept we can grasp without difficulty. Yet, for most of our working days we are sentenced to an environment devoid of the same care and attention you afford to your home.

St. Luke's is not a virtual office nor open plan for that matter. It does not employ teleworkers or run on flexitime. St. Luke's is, if anything, a 'resourceful office' or, more simply, a clubhouse.

When we designed it, we had to take note of our organisational and ownership structure. That put paid to Director's offices in one fell swoop. We considered two other important things as well – the work we do there and the barriers to getting it done.

The work we do is the supply of imagination, of commercial art, to our clients, who in turn pay us monthly fees. If we simply thought in the conventional Industrial Age paradigm, we would see the supply of this service as a product produced with a process. We would apply all the normal rigorous quality controls to the product development and be keen to ensure the process purred like a beautifully balanced Rolls-Royce engine. Our product would drop into our customers' hands immaculately from a conveyor belt developed and tweaked over decades of use. Perfect.

Our payment would be for services rendered.

But think again about this from the point of view of the Creative Age.

We see ourselves as intermediaries adding value to a chain that links customers and businesses by communication in the media. Our process is not linear, like a production line. It is digital. We apply as many heads as possible to the initial process of designing our communication idea – including our clients. Our clients are not our customers as such any more, they are part of the project development team and we work closely with them throughout all phases of the development of a creative idea. Their imaginative brains are useful servants to the end result, just like ours.

There is a co-operation between supplier and recipient that often makes it difficult to see where each makes specific input. It is in both our interests to get the best idea out, but we bring some specific benefits, in objectivity, craft writing, designing skills and intellectual stimulation. Communication is unlikely to be the single focus of our client's job spec, so we also bring single-minded dedication.

We therefore view the monthly fees differently. Instead of being 'for payment of ideas', or 'for services rendered', they become payments reflecting concurrent use of our resources, facilities and skills. The fee is the only source of income we draw from our clients and it is negotiated keenly.

In this way we see our office as more like a clubhouse for our clients. They pay fees and use such resources, facilities and skills as they please.

When you join a club, you do not expect to be kept waiting until your squash coach comes to meet you and escorts you like a jailed prisoner to your destination. You expect to be able to roam freely and use as little or as much as you like. You will know the rules and you will know if some services cost extra, above your monthly fees.

To achieve this, we had to make one simple decision. To give our clients, rather than ourselves, our office space. In that way they would always know where to go for their meetings. With a little experience of the place they would also know how to access all the other facilities, such as the libraries, Internet, CD-Roms and restaurant (in which they willingly abide by the rule to take their dirty plates back into the kitchen themselves, for we have no waiters).

Each client has its own purpose-built creative communication centre and the owners at St. Luke's have what is left – the open spaces, the restaurant's spaces, the crazy spaces.

You might think that we short-changed ourselves. Not a bit of it. We carefully considered what elements of office life were barriers to imaginative thinking. They were things like hierarchy or the owning of ideas – our ownership scheme solved that. Like hardened systems which created a strict bureaucracy – our organisational model solved that. And things like habit-forming routines.

You get up with your alarm clock and easy-to-digest radio/TV show. Wash, maybe eat, and jump in the car, on the train or bus (you might walk if you're lucky but only a tiny percentage do). Same route to work (perhaps a clever shortcut – but it's the same clever shortcut). A swipe of your ID card, a nod to the security guard, a smile for the receptionist, then it's straight to your post. Up in the lift maybe; same floor, same squared-off office/workstation/veal fattening pen. Coat/jacket off. Onto the back of the chair or onto a hanger. Sit down. Switch computer/ machinery on. (I sometimes think that 'logging on' has replaced cleaning your teeth as the totemic start of the day.) Ping! Your day has started. The way it has always started. And the way millions of others start their day. That is not a creative act by any stretch of the imagination. It is a mindless routine that working life has imposed on millions of people.

Not only did we give our clients the offices, but we disposed with our personal desks altogether. None of us has an office or a desk. We share everything, computers, pencils, crayons and others' working detritus! The whole building becomes everyone's working space. We roam from area to area as we like, changing where we sit to suit our changing moods. We have meetings in curious, outlandish, but somehow perfectly acceptable places, like corridors, kitchen tables and cubbyholes.

But ha! You now have to know what you're doing, before you know where to go. And this represents a fundamental shift in the way you work. It changes your work pattern from one dependent on geography, to one dependent on project.

To do this efficiently, we are linked together by a computerised project management/diary system to which everyone has access. Meetings are booked and the venues advised, and by accessing this system from any computer you know where to go and how to meet up with others.

Phones are no longer fixed to desks and hard-wired into walls. An internal mobile system allows our phones to go with us. Just like ordinary phones you can divert and you can put on hold.

Each person is equipped with a St. Luke's satchel, so that if they need to transport documents as they roam around, they can. Everyone has a locker to keep personal belongings safe and sound. We have them because we all asked for them. But they have become archaeological wonders. Weekly papers and books, jogging pants, scarves, video tapes and odd shoes pile on top of each other until the QUEST calls a halt, hires a skip from the local council and we consign the contents of the lockers (and the accumulated rubbish of old work in the project rooms) to the municipal rubbish tip.

An office like this becomes as tidy as the untidiest person. It used to really bug me, but after a time I realised that no one else seemed that upset. Certainly not the clients and suppliers who bustled in and out and certainly not the majority of the owners who felt comfortable with a certain level of messiness.

I was viewing the office as that graceful swan. The one I referred to earlier that swims elegantly around, looking smart, purposeful and well preened. We are an upside-down swan and the untidiness is part of the flapping feet that are on full display.

Fortunately, there is a wonderful (and wholly unexpected) by-product of the project-room system. Every piece of paper has a home. If the piece of paper refers somehow to, say, Midland Bank, it goes in the Midland Bank Room. If it is something personal, you can give it to the person, pop it in the relevant pigeon-hole or find the person's locker. If it is neither of these things, you can deposit it in the '5.30 Box'.

The 5.30 Box (there's one on each of our five floors) is a brutal but efficient system. Anything left casually lying in a general, all-purpose space is swept into the box at 5.30 and (in theory) is thrown away after seven days. I say in theory because I guess we are all too nice to each other and we leave things lying in the box long enough for it to be retrieved!

There are workstations everywhere. On each of our five floors. In corners, by stairs, in the restaurant, on smart purpose-built tables, on rudely manufactured trellis tables. Sofas abound, of all shapes and all sizes, including the notorious Porno Sofa, reputedly from a brothel in Brighton, that has been with us so long and is so shabby that we treat it like the family pet. One day we expect it to quietly pass away.

There are noisy spaces like the Egg Floor (so named because when we first took over the building, all creative work was approved for production from there; now that, too, happens in many different spaces). And there are quiet spaces like The Womb, a dark-pink, enclosed space with only one entrance. If you want to get away from it completely, you can sleep, read or be massaged in the Chill Out Room, where there are no phones or computers.

You can work literally anywhere, but whilst there are always computers available, the computer-to-person ratio runs at 64 per cent. With this system of working, you do not need a computer on every desk, which is a personalised statement and a private zone. And an expensive luxury. Computers for us are public property, like phone boxes. Useful, but with a 'take it or leave it' feel to them. We are not hooked on logging on. Every computer has Internet access and CD-Rom drives and, apart from specific finance software and top-level design packages, you can do anything from any computer.

The office space is painted in bright colours. Whilst some use of space seems strange at first glance, there is no sense of over-design, only one of human imprint. There is a wonderful story, maybe an urban myth, of an architect who designed a fabulous new building, set in a spectacular open green site, for a university. He had to have it completed by a certain date, on which there would be a grand opening. When the day came, the

Dean of the University rushed up to the architect and said, 'It's a disaster.'

'Don't you like my design?' queried the architect.

'It's wonderful, beautiful, fantastic, but there's one big problem, you haven't put in any paths.'

'Don't worry, I'll return later and do it for you.'

Left with little alternative, the Dean could only hope that the architect would keep his word. Many weeks later, well after the building was in full use by the students, the architect returned and built the paths where the students had naturally made tracks on the grass.

It was an inspirational idea and one echoed in the way our office is used. It has all the private anomalies of a house, with specific things being in specific places (like the pool table dividing the library, so that we have to have two), coupled with the more familiar 'bric a brac' of office life such as photocopying machines (though I fancy they lie oddly around the office like large grey beached whales).

In a fluid workplace like this, the 'grammar' of conventional office life comes under fire.

If you see someone lying on a sofa with their feet up reading, your initial instinct is to say they are relaxing. They probably are. But they might also be working. With no personal desk or chair, you cannot be found sitting in your squared-off zone, jacket on the back of a chair, computer humming, poring over a large stack of papers.

Reading a research report with your feet up is acceptable behaviour. We will take a look at culture later, but this informality pervades the office. It destabilises newcomers who misread the situation and think they can interrupt at will.

When describing the working life at St. Luke's, I often use the analogy of school and university or college life, and their differences. When you go to school, ding! the bell goes at nine o'clock and you go to your desk. Ding! it goes again at five and you go home. You eat and play in between. You have your desk and you stick with it. It will be full of books – geography, history, maths, you name it. At school, you all dress the same, either literally in school uniform or culturally according to the peer fashion of the times. You are given work assignments period by period. Your time is dissected up into small parts and handed back to you. Homework must be in on time. Your behaviour is codified and regulated. You make sure you are in the right gang. You are graded and checked regularly.

Then you go into further education and everything changes. You are not given a desk or dress code. You are not given detailed daily routines, you are given large-scale projects. You are given a quality standard and you are given completion dates. The college campus will have a refectory and will be subdivided into subjects. If you choose to do your project work all through the night, fine. If you choose not to discover the library and to skip lectures, that might be fine, too, as long as the quality is maintained. You are liberated to think. What you look like and what you wear are secondary issues.

Our working routine at St. Luke's is similar to that of university and college life and as different from conventional life as school life is from college. Actually, I would go further. After your further education, you return to the school-like world of conventional business life. The come down is terrible. Your freedom is severely curtailed. Your ability and requirement to think as a free-standing adult is limited.

It takes time to learn how to work in a place like St. Luke's. We learned the hard way. When we moved from our stylish Chiat/Day offices on Shaftesbury Avenue to the converted toffee factory in a much less fashionable part of town, we took a deep breath and jumped in.

We moved to mobile phones, no desks, lockers and client project rooms immediately. We were used to our own spaces and a wall area for photographs of the kids or invitations to parties. It was wildly dis-orientating and our first weeks in our new building were miserable. We had no one to turn to for advice on what we were doing. We were writing the manual as we were experiencing it.

But everyone was determined to make it work and now it is second nature to us.

Recently I was invited back to my old agency, CDP, for lunch. The office had since moved and was now in fashionable Soho. As I walked in, I was struck immediately by the effect of walls and corridors, closed doors and small personal offices. Everyone was packaged neatly and somewhat tightly in a small defined space. It looked really odd. And I felt as I do when I am at the zoo and see beautiful animals, reptiles, birds or insects caged in squared-off cubicles for everyone to gawk at.

⑱   Culture

Do you work somewhere that has a strong company culture?
What do I mean by that? 'Company culture'? Actually, it's quite a vague concept, weightless yet omnipresent, ardently defended yet invisible.

You will know if you have a company culture. You will know because it will be referred to by your co-workers ('Don't worry, it always takes a few weeks to get into place'). You will know because you will *feel* acceptance or rejection ('She's just not one of us. She's too ... um ... er ... you know'). You will know because your boss will tell you ('It's OK, what you're doing. Don't get me wrong. It's just that it's not the way we do things around here').

All workplaces have codes of conduct, histories, habits, routines, nicknames, catch phrases, myths, mission statements, Chairman's statements, objectives, strategies, systems, procedures. Merge them all together and you can get what might be passed off as company culture. But the real thing is decidedly different and is distinctive from the many false cultures that can be found operating deep within companies. These false cultures come in a number of forms. Below I describe five that I can instantly recognise.

I guess at this point I should assert my own definitions. I think a culture is very different from a vision, and both of these are very different from a mission. They ought to be defined, because then their role is made clear. By that, I am not suggesting that all companies need a vision, or a mission, or indeed a culture in order to be successful. I would, however, say that with them, you are likely to be more successful.

A vision is something you aim for. A long shot that you know you will never fully achieve. Or if you do, it would dramatically change the company you are in. It is an endless pursuit. Our vision at St Luke's is 'To Open Minds'.

A mission is the method by which you aim to reach your vision. Ours is 'By Creating Fascination'.

A culture is ... well ... I like how Ralph Stacey defined company cultures in his excellent book *Managing The Unknowable*:

> *'Culture is a set of beliefs or assumptions that a group of people share concerning how to see things, how to interpret events, what it is valid to question, what answers are acceptable, how to behave toward others, and how to do things. The culture of a group of people develops as they associate with each other. The most important parts of it are unconscious, and they cannot be imposed from outside, even by top management.'*

This is 'proper culture' for me, because it is honest in what it describes and practical in how it affects a company. Personally I fear cultures that will not change, have to be constantly articulated or which cannot thrive invisibly and instructively in the hearts and minds of every employee.

Stacey's culture is based on beliefs or assumptions that you all share. But not all types of businesses can be bothered with beliefs or assumptions unless they belong to the boss. 'Stop pussyfooting around and give me the sales data. I didn't get where I am today by believing in beliefs and assumptions,' the fictional CJ, head of Sunshine Desserts, might say. In fact the pursuit of the bottom line not only drives culture into a corner, it also dangerously and dismissively reconfigures it as nicey-nicey, soft stuff to 'keep the troops happy'.

The presence and/or prevalence of the culture in your workplace is defined by the type of organisation you work for. Figure 3, first shown to me by Dr. Bart Sayle, provides a useful tool to plot how individuals in society prefer to conduct their lives and manage personal strategies within their work. It has a simple premise. You either work alone or in groups of two or more. And you either like to be bound by specific rules or prefer to make agreements and unwritten laws bound by common consent.

How do you square up? (And there are no right or wrong answers.)

Are you the sort of person that believes in groups of people, teams maybe, or departments? Do you like to know exactly where you are going and how things will pan out for you? You will find yourself to the right of this diagram, if that is so.

Or are you attracted to the personal charisma and skill sets of one person, like Richard Branson or Bill Gates, or the person whose name is on the letterhead (*Tom Rooney Esq – Master Carpenter*)? If so, you will find yourself on the left of this diagram.

Do you like to have a written handbook of 'do's and don'ts'? Are there fixed procedures for doing things that you can recite? Do you have rigid salary grades and enjoy them, not least because everyone is treated with systematic fairness? If you do then you will find yourself at the top of this chart.

Or do you make it up as it goes along? Do you feel that there are 'different strokes for different folks' ('Let's all take a half-day off on all Fridays from May to September. Everyone agreed?'). Do you change your views and systems according to the market, the weather, the people you have around you? If you recognise this kind of environment, then you will find yourself at the bottom of the chart.

Figure 3: Cultures are Defined by Groups and Rules

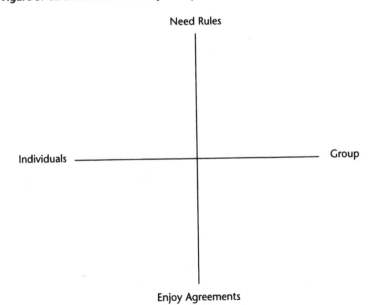

If you are in the top right corner, you enjoy hierarchy. This corner is the definition of a group of people joined by rules that they, or their superiors, need to have in order to retain direction and control. The rules will be a mixture of legal requirements (by the way, there are very few legal obligations a company has to meet) and company codes (there will be hundreds of these). What time you start in the morning and what time you clock off. Who can make what decision and who can commit what budget. Who reports to whom, when and where. And so on. These are codified and logged, and handed out to you the day you join. Most companies are in this top right corner, as are most democracies.

Democracies, in fact, pride themselves on a system of government that is preordained and inoculated against abuse or miscarriage of justice. The rules that establish exactly how, when and where you vote, for example, are well laid out. Whilst everybody may not know or care about the detail of the rules of the organisation or government, the broad disciplinary procedures are usually well known. The companies in the top right corner create lines which you may or may not cross, depending on who you are within the system. For some the lines are thin and can be debated or crossed for individual, specific reasons. For others the lines are thick and send out messages – 'Cross this line at your peril'.

These companies may flourish in this corner of the diagram, and individuals within them may enjoy sharing the same love of highly systematised procedures, but not all will. There will be those individuals who occupy different corners of the diagram from the company they are in, and the company of friends and associates they keep in and out of the workplace. Being a fish out of water in the workplace is a terrifying, but widespread malaise. Most of the time you keep your deeply felt differences to yourself, until you feel you can make a successful challenge, or until you can make a successful departure. Doing this puts you under enormous stress.

If you are personally in the bottom right corner, you would want to seek out a company that others (and possibly you as well) will call a 'cult' or a 'sect'. Companies here are not hierarchies, they are organisationally much flatter. Instead of rules, companies in this corner subscribe to beliefs and abide by agreements bound together by trust.

Interestingly there are no real positive words for companies like this.

'Sect' and 'cult' are pejorative and other possible words like 'family' or 'clan', used outside of their first and obvious meanings, suggest zealous religious groups, or conjure up images of Bringham Young (who led the Mormons out of Illinois in 1846 and established Salt Lake City as the base for Mormon colonising), or the Cosa Nostra even. Apple of the early 80s was a company like this. Steve Jobs would tell his fellow workers that they were going to create something insanely great. Insanity is fine in this corner – if that's where the leader is leading you!

If you think you live in the bottom left corner, you are in a personality driven organisation. Hierarchical or flat, it makes no difference. Entrepreneurs and dictators are to be found here. Sometimes the dictators are benign, sometimes not.

The personality will infuse and infect the whole organisation with their dynamism and entrepreneurial flair. Rules are pointless. People here make it up instinctively as they go along. Intuition replaces information. Virgin is like this. It is Richard Branson's company whether you like it or not. And if you don't, maybe you should leave, because things won't change. If you do, you will flourish. You will be well looked after and made to feel 'one of the gang'.

If you are in the top left corner of the diagram, you are probably in the worst of all places. You are an individual who conforms to a set of personal guidelines or a personal interpretation of the company's rule book. You are a 'Jobsworth', as we say in the UK. 'Oh, I couldn't do it like that, it's more than my job's worth'. Severe cases here are lonely and depressed because they wonder why they are amidst people who adhere to different rules, different principles even.

Are there any organisations like this? I think so. Public services companies, particularly the National Health Service (NHS). The NHS is Europe's biggest employer, with over a million staff on its books. Despite a requirement to provide health care, it does not have an overall mission statement. It is often down to individual medical practitioners to make up their own rules. People in the NHS are often there out of a sense of duty springing from a personal desire to help. The same duty-driven people complain all the time about the NHS and individually hold different ideas of how to improve it. Take the issue of funding, for example. It will set chief executive against consultant, doctor against nurse. Voters in an election will hold a view, patients will speak first hand, the government will take a different stance.

This diagram cannot represent tidy compartments. Human nature does not so easily conform to these stereotypes. Rather, the diagram operates best when seen as a series of 'magnetic pulls'.

The Body Shop is emotionally centred in the bottom left corner. Its staff pull it to the bottom right and the City of London's rigorous financial requirements pull it to the top right. (There is nothing more unnerving to a finance man than constantly changing rules!) An individual in one corner may belong to a company in another and may do well as the 'rogue gene' or 'token maverick'.

Where you and your workplace are centred, the directions you are pulled define an atmosphere of working conditions that sometimes add up to a culture. But if your company is pulled in more than one direction, one man's culture is another man's stricture.

Nike's culture was for years centred on its slogan 'Just Do It', which is a kind of encouragement for everyone to join them in the bottom right corner. Apple's culture of the 1980s was that of David versus Goliath. The small (but smart) guy who was up against a brutish dominant force (IBM, the Big Blue). Virgin employees are sent by 'Richard' to execute his next brilliant idea. They are entrepreneurs in his image – restless, slightly disorganised, creative, intuitive and almost always successful. Virgin is a winning brand concept.

Cultures that are badly assembled, or wafer thin, fall prey to the vagaries of my simple diagram. They are quickly vaporised when different agendas come to the fore (profit generation versus ethical purchasing, for example) and are equally quickly invoked to smother a low-quality product ('We're a distribution-led company, we've got to keep the lines moving and keep the salesforce happy; there's always someone out there who will buy our product').

Ralph Stacey's definition of culture clearly places an emphasis on shared views. Strong cultures are like the wind. Invisible, but you know when they blow and everyone feels the same force, from the same direction.

I find it important to remember this as I ponder what I call the 'Five-P' types of unreal cultures. I see manifestations of these 5-Ps a lot (and at times in St. Luke's), and I like these manifestations much less than what I choose to call the 'Proper (or Pure) Culture' – i.e. Stacey's. In fact, I worry about them, because I see companies adhering to a cultural mantra that is inconsistent with its present stakeholders or trading environment. These cultures are designed to protect and serve the community of people in the company, but more often they dupe and debilitate them. They are insidious cultures, because they can all live in the body of one company at the same time.

The 'Five Ps' are : Past Cultures, Pile-It-High Cultures, Prescribed Cultures, Pseudo Cultures and Precious Cultures.

Past Cultures

You will experience the company living with a past culture the day you join. 'When this company was started (back in 1882 maybe, or even 1997), we believed in honesty. Honesty Is The Best Policy. That's why we were successful. It worked then and it'll work now.' The culture will be firmly etched in stone (probably in a stone laid in the wall of the reception).

Like the enormous stone plaque which greets you as you enter Broadcasting House, the original site of the BBC. It looms over everyone, employees and visitors alike, and bellows a paternalistic vision of the edifying properties of quality broadcasting. And it is in Latin. This cultural icon was not made for ordinary people. It signifies broadcasting of the educated people, by the educated people and for ... well everyone.

A culture like this is nervous of the temperaments and requirements of 'new blood'. New blood is an obvious and inevitable consequence for all companies. Yet, a culture rooted in the past runs counter to that biological certainty. Cultures like this are taught, not caught. They are not like the wind, they are like a prescription. They are not weightless, they are sonorous. They are not relevant, they are annoyingly and cloyingly archaic.

They can be ignored. But be careful. There is always someone who can invoke the right sentence at the wrong time, for you.

Past Cultures haunt companies like the ghost of Julius Caesar, who haunts the full five acts of Shakespeare's play but who appears only in the first third. They are spoken about as if they are living, whilst everyone will really know they died a long time ago.

Do you remember my story about how CDP was haunted by Frank Lowe in this way? Even though he left in 1982, he was still spoken about in 1990 and I suspect still is even today. He left his mark, a specific culture based on Total Creative Focus. The creative people were isolated specialists who delivered highly polished jewels. Everyone, including the client, were slaves to a process which religiously and rigorously crowned each piece of work. To reject work from the creative teams in this culture was simply not done.

Past Cultures drag on companies and slow them down. They alienate new people and they make old-timers feel comfortable. They are often found on the top right corner of the diagram, where they can sit and vegetate, and probably do no more harm than make many employees feel as if they do not really belong – as if the company really belongs to someone a long way off. Sometimes you will find them in the bottom right corner. Here they are debilitating and dangerous. They become a creed. Getting emotional sign-on to the creed is like one long hazy bar mitzvah with a distant (and often unrecognised) reward of adult entry into the community, sect or cult.

Pile-It-High Cultures

Successful companies which grow fast often don't stop to assess what they really stand for. Consequently, what the company was doing in the time segment you joined and what you personally believed in at the time become the overriding factors that determine the culture. Large groups of people will each have a different spin on the culture through-out the year, until the annual get-together tries to 'wire' all the different segments together in one glorious, all-encompassing speech.

Apple Computers is an example of a Pile-It-High Culture. It is Steve Jobs, it is a couple of poor students in a garage, it is a piratical attitude, it is David versus Goliath, it is creative graphics, it is 'for the rest of us', it is big business, it is John Sculley, it is not Microsoft or Bill Gates. All of these are good qualities. Some are exceptional. Some were unique. Others are to be found in the most humdrum organisations. But they do not all seemlessly connect.

Because individually they have a history, a story and a value; they are piled on top of each other like children's bricks. And like children's bricks, when one falls others come down, too. A contemporary culture cannot be made up of everything that a company ever was. That is possibly something else – the DNA maybe. A culture must develop as associations develop and as the future reveals itself.

Pile-It-High Cultures are rarely found in the top of the diagram because they do not thrive in systems. It is systems which save companies from this type of culture, because they process out and constantly refine company propositions. The illogicality of a culture being made up of discrete segments forming the time-line of a company would somewhere along the way be spotted and ousted. No, this occupies the bottom of the diagram, where strong individuals and close groups hang onto experiences, safe and secure in the knowledge that they shaped and informed them but blind to the knowledge that they are in fact cumbersome, confusing and not at all contemporary.

Pile-It-High Cultures do not add focus to a company and consequently lead to endless internal navel gazing or double guessing. The humans in a company like this will often talk at cross purposes without realising it. Multicultures lead to multilingual conversations, with not everyone proficient in every required language.

Proscribed Cultures

These leave no room for debate. I have an example that is close to home. For a while in the early 90s at Chiat/Day London we had a flag which read: 'God, Guts and Creativity'. In the Los Angeles office at the same time they were wearing T-shirts that declared: 'Innovate or Die (and death is not an option)'. In New York and Toronto they were fond of an older Chiat/Day T-shirt that stated: 'Good Enough Is Not Enough'.

Proscribed Cultures tell you what to do and how to do it. They dictate what you will believe in. They are to be found to the left of the diagram. They are not often found in hierarchies, although you might expect an authoritarian perspective to belong there. That's because Proscribed Cultures are not part of group life, they are handed down, like Moses' Commandments, from one well-defined source – normally your leader. Hierarchies and cults treat Proscribed Cultures as witty aphorisms and useful slogans. They have limited motivational use.

But for companies that are individually driven (as Chiat/Day was, by Jay) they are often everything, and they are backed up by large-scale internal PR. Badges, T-shirts, posters and videos all proclaim the culture of the moment. 'Just Do It' is an example. It is one mighty culture neatly defined in a tiny slogan. Perfect.

But cultures like those gain superficial buy-in. They allow employees to articulate a culture in neatly wrapped parcels. They are mistaken for passwords that let you into a magic kingdom full of cultural nuances and resonances that are easily deciphered. In truth, they are simpler than that. They are what they are, just a handful of words, crafted or accidentally discovered by small coteries of people who invested the words with their own inner-meaning.

Language is full of such annoying and misunderstood shorthand. 'The Dunkirk Spirit' has come to mean a spirit of endeavour and derring-do. A 'knuckle-down' and grit your teeth, 'we're all in this together' attitude. But actually it referred to small, individual acts of uncommon bravery to snatch and salvage something, however small, from the jaws of defeat. Dunkirk was a disaster. The spirit refers not to the army but to the civilians who came out in tiny boats and rescued the troops. To say a situation is someone's 'Dunkirk' means a complete abandonment of one's position, whereas for many it wrongly means an example of heroism.

Similarly, 'Good Enough Is Not Enough' was read differently by different people. For some it meant that mediocre work was not to be accepted, for others it meant the constant generation of creativity to find the best. For most it was an authoritarian injunction, based on a negative, that somehow made one feel permanently reprimanded.

Proscribed Cultures are an alternative reality. They are not like the wind, they are like the weather forecast – 'Rain Tomorrow'! They exist only in the workplace and are awkward outside of it. They do not readily chime with the personal value systems of employees and are usually exercises in sloganeering designed to 'rally the troops'. As such, they fail to harness and mobilise the true potential of the workforce and live more comfortably on T-shirts and posters than in the hearts and minds of employees.

Pseudo Cultures

Pseudo Cultures are a simple misrepresentation of the word culture. They are not shared beliefs or assumptions, they are things like the *modus operandi* of a workplace, the systems, the management style. They define an aspect of life in the workplace but they go no further. They are easy to spot, because they elevate almost everything else above humans. They are cultures that like to focus on process, performance and product rather than beliefs, assumptions, attitudes. In this way, Pseudo Cultures belong firmly to the Industrial Age, rather than the Creative Age, because they display a production line and distribution mentality. They ring-fence the internal workings of the company to the exclusion of all other possible stakeholders.

There is nothing wrong about basing your company in easy-to-understand processes, it is just that when you pretend they are more than just process, you fake the effect the workplace has on people. Cultures move people to *behave* in a certain way. By misrepresenting the notions of culture as a process, you create an environment where employees become uncertain about the actions and expressions they deploy to endorse the corporate culture. In short, you have the opposite effect of what a culture can achieve. Uncertainty.

Advertising agencies often say they have 'creative' cultures. What they mean exactly is unclear. For some it means that there is a quality control process in place which makes sure that key, valued, skilled people put their signature, literally, to the work that is produced. In so doing, they stand behind the work and defend it. They stand in defence of 'creativity' and will assert certain rights like, 'We know best'. In truth the only defence, should the product come under question, is 'Trust us'. The culture does not travel beyond the notion of trust (which is a variable quotient), because it is not based on anything substantive that all humans involved in the transaction can buy into.

For others the creative culture is an adherence to a type of creative product. It is a regimen, a prevailing system or set of conditions that produces a consistent style. It is the view of the owners at St. Luke's that the creative award ceremonies propagate this style and creates an atmosphere that deludes employees throughout the industry into thinking they have joined a recognisable culture. There is a mantra to this Pseudo Culture that revolves around the words 'Relevant', 'Distinctive' and 'Effective'. They fail to describe truly the shared beliefs of the workforce.

Other industries are similarly deluded and would do better to reassess the value of the expressions they have. The pursuit of Pseudo Cultures is a major reason, I believe, why there is little to differentiate companies beyond price, design and quality, all of which can be emulated. Perhaps there is no need to differentiate – but if so, why do so many companies try so hard to be different? Difference in itself may not provide competitive edge, but it certainly provides fascination.

I asked 40 senior managers from a recently privatised energy utility if they had a corporate culture. It was ingrained from the top down they said; what's more you will find it in the company report. It was a culture of fairness they said.

I was naughty. Half an hour later, I asked them to write down ten adjectives that they, their associates or their families and friends would use to describe the working day in their company. General words like stressful, exciting, active, competitive, confusing, busy, all came up. There were some specific adjectives, too, that were applicable to their organisation: legal, red tape, international, complex, hierarchical.

Not one of the 400 words that were generated (there were 150-plus different words and many repeats) was 'fair' or 'fairness' – i.e., the company report did not chime with the cultural expectations of the employees.

'Fairness', in the company report, related to transactions with stake-holders, many of whom were foreign governments. There was an obligation with this company to strike a two-way fair deal with a multiplicity of suppliers and partners. It defined the way the company felt it should deal, but it did not define a culture and if, given the words that are generated, it tried to, it would come up against a barrage of problems. 'This company is not fair to women', one said, 'it's a rough, tough male environment'. A woman responded (there were three); 'that's because you make it a rough, tough male environment'. You see the application of a notion as a Pseudo Culture can lead to uncertainty and disgruntlement.

Pseudo Cultures can be found anywhere on the diagram. They are the cultures that can lead individuals to believe they are acting in accordance with company desires, when in fact they are acting out their own personal view of the culture. They can be found in large companies that participate in internal communication programmes. Cults can drum up support easily around a Pseudo Culture, because they are groups that respond readily to mantra. And entrepreneurs can find themselves in a Pseudo Culture that is maybe even not of their own design – a culture that is foisted upon them by eager acolytes.

Precious Cultures

Some companies hoard their culture amongst a few people greedily, as if deployment would somehow vanquish or certainly diminish it. It is kept locked up in the boardroom or is secretly administered as if from a corporate chalice to the chosen few.

This culture will very ably define a company culture, but it will define a company that only the chosen few believe they belong to. It establishes a two-tier system. A true culture that bonds the inner-circle and a secondary layer of employees whose ability to grasp and be motivated by the culture is of little consequence.

In companies that have Precious Cultures, few people really matter. In companies with Precious Cultures, the workforce will constantly change. Precious Cultures not only divide companies, they create long-term instability. The more the inner-circle understand, relate and respond to the culture, the more alien they will become. The more alien they become, the greater the staff turnaround.

Family businesses are often examples of this. For example I know of a large, well-known retailer that has a well-defined culture at the top of the organisation. It is a true culture and one to be respectful of, because it has enabled a family firm to spread to a worldwide organisation. Those who manage the company are synchronised in their empathetic understanding of how the company works. This understanding per-meates through the company only so far (local senior management) and then dries up. The tellers and store assistants are not party to the culture and consequently do not have the same degree of involvement with the company.

Precious Cultures most regularly live in the bottom left of the diagram. They are the constructs of successful entrepreneurs who operate with a loyal and diligent coterie of close comrades. Surprisingly, these com-panies can more easily succeed in developing a set of shared beliefs company wide.

It's so easy to create a Precious Culture, and it is this type and Pile-It-High that I am most mindful of when I reflect upon the culture of St. Luke's. You see, all cultures can be pernicious in the way that they brutally reject non-conformists, but these two are the most easy for a company like ours to adopt.

St. Luke's is obviously in the bottom right corner of the diagram. It's a company based on a set of beliefs. We are nearer the centre, rather than on the outside edge, because we do have some rules. They exist in the Owners Manual which is issued to everyone who joins the company. It outlines important things like the maternity policy and the protocol for taking sabbaticals. It is also full of advice such as why cynicism is like a factory fire for companies based on human capital. Or thoughts like Tom Peters' fabulous 'Profit Is Like Health, We Need It, But It Is Not What We

Live For'. It is a thought-piece to remind us of the role of money-making. It starts and stops there. The culture of St. Luke's is not about what we do with our money.

(Cynicism comes from the ancient Greek, κύων, meaning *a dog*. It referred to a sect of philosophers founded by Antisthenes, a student of Socrates, who were surly and showed contempt for the enjoyments of life. Their contempt was often showed by public displays of urinating against the wall. Like dogs. Cynics, then, are people who piss on ideas. And in a company which grows ideas, it stands as a first-class felony.)

But there are lots of unwritten rules, too. Another is the dress code. People dress as is fitting for them and the occasion, not as part of a theatrical business device to display orderliness. For example, we do not have secretaries. It is generally understood that we can do our own 'menial' work – although this can often be irritating.

For example, we self-regulate as much as possible. We self-regulate our personnel requirements through an outside consultant. St. Luke's pays for a service that anyone can access whenever they feel the need. The consultant advises on relationships, careers, personality clashes, etc.

We self-regulate our salaries. St. Luke's sets an overall target, but as individuals we approach our reviews with an idea of what we think we should be earning. This process has been glamorously described by the press as 'Set Your Own Salaries'. The expression is fine, but has to be read within a context of the overall financial ecosystem, of which everyone is aware.

At St. Luke's we see things differently. We see our input as belonging to ourselves, but that we in turn are contributing to others' and the welfare of the company. We understand the need for personal responsibility in all our actions, particularly with regard to other people. We see cross-fertilisation and reinvention as critical to remaining contemporary and intellectually active. The combination of the way we are owned and managed, the way we work, the way we use the office, the way we create our product, and the look, feel and effect of our product are second nature to us. Journalists write about them every week. We have been constantly filmed, by the likes of Tokyo TV, BBC, CNN or Channel 4. We are in magazines around the world. Our office appears in architectural digests everywhere. We are even 'required reading' for business management degrees in the USA and other important academic institutions.

Yet we hardly talk about these things internally. In this sense, what we do and how we associate are invisible. These things to us are like the oxygen of our environment.

What do we talk about? We talk about our product and its effect. We talk about developing the company. We talk about squabbles. In other words, we talk about the engineering of the company.

The QUEST is the cultural barometer of the company. It contains a cross-section of people (all voted in by the employees). Their watchful eye on the culture of the company is not forced upon them from a 'top-down' perspective. They are the culture. The QUEST itself is part of the culture. We feel the culture of the company like a wind blowing through our bones. Sometimes it is a chill wind; then the QUEST warms us up. Sometimes it is a torrid wind; then the QUEST cools us down.

Newcomers are treated to 'Culture Club'. I sit down with them and the first thing I say is: 'This is your company, you own it.' I am thrilled when I meet our new owners, because I know that they have the greatest potential to take us forward.

It is a culture that makes growth exciting. Perfect for a movement.

⑲ Technology

There is a general disinterest in technology at St. Luke's, which is odd for a company whose owners spend 15 per cent of net profits on upgrading it each year and whose working patterns are dramatically changed by it every day. Let me explain.

The technology in our office comprises two essential elements. The telephone and the computer. Both have changed the way we work. The telephones are officially classified (by those in the telecommunications business) as an internal DECT mobile system. They are just like ordinary desk phones: you can divert, put on hold and memorise a handful of numbers. But they are internal mobile phones, which travel with you wherever you are. (This can be embarrassing at times; phones are rude instruments which interrupt thoughtlessly whenever they wish.)

The computers are all slaves to a central server – the Brain – which operates a Lotus Notes system to provide each terminal with electronic diary/project management, e-mail and virtual entry to the filing cabinets in each of the client project rooms. There are computers everywhere, on desks, ledges and kitchen tables. We choose one we fancy, sit down and get working. When we've finished we sign off and move somewhere else.

The phones and computers enable us to operate the flexible working patterns we desire. Patterns which are disruptive and anti-routine. By changing the way we work, we are changing the way we think, about business, the nature of work, creativity and also technology itself.

In my working life, I have seen technologies both overhaul huge business institutions and change domestic life as well. The story of how technology has evolved since the late 70s is a famous one. But my story is about how wanting to work differently has led us into a new understanding of these technologies. I believe both the phone and the computer have entered a new phase and given impetus to the Creative Age. But each in its own way.

I remember walking down Praed Street in Paddington, London, on the morning of my first day in advertising. Praed Street hasn't changed much since 1978. It's a street that serves a major railway terminus, Paddington Station, and like so many in such a vicinity, features low-grade retailers, smutty newsagents and tacky souvenir shops.

In a shop selling large gaudy watches, executive toys and office stationery I saw my first-ever pocket calculator. It was branded 'Texas' and has bound Texas Instruments to this technology forever in my mind. It was a large calculator, about eight inches square. Below the price (they ranged in this shop from £18 to £22, which makes them nearer £50 to £60 today) were the words, 'Complex mathematical calculations done in a second! With LCD!'

It was pure magic. Two years later we were all issued with these calculators and I quickly unlearned my mental arithmetic and so sentenced myself to a life of key-pad pushing. I showed my friends the LCD. 'It's a liquid crystal display,' I would say and proudly awarded myself another life sentence of computer jargon that would inexorably lead to expressions like 'virtual cyber-space reality' falling from my lips without so much as a thought for what I was really saying.

The pocket calculator was the first sentinel of technological revolution in the workplace, but although it was magic, it wasn't surprising. It was a trick I had seen before. Ever since Stanley Kubrick's masterful *2001*, I was ready for computers that would change, maybe dominate, our lives.

The film had set me up for videophones as well, but I had to wait until the early 90s for these and even then the technology was limited. The phones we used in the late 70s were made of heavy plastic and had dials instead of push-button pads. They belonged to a post-War generation of Bakelite and Tupperware.

Written work was performed by secretaries with fast typewriters. They were electric, but they were not the sophisticated word-processing typewriters that emerged five years later. The office stationery cupboards would hold small bottles of correcting fluid with names like 'Tipp-Ex' and 'Snowpake'. This was Dickensian, although we didn't realise it. I shudder when I look back and think that in those days a man had already walked on the moon – ten years earlier.

Our office eventually got a computer. I remember the day it came. It sat in the basement in a special perspex air-conditioned box. There were large palettes of computer printout paper surrounding the computer and small boxes of floppy disks.

We then hired our first computer controller. He was a new breed of executive, the like of which I had never seen before; slick, intelligent, debonair even, with a convertible BMW. He administered to this machinery in a mysterious way. No one really knew what he would be doing, but he spent hours doing it. When he emerged from the basement, he would appear like someone from a different planet.

The computer was bought by the company, but it really belonged to him. No one would be allowed into the basement without him. He`had a special security system installed, not because he feared it would be stolen (it was the size of four washing machines), but in case uncouth business barbarians would inadvertently wreck it as they pored curiously over its glistening wires and shiny metal plates.

He said it could do anything. 'You just programme it,' he would say, as a stock response to any question about its capabilities. Computers at this time were very *private* machines. Long before the operators became Nerds or Anoraks, they were revered like trained priests who had learned holy languages like BASIC and FORTRAN.

In secret places, new acolytes like Bill Gates and Paul Allen were writing their own special versions of BASIC to transform the MIT's Altair 8800 mini computer kit into a more usable, human-friendly machine.

Computers were for boffins, for the finance department, for inventory management, for regulating machinery and the great question was, 'What have they got to do with the rest of us?'

In 1984 we found out. Steve Jobs rescued us from the private world of computers and introduced the Apple Macintosh, a computer for the rest of us. Computers became *personal*.

The launch commercial for the Apple Mac is the most expensive ad ever produced. Directed by Ridley Scott, who made feature films such as *Blade Runner* and *Thelma and Louise*, it was based on George Orwell's book *1984* and showed uniform ranks of drone-like people liberated by the arrival of the iconoclastic Apple Mac. The ad cost $600,000 to make and $1,000,000 to run. It ran only once. It was an act of sheer bravado for a company brimming with entrepreneurial flair. The advertising agency was Chiat/Day Los Angeles.

The launch of the Apple Mac was a sideswipe at big bureaucracies (like IBM) and ushered in a whole new attitude to computers. That year, so entranced by the individual power of these computers, Jay Chiat overnight threw out all the electronic typewriters and placed an Apple Mac SE on everyone's desk. They became a symbol for entrepreneurial, individual performance. The graphics were simple. They were intuitive. Hey, even kids could use them. The Apple symbol became a clarion call for a whole new generation of businesspeople to embrace technology and access its power for personal liberation.

The Apple Macintosh SE has been superseded now (although that's what we were using in the London office of Chiat/Day as late as 1994). If you wanted to see one now you would have to go to scrapyards or underfunded schools or to the top floor of the Museum of Modern Art on West 53rd Street in New York where an example of one sits quietly in a corner, a silent display every bit as pensive and meaningful as one of those statues from Easter Island.

Throughout the 80s I was never acquainted with personal computers. At CDP, where I worked from 1983 to 1989, the only computers I knew about were either in the accounts department or were grand calculators assessing volume discounts on TV airtime. We worked in our own individual small cubicles and communicated via secretaries.

At some time the utilitarian phone received a make-over and digital tone dialling emerged to take over from the old pulse method. The phones felt lighter, flimsier, more worthless, but the features they offered were getting more useful. Speed dialling was the buzzword of the late 80s.

When I joined Chiat/Day I joined the computer-literacy set. Friends from other advertising agencies used to visit me just to look at how I had learned to master this unique skill. When I showed them how I was receiving and sending e-mails from around the world, they were positively astounded.

The City, of course, had already embraced computer technology, but outside of specific, complex trading situations, PCs were rarely seen. In the 90s they moved slowly into the general workplace out from the bowels of the accounts department, through secretaries to everyone's desk.

The idea that a PC sits on everyone's desk has caught on and it joins the ranks of other personal business paraphernalia like your briefcase, Rolodex and in/out tray. It has been folded into office life unquestioningly. It fulfils a number of tasks and has added another dimension at the same time. It is a superb word processor, but it is also the provider of e-mail. Before e-mail there were memos, announcements and notice boards. These still prevail, but e-mail has added a conversational level to formal messaging.

Offices have become reliant on PC applications. They have become extensions of human workers, electronic tendrils that reach out, touch and communicate in a variety of ways. Our dedication to their power has made us wonder what life without PCs was like. In one sense they have connected us even more to each other in the workplace, but in another they have become alienating, lonely places, that pass on electronic versions of our word and voices. Hunched over our keyboards, the sound of tapping keys has become a symbol for industry. A silent computer somehow registers a lack of enterprise.

In fact an over-emphasis on the abilities of our computer technologies has created many curious syndromes. For example, it has put us in awe of our children, whereas we used to be in awe of accumulated wisdom. Our children take to computers like a fish to water; old folk seem so much older now – what do they know? But in our haste to worship the computer skills of our infants, are we not forgetting the extraordinary achievement of learning to speak or ride a bike, and the equally extraordinary value in the sagacity of our elders?

It has created a dependency (like a pet). The Tamogotchi are merely childish commercial objects that act for me as metaphors for our indulgence in the technology of personal computers. Some are incredibly personal. Complex passwords, custom-made screen savers, personalised search engines, e-mail, computer games. All these have created a relationship with computers beyond their actual function. At Chiat/Day, where we had a computer on every desk, there was a greedy hunger to see who had sent you e-mail and there was a cosy comfort in seeing information being displayed exactly how you like it, day in, day out.

The computer has created the IT department. IT stands for Information

Technology, but that's not really what our computers at work are doing, is it? They don't provide information unless you search for things on the Internet or subscribe to information services like Reuters. It should be called the LT department – the Liberation Technology department – but it borrows its name from the fancy that we live in the Information Age and that information is power. It isn't. It's a burden. Hoarded and meted out secretly and selectively, information is used as a weapon for control.

We live with more passwords and key numbers than ever before. For our computers, our homes, our car radios, our banks, you name it. We fear anybody knowing too much about ourselves, because that means we have handed over information, handed over power. Information that you have, but will not share, is a power move.

This is crazy. Think about the value of a secret. It has no value whatsoever until it is told, at which point it ceases to become a secret and becomes selective information. But if you can persuade someone to think you hold many powerful secrets, you are in a dominant position. How often have you walked into a room where two senior people are chatting? They stop dead. Were they telling a blue joke or were they sharing information about ... huh! ... *you*? Personal computers have become burrows for stored secrets. Thousands of them. But at St. Luke's we view them differently.

When everyone owns the company, there are few secrets, if any, that are needed. Personnel issues of a sensitive, say, medical nature are a secret. Your bank account, too. But information about your own company cannot be kept a secret. At St. Luke's you are allowed free rein into the company's computer 'nooks and crannies' to find out whatever you wish, including that greatest of taboos, salaries.

Computers for us are clearly not *private*, but because we don't have any dedicated to individuals (there are some specialist design computers and some with specific accounting packages that are different from the other computers, but they are still available to anyone who needs them), they are not *personal* computers either.

Computers for us are *public*. This changes our attitude to them dramatically. They are like public phone booths, roads, traffic lights or public libraries. They are incredibly useful when used, but totally redundant, and in fact somewhat ugly, when they are not.

Through the the gift of microprocessors, computers (and many other domestic and business goods) get better and cheaper, thereby defeating our preconceived notions that better things are more expensive. They serve us well and add value to what we do, but in themselves are too readily obsolete. They are like the casual acquaintances you meet while on the beach in summer. You like them, then, in that place and enjoy their company. You promise to meet again but you never do (only really special ones) and you happily pick up newer, fresher, more interesting associations the following year. As the years go by, your ardour for the relationship cools and eventually you scrub the people from your address book.

Overall we at St. Luke's have a coolness towards computers and pride ourselves in only needing 70 for the 105 employees.

Using technology creatively saves money we exclaim at St. Luke's. But that's not the real reason we do it. It's a happy coincidence that technology for us is more cost effective than other places, but the real delight is in knowing that our capital investment in this superior race called 'Technology' (chess Grand Master Gary Kasparov was beaten in a six-match chess series in 1997 by $3\frac{1}{2}$ points to $2\frac{1}{2}$ points by IBM's Deep Blue supercomputer. Deep Blue can look at an average of 200 million positions per second – that's superior in my book) runs at a lower percentage than our human capital.

We are cool towards our computers, but, curiously, we have befriended our phones. Phones for us at St. Luke's have moved up the evolutionary relationship scale as computers have dropped down.

It was unplanned. Visitors to St. Luke's make a bee-line towards what we call the phone table. It's a purpose-built construction designed to carry all our personal mobile phones and chargers. I laugh when visitors ask questions about it, which they surely must, because it's an odd piece of equipment, but one all future offices will one day have. I laugh because I see a smirking journalist on a TV programme in the future standing by our phone table saying, 'In the old days, phone tables looked like this!'

Our day starts neither at a preordained hour nor at the moment you log on to a computer, but when you lift your phone from the phone table. At that moment your one trillion brain cells are potentially linked to the other 104 trillion in the workplace and any other sources of stimulation you enjoy.

You may argue that fixed-wire phones link people up in the same way, but there is difference. Fixed phones fix conversations: 'Get me our New

York office, please, Miss Jones.' Fixed phones fix locations: when I am talking to my mother, I see her standing in her hall; even if she has a cordless phone I still see her in her house.

Without desks we are not located. Yet the conversations do not begin with 'Where are you?' (as they so often do on cellular phones) or 'How are you?' as they do on fixed phones. They start fluidly as natural conversations start: 'Hi, Kate, are you and Tim free for five minutes?' They create little oral-electric conversations of the same weight as the oral-only ones.

Alexander Graham Bell invented the telephone, it is said, to improve his wife's hearing. The conventional phone conversation speeds up and amplifies the human voice and transmits it over huge distances. Our phones do the same and more. They improve our ability to connect digitally, to make serendipitous discovery, to keep close together.

This multiplicity of inter-connectedness via our internal mobile phone system improves our thinking, because it opens our minds, through our ears, to omnipresent conversation. The phone is no longer a dumb plastic mould, it is an intelligent object. We personalise our phones as if they are part of our make-up. Occasionally one gets lost, or someone borrows someone else's without asking. There is a furore. A huge one. The angriest e-mails are sent about this; it is deeply upsetting.

A new arrival remarked at this: 'Haven't you all got better things to do than moan about a lost phone?' From where she came, a phone was a light plastic mould full of wires and was of little value beyond its obvious utility. 'Missing phones dismember us,' I replied. 'Without your phone you are like a limb without ligaments.'

Technology can and should change the workplace.

It can allow you to redeploy your talent for greater added value

For example, it can promote secretaries out of the typing pool into real added-value jobs, where their brains as well as their fingers are put to good creative use. Word-processing packages are incredibly simple, but managers shy away from using them because they have it in their heads that typing is not their job. The thing is, it isn't typing. When NASA bring down Challenger shuttles with a series of tiny electronic gestures on a keyboard, they are not typing. A keyboard is not a typewriter, even though it closely resembles one. I see them as very distant cousins, like man and apes: some core similarities, but many more practical and behavioural differences.

A comment I get a lot is, 'Don't you have better things to do than type your own letters?' My response is that I can usually create a memo, letter or document faster than I can dictate and check it. I'm not boasting. It's just that technology affords me that privilege. And at an average of £3,000 per computer, it's a privilege I feel is right to take up.

Other people say, 'But who organises your diary?' I self-administer my diary via a computerised diary management system. It's wonderful. I decide when I want a meeting and with whom and a few punches of the key pad later I can either set the date I want or automatically reschedule to a suitable time if I see that someone cannot make it.

'Who fields your calls?' I do. If I'm in, I'll take my calls or leave a voice-messaging service, or make sure The Hub (our central reception/ switchboard, meeting and greeting place run by 'Hubsters' who, like air-traffic control, count us all in and out, and monitor our movements) send me an e-mail stating who's called. I can switch my phone off if I do not want to be interrupted and I can divert it to a colleague if I am expecting a specific call. We can all do this. Why do I need special treatment when technology is such a universal provider?

I'll tell you why. It's a difficult concept for so many people in the workforce to comprehend. It's because businesses have built up a 200-year-old 'grammar' that it employs to uphold theatrical conventions it feels is so necessary. It's a theatre that protects an old regime and old thinking. It's a pre-computer grammar that ensures the boss is treated regally and that the juniors are made to feet insignificant. It's an Industrial Age concept of barons and serfs.

At St. Luke's technology is a great leveller. Beyond the skill of programming, the use of computers is a fair and democratic process. That's good, because it means that work's greatest enabler is available to any and every human, regardless of who they might be.

Technology can make valuable new connections – if you let it

I was talking to a large supermarket retailer one day. He was thinking of moving his headquarters and seized upon the opportunity to work in a more contemporary way.

'How does it work at the moment?' I asked.

'Well, we are organised around our various categories. We have buyers and quality controllers and merchandising teams centred on mothers and babies, off licence, fresh fish and so on. At head office the Directors all have their own offices, each with a secretary sitting outside, and the remainder is organised around business groups.'

'And Finance?'

'Finance is separate.

'Distribution?'

'Separate.'

'Advertising and Marketing?'

'In a world of their own, but they get their budgets and instructions from the business divisions. The Marketing Director has her own office, with a secretary outside.'

This company's technology served and reinforced this system. It was decidedly not there to interrupt or challenge it. The separate divisions were profit centres. If 'stationery' started to lose money, then there would be a discrete, surgical examination of why. Was it placed incorrectly on the shelves? Was the product range wrong? Were the customers simply too concentrated on buying food? Were the stationery team at head office no good?

Technology could help answer many of these questions by doing comparative analyses or by looking at costs, consumer behaviour and 'traffic flow' (how the customers actually walked around the stores). But technology in this instance was serving a set of preordained assumptions about how the business operated.

'Supposing you organised yourselves around your customers? You could have a male-only group, female, baby, kids, teens, pensioners ... you name it. A reconfiguring of your technology and a retraining in the way you use it might enable you to make some extraordinary connections.'

The retailer was worried that this could mean a total staff reorganisation. But it doesn't necessarily (it might eventually if you wanted it to). What it would definitely require is a greater commitment to the idea that technology can change the way you work and think, and by so doing, provide you with a potentially distinctive point of difference.

Technology can provide brain food for starving, or just lazy, minds

There are over 150 million separate items stored in the new British Library on Euston Road, just 200 yards from our office in Duke's Road. These items include books, patents, manuscripts, magazines, journals, sound recordings, video recordings and stamps. Every known language on this planet is represented and every subject is covered. In a blaze of publicity and with much justifiable pride, the Library, which was planned over 20 years ago (in the Communication Age), sprung to life in 1997 (the Creative Age).

In this one building there is so much learning from so many centuries that browsing is impossible. Indeed, at face value, it is a pretty strange library because one is hit immediately by the realisation that this building has few books and few shelves. The Library's collection is held in stores deep underground. They are accessed by on-line catalogues and an automated ordering system. The tables are all numbered. You log in your number and a light comes on when your order is ready. You read what you have and you study long and hard. The books are then returned and travel back, deep into the bowels of the Library until one day, someone else asks to look at them.

The British Library digs you deeper into what you already know or nearly know. It will most likely deepen your existing understanding of a specific subject, rather than broaden your thinking and take you somewhere entirely new. It is 150 million items of things you know you can discover, because they already exist.

I have a copy of *The Times* newspaper at home that I have kept safe since I was a boy of 12. It is the edition of 6 January 1969 and the headline reads, 'The Colour of Space'. I loved this picture. I still do, but for different reasons.

Then I loved it for the sheer majesty, the achievement of showing earth in all its glory as a blue, serene planet. It wasn't the whole earth, it was an 'earth rise' from the moon's perspective. Neither I nor anyone on the planet had seen earth like this before. It placed us humbly in the long line up of planets in the solar system, but it also united all earthlings and showed us in one photographic shot the small rock that belonged to us all. It made us more 'inner-directed' as a species. It made us think differently about our planet, even though we knew we *were* a planet.

Now I like it for the shocking ego trip that it really was. There was *Apollo 8*, with its dashing astronauts, Frank Borman, James Lovell and William Anders, driving forward into space on a journey of discovery, and the only thing that was truly fascinating was a photograph of ourselves. I guess I am still thinking about that photograph.

You have to work hard to look round corners others don't look round, and you have to work even harder to know what to do once you're there. Life for most is simpler with routines and systems that we are accustomed to. But it's also duller.

If you wish, you can always sit next to a different person at St. Luke's. You can sit next to the same person all day as well, but in different locations. Not everybody makes the jump from fixed to changing location very easily. Some do it in a day, others take a year. A tiny percentage are growing roots. Those who do move around love it. In fact, the thought of being in the same place all day fills me with horror. I know that I and others won't make the connections that we now know we can. I was sitting next to a typographer once. He was in his early 20s. We chatted perfunctorily to start with, but knowing I was writing this book he said, 'I saw a great book on modern office architecture the other day, I'll bring it in for you.'

I did not know this book existed and I cannot be sure that any other connection I may have more conventionally made would not have bought it to my attention. Actually it doesn't matter. The connection was made.

This connection was not of the general coincidental nature. As owners of the same entity we are bound to hot-house subjects of mutual interest. Invisibly throughout the day we are working out ideas and cross-referencing items that make sense to our business.

Telephone and computer technology allow us to do this. But add one other thing. The Internet. Each computer at St. Luke's is linked directly to the net. Idly surfing or diligently looking, we are all 'out there' making more connections.

The speed of association has put our human capital into a different kind of spaceship; one that travels at the speed of light without so much as a rumble of movement. It is rewarding and liberating. The randomness of the associations we make and the speed at which sentiments coalesce to form a consensus view are extraordinary and exhilarating.

The British Library, with its millions of well-ordered stacks of information on 600 kilometres of underground shelving, its serried ranks of beautifully manicured study carrels and its astonishing architecture and design, now, barely six months after its grand opening, seems weirdly and sadly confined to very specific types of discovery. It will be subject-centric and analogue in form. Sure, the human brain will make its own connections with what it reads and will assimilate data from hundreds of pages flicked over and annotated as fast as a human can write. But it will be a sequential form of study, methodical and set against a specific aim. It will not be digital in form, it will not match the speed of technology, it will not permit absurd, serendipitous or random connections. Conceived in one age, pregnant for too long, it was unexpectedly born in another.

Today, billions of people in almost a billion homes can exchange views with each other. A billion people can attend a funeral. But this interconnectedness is also breeding an array of shorthand messages that in their own way render ideas into tidy parcels. It is annoying that we do this. Interconnectedness is a journey, not the discovery of a new place. Most ideas can be communicated with icons; clichés package inventiveness into tidy packages – think of a cowboy and you think of a cowboy hat, waistcoat, gun, holster, boots and spurs. Get shown the real thing and the gap between perception and reality opens fast. Media imagery tends to close down outward thinking as it shorthands concepts for instant delivery.

The very technology to open minds closes them. To allow technology to take you somewhere, I guess you must want to travel in the first place. We all did.

㉒ **Output**

n this, the last of seven chapters looking at what happens to the shape of a company when you really do put humans first, I can show you what happens to the product we make as a result of our model of ownership, our organisational structure, our culture, our way of working, and our attitude to and use of technology.

All these combine ultimately to focus on what we make and earn income on – creative communications. All of us have at some stage in the past discussed what sort of company we would like to work in, but when it came to assessing the impact that this would have on our work, we were in unchartered territory. We had removed many of what we felt were conventional hurdles to producing innovative work – habit-forming routine, ego, greed and narrowly defined creative ownership and control, for example – but we did not know what the effect this unshackling would have.

Whatever business you are in, you will be bound by rules that determine what sort of product you make. You will carry on making the same thing as your friend in a competitive company is making until someone changes the rules. Until James Dyson came along, every vacuum cleaner was the same; until Pret À Manger came along, sandwich shops were just sandwich shops.

This chapter is a detailed look at how advertising is produced. It is the main thing we produce at St. Luke's. But not the only thing. We have made a documentary and a short film. We are creating an event attended by children from all over the world to express their imagination. We have produced live theatre. In fact, we have groups with creative producers who do no advertising at all.

Although it is about the production of advertising, ask yourself whether there are any similarities with your business. I know there will be.

Now, conventionally speaking, I am not a creative person (see below, for what constitutes a creative person). But the St. Luke's people I will quote in this chapter are. The difference is they have ceased to ring-fence creativity and have become ambassadors and proponents of an art form which is not finite, but is never ending. 'Creativity at St. Luke's is like a constantly running tap of ever flowing ideas,' says one of our creatives, James Parr, an Art Director by training. 'We don't bottle it and package it. We constantly bathe in it.'

The word 'creative' has a special meaning in advertising. The output of advertising agencies is called 'creative work'. It is produced by 'the creative department', which is organised into teams – 'creative teams' – always comprising one art director and one copywriter. This system has been in existence for over 40 years and was established to cope with the increasing demands of a brand-new medium – television. Advertising folklore has it that it was Bill Bernbach, an American creative working in New York, who invented this team structure.

'Creative' in the world of advertising means having the power to create, to be imaginative, original, to write, make TV commercials. It means you associate with film directors, photographers and art studios. You might get to make a commercial with Ridley Scott or a famous actor, or a clutch of super-models. The training for this job comes from Art College or the School of Communication Arts. If you are a copywriter you may have a degree, probably in English, or you may have attended one of the schools of journalism in the USA. (Of course, as in any industry, there are stories of great creative people who started out in the post-room and clawed their way to the top through sheer ingenuity.)

Creativity is formally assigned to these creative teams and is preciously and jealously guarded. The Creative Director is the creative supremo. What he says goes. When the advertising agency grows big and unwieldy he may employ some Creative Group Heads to help filter the ideas before he sees them, but even then he has the ultimate power of veto.

Creative departments are more like creative compartments. They are self-contained, on their own floor or in their own section. Each team is further compartmentalised into their own office. Tom Childs and Ed Morris, a new team at St. Luke's, described this system to me. They had previously worked at two different advertising agencies. This description was of their first experience. 'The Creative Director had the biggest office. It was a corner office with sofas, a drinks cabinet and a stereo. The offices got progressively smaller as they went down the corridor, depending on status. Eventually you got to our office. We were the most junior creatives. It was the size of a broom cupboard.'

They explained the set-up further. 'One day we asked for a shelf to put our books and knick-knacks on. We had to wait for weeks and weeks. Because we were junior, our request was perceived to be junior too. People said, "Why do they need a shelf – are they allowed a shelf?" Eventually we got the shelf. Then we asked for a Hi-Fi system so we could listen to music demos. They said, "You have a shelf, what more do you want?" ' The request was turned down.

Creative departments are zany places, in strong contrast to the formal businesslike floors elsewhere, full of the flotsam and jetsam washed up from filming commercials or shooting press ads. Fun stuff, like pictures of famous people larking about with the creative team, or toys from a shoot for a children's product. You will find pool tables, juke boxes and table-football games. There will be music, different sorts from different offices. The creative people will wear clothes that suggest they rebel, as much against the conservative aspects of the people they have to work with, like clients and account handlers. (Male account handlers are nicknamed 'Suits' by the creative department and the females are called 'Frocks'.)

The Creative Floor seems unwelcome to most of the remainder of the company. Suits and Frocks step lightly and aim to please. A creative team's office bellows 'Go Away'. Kola Ogundipe, one of our Copywriters, described the sensation. 'Account handlers would walk into the office, but they weren't really in. They were always half out. They were poised like ballerinas with one foot pointing in, and the other foot desperate to make an exit. A rejection of any aspect of our work would be likely to offend, so a quick escape would be necessary. All the time they were there they would be wanting to leave as soon as possible.'

The year begins and ends for creative departments in the spring, when the creative awards ceremonies begin. And there are many. D&AD, The

British Television Awards, The Creative Circle, *Campaign* Press and Poster, Cannes Advertising Festival, The One Show, Clios (that look a bit like Oscars), and a multitude of European ones. They cost a lot of money to enter and even more to attend (particularly Cannes, where flights, black-tie dinner and overnight accommodation is £2,000 per head). Creative departments are obsessed by them.

Winning creative awards is everything. Ads get changed to make them more understandable to juries who are judging them. Careers get built and demolished by the number of awards won. Creative departments urge their companies to win charity accounts and low-spending clients that want 'good creative', so that they can do some nice work and win awards. Every year, one agency or another is reprimanded for entering creative work that never ran (it must appear in the media to be eligible) or cautioned for entering work that only ran once in an obscure magazine or small TV station. The number of awards is important; ideally you want to scoop them all. Even better would be to win the Gold, then your peers would really be impressed and think you more creative.

The more awards a creative department garners, the more creative it is. It's a simple, industry-made equation. The awards are judged by the creative people in the industry. So winning always means success amongst your peers.

Most creative agencies set a style for their work. Indeed, there are industry-wide standards for 'classic' looking advertising. Often, you can tell which agency has produced what, although as agencies suffer break-aways and new ones are formed, you have to work harder to trace the creative lineage. The creative gurus who set high standards in layout, look and copy style are, for example, Bill Bernbach, Lee Clow, David Abbot, John Webster and Tim Delaney. There are others, of course, but my point is that I can name them. These are schools of creative style that permeate through the industry, through generations. If you are a creative person in an agency which in some way pays homage to a particular school, your work is amended to make it fit.

The relationship between the creative department and the other departments is like one of a permanent truce, with a feeling that hostilities can break out at any moment and possibly for no specific reason. The stories of creative people throwing things across the room in fits of anger are legion.

The managers of the company (CEO, Chairman, MD, for example) manage this relationship across a spectrum of styles, from 'total obedi-ence' to 'forced compliance'. 'Total obedience' to the creative department is the positioning of a creative advertising agency. 'Forced compliance' is a state whereby the businessmen at the helm ultimately hold sway over the creative product, even at the expense of losing experienced creative talent. The former will assert that creative advertising does better for its clients; the latter will bend with the clients and argue that it is only commercial art after all. The thing to note here is that creativity is deemed to be a specialism and is defined by the total ownership of the development and implementation of the creative thought.

Copy writing is a skill, so is art direction, but you may be surprised to know that many Art Directors cannot actually draw or paint. I don't know what the percentage is, but my guess is that it is over 50 per cent. And not all copywriters are specifically trained to write copy. Over the years I have met many who cannot spell. Some discover a gift and pursue it, others just assert their love of the written word. No, the real skill of the creative team is to invent jointly a creative idea. They can brief others – photographers, film makers, even authors if they wish – to execute their ideas. They need no demonstration of specific art skills or training if their creative idea is superb.

Creative work is produced to a specific rhythm. First, the team is briefed. Then they are left alone for approximately three weeks. They show their work to the Creative Director. In a creative agency, he can reject it and insist on more time from the Suits and Frocks (who in turn plead with their clients). Once the Creative Director approves it, the work is carried along an invisible conveyor belt of approval. This might be long (at CDP there were four signatures to collect before the client saw the work; showing the client unsigned – i.e., unapproved – work was a firing offence). Eventually the client is presented with the creative work, not normally by the creative team, possibly by the Creative Direc-tor, more usually by the Suit or Frock. If the client has any questions, they will be relayed back through the system. If the client rejects the idea, the process has to start all over again.

Does this sound long-winded to you? Of course it is. Some agencies will protest that they shorten this system and collaborate more, but even HHCL, a company I admire for its innovative stance on creativity had, until recently, all its creative teams in glass boxes with everyone else working more freely in open space.

This is a creative organisational model based on a production-line manufacturing system. Indeed, folklore (again) has it that CDP, which formalised this system and revered its creative department in an almost godlike way, simply borrowed the creative production system from watching how Ford (one of its clients) made cars. They instituted a quality control system that aped the quality controls implemented for the production of cars.

It is an Industrial Age model. It is anachronistic and it is out of kilter with where most businesses are heading. Even cars are not produced in this way any more.

It was obvious that our way of working was going to affect the way we produced our product. But was it going to affect the actual product itself? Could changing the way you work and changing the way you think actually change the product you produced? If so, was that right?

I was strongly advised by friends in the advertising business that breaking the sacrosanct relationship of those in the creative department with everyone else would weaken the quality of our product and destroy our creative credibility. And there were real lessons to be learned from the early days at Chiat/Day. Too much experimentation and collaboration befuddled the creative teams, who demanded more private time and less fingers in the pie. 'Too many cooks spoil the broth,' Ken Hoggins, the first Creative Director at Chiat/Day London, would say to me, when we were struggling in the early days of 1990 with a new Chiat/Day creative proposition.

Dave and Naresh paved the way for the St. Luke's generation of creative teams to feel comfortable with a cataclysmic change to their working routine and to feel ownership of a new Creative Age model of working that would wholly reject the 'creative compartment' culture that seemed deeply rooted in the heart of every single advertising agency in the UK (and in the USA, and in other markets too, actually, which have emulated the style and *modus operandi* of the more mature UK and US industry).

We felt it was right. We wanted to produce a different product. We wanted to create something that 'drew back the veil', relieved the business of artifice, that genuinely worked for the good of our clients and at the same time contributed to the culture of the country. Creativity we felt was a force for good. Being spiky, breaking taboos, not following set styles was beneficial because it would provoke debate and refresh a medium littered with stolid art direction, situation comedy sketches and puns a-plenty.

'We are a powerful practitioner of our medium,' Bono said to me recently. 'We have a responsibility to take it seriously.' How our competitors would have scoffed. Coming from a company called St. Luke's, we knew we would be ridiculed for our apparent pomposity. We decided to just do it.

The difference in what we do can be described as the difference between 'creativity as work' and 'creativity as life'. The former is career creativity, the latter is cultural creativity. Look at the differences across a number of 'conventional aspects'.

Creative awards ceremonies

Where you are assigned creativity as your daily task, as a specialism you must deliver, you defend the spectacle of an awards ceremony as a ritual of success. You value yourself by awards because they are tokens to be collected which if displayed represent authority and if cashed in represent monetary value – you can leave for a better job as a 'top' creative, or be persuaded to stay with inducements of financial and status increase. It is an example whereby a company feeds you with something that has as much, if not greater, value outside of the company itself.

The idea at St. Luke's was to create an environment whereby personal development, transformation even, occurred. 'We value people as human beings,' says Creative Director Al Young. 'We look at each other and say, "What good things have you done today?" If you value yourself externally by awards, you seek approval from outside the company you own.'

Creative people, as with everyone else, are rewarded by the people who add value to the business they own – their clients and their co-owners. Copywriter Andy Lockley and Art Director Jim Gillham explain: 'We don't look to our peers, we look directly to the people we are selling to. In that way everything is original.'

But the greatest award at St. Luke's is to have transformed yourself. To have liberated yourself to produce something you never thought you could have produced. 'I'm doing my best work ever, here,' says Creative Director Kate Stanners. 'St. Luke's pushes you to go to places you've never been before.'

And the team structure means that idea origination is hard to pin down. Sure, the craft skills of the copywriters and art directors play the major role in creative development, but Naresh will tell you that it was the strategic planner, John Grant, who originated an idea for Boots.

The system does not permit whole teams to win awards. And the system requires the imprimata of seasoned experts in an Industrial Age production model to bless the work.

On the last Friday of each month, we all gather in our café to see the work and hear from people in the team about how it was developed and what effect it has had. Everything is shown and the applause is stronger sometimes than others. There is no greater spur to a team than to witness lesser applause, particularly when it comes from a wide body of co-owners who relish innovation and originality.

Creative styles
If you are the only 'creative' person amongst a group of owners of a company (the other owners are of other specialisms – strategic planning, sales, for example), you can assert your creative will over the company with ease. You may be able to do it benignly or you may choose to be aggressive. Those you employ will get the message either way.

The organisational model at St. Luke's joins creative teams with the whole operational team, including the client. Then it breaks groups down so that early creativity can come from the whole team and is not lost in the bureaucracy of a large, systematised organisation. There is not one creative mantra, style or focus. There are currently three sets of Creative Directors. There will be more. More like Alan Young and Julian Vizard, for example, who have undergone a personal transformation and seized an opportunity to create their own creative entity after four years with the company. Or like Kate Stanners and Tim Hearn, who chose to reject the conventions of the advertising industry and change the way they work. The work is developed in concert with clients and early work, not ripe for formally selling, is also discussed. These meetings, which take place in the project rooms (on neutral territory if you like), elicit early views on any number of potential routes.

It is impossible to implement a system whereby all the creative work follows a company style. Each team has their own view and there is not one overriding creative guru to gently knock back work that looks roguish or odd.

The result is co-operatively produced advertising, sourced from a digital process, that gets tightly bound teams to be inventive early. Before even the brief is issued, there will be brainstorms around the product or service to be communicated. The team will, together, look at competitors. They will look at what is going on in the culture of the consumer to whom they are addressing themselves.

Right from the start the work will be stamped with a creative dye that comes from a joint collaborative experience. Does this mean that anything goes? Well, yes. But there is no owner who wishes to produce badly thought-out work. When the output is entirely in your gift, your responsibility for its quality rises dramatically. It is a company full of individual Creative Directors, if you like. Everything you do, you passionately strive to make perfect.

There is no common style, yet the work of every single client has been commented on in the national press. The power of individually directed, tight entrepreneurial creative entities is such that everything is important. Every client, every piece of work, every detailed point. It is important because it is produced by the company we own.

Where creatives work

'When you work in an office', says Andy Lockley, 'you spend perhaps three hours a day physically working and the rest of the time lounging around looking at all your personal stuff, mementoes and souvenirs. At St. Luke's, the rest of the day isn't wasted. You have 100 other people's souvenirs to look at. You talk to anyone and everyone. In an office, you speak to people on a need-to-know basis. Here you speak to people on a want-to-know basis.'

Something curious happens in a personal office. Your visitor enters your space and speaks to you in a confined, self-selected way. You are spoken to within a framework of possibilities. It will be about work, your work, or about you. It is very unlikely it will be about anything else. If it is, it will probably be gossip.

The limited office conversation is uninspiring, as is the office itself.

'Without an office you have to find your own inspiration,' is how Bono puts it. He goes on: 'The office makes me better. Your eyes are open all the time to the way you think. I can understand more when I'm not cooped up in a room.' Bono remembers how important offices were in another large agency he worked at. 'Creatives would strive for the "dual aspect" office – which means it's on a corner with windows looking both ways. It made being a creative like being a nine-to-five creative. The office in which he sat made him creative. What happens, he'd go home and watch TV and stop being creative?'

'Everyday I look around and realise that this place is bigger than just you. I see that ideas can come from all over the place,' says Kola. 'Where I was before, all the creatives had their own offices because they said they needed space, peace and quiet. That's because they worked alone.'

If you see yourself as the central provider of creativity, you establish an isolationist principle that you carry over into architecture. Your mental empire, your status empire, are mapped out in square footage. Your office provides a ready-made routine – same view, same chair, same picture on the wall – which you only break out of at the moment you have invented your creative product and handed it over to someone else – a director or photographer. Offices are boring places to hole up in. You acquire narrow habits, when what you really need to acquire is wide knowledge.

Creative systems

The belief in a system where one person controls the creative output is almost unthinkable in any other business. That the system is borrowed from previous generations is even harder to imagine. But when you consider that the rules by which creative directors judge the work are as limited as can be, you begin to wonder what sort of archaic production line is actually at work here.

James Parr noted that in these kinds of advertising agencies, 'you learn craft from your boss, you think it's a syllabus. There is a way of doing and approving things. Here you learn to find your own landscape. And because only you define the limits, it's never ending. It's addictive. It's that good.'

This is a challenging set-up. 'Lowe Howard-Spink has a definite system and style. In some respects it's harder here because we have created an environment where we are constantly performing at our optimum level. And everyone is looking at you all the time,' remarked Colin Lamberton, who with Seyoan Vela created a brilliant short film for BBC Radio 1. Seyoan carried on: 'I am able to do much more here. I can explore my own ideas, not rethink every time my boss tells me the tone is wrong.' 'Yes,' takes up Colin, 'you do a lot of work here and you feel it's your own work. This makes us feel braver and, consequently, we attract braver clients. Even better, we get to talk to the clients. That never happened before.'

Jim Gillham picked up the same thread: 'We have ideas about other people's work and we don't feel we shouldn't tell them. There are no set rules here. Nothing is blocked by Creative Directors who have their own view. St. Luke's is more about what you want to do.'

The fact that we have strict timing plans, huge budgets and specific consumer requirements to cater for, means that creatively we are already in the realm of commercial art. We have to deliver, but we want to deliver originality, not stereotypes, clichés or puns.

Julian Vizard knows that systems can over-regulate your work: 'We can try things here and then change our minds without people thinking that change represents some kind of loss of direction.' Alan Young chimed in: 'You can lose direction, too, if you want.' Julian continued: 'There is no advertising pattern book here. In my old place, systems were a block. Here, if we create a system and don't like it, we can change it. Each client has a different system.'

Alan and Julian are part of the Fox's Biscuits team. Biscuits are not treated seriously by advertising agencies – they are frivolous, small incidental items. There is a long history of biscuit advertising that features cartoons, jingles and situation comedy sketches. The work is all too often light.

The team did not bow to any of these previous well-played formulae. They risked their reputations and took biscuits into a totally new area. The outcome is simply astonishing – an assertion that Fox's can unite communities, can get people talking to each other, can turn strangers into friends. Why not?

'Everything should be interesting in its own right,' Alan explains. 'It shouldn't have to borrow from a previous creative life form. I want our work to always say something. So much advertising is demeaning. It's pollution. There's so much advertising that people today see through blatant product claims. They see through the advertising and if they don't find something real, like "meaning", then they will think less of you. Since I worked with less creative structure, I have never been more confident of my own creativity.'

'There is no system as such,' observes Ed Morris, 'but it's one of the most supportive places I know, because you know you've got a whole team behind you, including the client. Consequently, people have more faith in each other. A few days after Tom and I joined, Al and Jules said to us, "You're here because we want you to do what you want to do."' Barely a full year in the business, Tom Childs and Ed Morris found their team was to develop TV work for Teletext. Teletext is an information service delivered coldly on TV, but the work is so refreshing. They imagined it as warm and friendly, seductive even. The work they produced has an almost Zen-like quality to it. 'We feel more confident than ever here. We feel stable and we feel wanted.'

Ed's description doesn't sound like he's working in creative anarchy. But he is. It's anarchy and chaos, and it's the trademark of a company operating in a new age, with new strategies for success. 'Our methodology doesn't make sense to most people in this business,' summarises Bono. 'And that really frustrates them. They know what we are doing is great, they know our product is great; I mean everything we do is talked about – Midland Bank, Eurostar, Boots, IKEA, Clark's Shoes, Teletext, the Government's New Deal stuff. Everything. They know it's good, but they don't know why. They think we have a secret formula. Like Coca-Cola. Everyone loves Coca-Cola, but no one knows what's inside. All they end up saying is that we're like the Moonies. Fine. I like that.'

We are all creative at St. Luke's. Because we are all human beings who have given ourselves the freedom to operate creatively. The head of IT, Gidon Cohen, was our 'Person Of The Year' last year. 'St. Luke's is the only ad agency that would make the IT guy Person Of The Year,' he said when handed the award at the Christmas party. But the work he had done was wonderful. He has stretched himself into any area of the company that was needed. One day he would be redesigning the entire software system, the next he would be on all fours inside the Cabinet rooms behind Downing Street, setting up a technology show that would spellbind Gordon Brown and Peter Mandelson.

I think the copywriters, art directors, graphic designers and typographers at St. Luke's are more creative than elsewhere. Sure, there are good ideas from elsewhere, but the people at St. Luke's are more flexible, more adaptable, more willing to hear another's point of view. They are more original in the way they construct their ideas and they deliberately seek out new ways of doing things. They have turned their backs on the existing system and are happy to be considered outsiders. They do not belong to any of the stylistic schools; they are not compartmentalised into protective shells; and their work is not mechanically processed in the conventional, analogue, sequential way. Consequently, their minds are more open to more possibilities than even they could have dreamed of.

Jason Gormley and Steve McKenzie have the last word: 'In many ways it's much harder at St. Luke's. The company makes you think a lot. There seems to be a higher principle. It's as if you don't get briefs to work on, you get missions to achieve. It's awesome. It's an awesome responsibility. And you can see it in the output. It has such ... veracity. The work we produce, all of it, comes to you, it's challenging, it confronts you. It's truthful.'

PART THREE

Crash Test Dummies

㉑ Accidents And Emergencies

'This is a fucking disaster. A fucking disaster.' Jonners was not happy. As the last man out of Jay's designer dream offices in Berkshire House, he had witnessed the elegant open-plan layout being disassembled, piece-by-piece, until he was left alone sitting on a bright-blue plastic packing crate trying to appease anxious suppliers who were worried that the move was causing a communication breakdown, or, worse, that it signalled a company on the run.

Berkshire House looked like a tornado had been through it. Where there were once neat rows of workstations, each with its own Apple Mac, fabulous open meeting rooms and an electric atmosphere that hit you like a train as soon as you walked in through the front door, there was now a wasteland. A few sticks of broken furniture lay strewn randomly around. Everywhere there were bits of pencils, pen tops, paper clips, defunct documents, advertising concepts ripped and yellowed by time and faded Post-it notes.

We took everything we could reuse and sell and like some absurd larger than life 3-D jigsaw puzzle, reassembled it all in the toffee factory in Duke's Road. Were most of us not high on the thought of building our Utopian Dream, we would have shared Jonners's far more realistic view of what was going on.

The idea to recycle the old office seemed like a good one at the time. It smacked of a common-sense logic both financially and environmentally. In fact, it became the first of a long list of crazy actions and mishaps that, hour by hour, day by day, week by week, conspired to sap our energy and drive down our spirit until ultimately we questioned the whole idea of working in a totally unique way. Every day, anxious individuals or pockets of colleagues ganging together through some common frustration would opt to reassess all of the ideas which we forced into the move – giving up our desks, roaming from computer to computer, utilising the whole office as a resource, giving our clients their own individual, customised office space, and being heavily dependent on technology.

In truth we had no plan. There were no lessons from Jay's American offices which, since the merger with TBWA, were preferring a more conventional use of their space. There were no books or management texts on how to slough the skin of 200 hundred years of 'doing it the Industrial way' and instantly assume the guise of a 21st-century 'new model Creative way'. We made it all up as we went along. And it hurt.

Some of the things we did were just plain crazy. For example, not content with simply reassembling the furniture as it was, we were determined to create hybrids out of what we had demolished. When everyone arrived on the morning of Monday, 11 December the place looked like Attila the Hun had taken a chainsaw to a post office sorting room and asked Heath Robinson to put it back together again.

It was awful. OK, there were workstations to sit at and the computers were up and running, but only because Sally, Smudger, Neil and Rachael worked around the clock to reassemble everything into some kind of working order. But it looked like bedlam.

The reception resembled a down-at-heel taxi cab company's waiting room, and to get to it, you had to muscle past heaps of furniture piled dangerously high. David and I would create open spaces by moving the piles of furniture around, only to find someone else had moved them back again to create a different sort of space for themselves.

People would roam around trying to place their files somewhere safe. With no code of conduct in the Project Rooms, there was a scramble to use them and hide in them. Without desks there was nowhere to place your Rolodex, pin up your 'to do' list or place your diary. A diary? What use was it when you had to drag it around with you all day long? Documents were mislaid, meetings were missed and messages vaporised as no one knew how to pass them on.

In the chaos two burglars walked in, calmly introduced themselves as window cleaners, asked for coffees and walked out with a couple of portable computers and my briefcase containing my house and car keys, passport and the entire negotiating history of our deal with Omnicom.

A dedicated team comprising an architect, his son (an interior designer) and a joiner were charged with the responsibility of making all the furniture fit together. Undeterred by the size of the task and unfazed by the growing restlessness in the company, they assembled the giant jigsaw as fast as they could. Soon they had begun to create some order out of the chaos. They constructed The Egg, a large ovoid table where you could stand and assess the work before it was finally delivered to the publications or TV stations, and worked tirelessly to construct meeting tables and as many workstations as they could muster.

One morning Neil received a phone call. An advertising agency had gone into liquidation. Without blinking, he grabbed the company chequebook and by the end of the morning had bagged six large Apple Macs, some small tables, chairs and a refrigerator, complete with someone's diet yoghurt, a cheese sandwich and a can of Coca-Cola. It was as if the move had made us literally free to behave as differently as we wished and we were pirates plundering what we could, whenever we could.

By lunchtime on 14 December, all the computers were wired in and humming to life. By the evening, every single one had stopped working. Sally worked through the night with the suppliers and by morning they were up and running again.

Lunchtime the following day they went down again.

The next day, we all assembled in the café in the basement for a ritual that would rekindle some faith in what we were doing. We voted for the first QUEST and I, Sarah Sanderson, Sarah Naughten (Naughty) and Smudger were duly signed in as the agency's first Trustees. At that time only two Questors were voted in by the shareholders (Smudger and Naughty), as was legally required – Sarah Sanderson and I were management appointees. We sombrely handed round the share certificates and supplied everyone with a St. Luke's canvas bag, T-shirt and bottle of bubbly. The formal proceedings came to an end, and putting all the disasters behind us, we made merry and laughed together again at how ridiculous all the self-imposed problems were.

The following Monday, the architect and his team had assembled every piece of furniture. They had done their job, but the place looked ludicrous. Why on earth didn't we just go to a good furniture retailer and make life simple for ourselves?

'Because we like to make life hard for ourselves,' said Smudger.

Then IKEA rang.

It was mid-December and they wanted to put together a shortlist of advertising agencies with a view to pitching in February. With the office looking like it did, we were nervous that they would think we were unprofessional. And being IKEA, the epitome of cool, chic Swedish design, we knew that our do-it-yourself office would be inexplicable to them.

We asked if we could meet in their offices. They agreed. The next day Bono, Charlotte, David Abraham and myself made our way to the IKEA store in north London and met with the clients.

We hit it off immediately. They were a company with an idea, who liked to behave and communicate differently. They were as different from other furniture retailers as we were from other ad agencies. We felt comfortable in their company and struck up a spirit of camaraderie based on mutual appreciation.

We returned to the agency. 'They think we're brilliant,' I enthused.

Rachael and Neil were on their knees staring blankly at a box of wires. 'We're not that brilliant,' said Rachael. 'The effing phones have all packed up again.' Our oh-so-clever internal mobile-phone system, so painstakingly put together by Rachael over many weeks, had completely failed.

And we were unable to install fixed phones immediately. We had consigned most of them to the rubbish bin and what were left hung onto life by a thread of wire. Fixed phones were a thing of the past in our new way of working. They represented a certain stuffiness and slow, sequential, industrial style of operation. At this moment in time we would have died for the old-fangled technology.

'Right', said Charlotte, 'we'll use our own exterior cellular mobile phones. Let's phone all the clients and suppliers and give them our mobile numbers. To make a call we'll have to stand by the windows, or better still outside. Keep your mobiles on you at all times.' It was the best we could do. It worked for a few days until the phones were back in order (although they were to crash a couple times more in as many weeks).

Later that day the computers crashed for the third (or was it the fourth or fifth) time. The ethernet cabling was faulty. Now we had lost our diaries and e-mail service.

Anyone visiting our office at that time would have thought our new way of working was odd rather than innovative, as clutches of people stood by open windows amongst curious furniture, or stood outside in huddles wrapped up warm against an icy winter that had descended the day we moved in.

The following day, fresh from the paper's Christmas lunch, we were visited by Diane Summers, a journalist from the *Financial Times*. David and I had hurriedly tidied up, but the office still looked shambolic. She quizzed David and me hard about the idea and ideals of the company and noticed only too well that we were only just getting to grips with the ownership, organisational structure and use of new technology, not to mention the DIY furniture. And she came with a photographer.

We had no real experience of dealing with the national press and remembered warnings from our years in advertising that journalists could trip you up if you gave them the opportunity – 'No one owns the media,' Jay would regularly intone to me. But we were really proud of what we had achieved and what we planned to achieve in the future. We gushed our thoughts and showed her around. We said to each other, 'You can only be who you are. We have nothing to hide.' She left saying she felt she had enough to write something interesting and that it would appear the following week on Thursday, 21 December.

It seems almost impossibly bizarre, but just as the office was starting to look tidy, workable and fairly organised, Tessa Wire, Kerry Newman and James Wood ripped it all apart. It was to be temporarily redesigned for a spectacular party.

The architect was utterly speechless. He couldn't believe his ears or eyes. The three started to move furniture and television set-designers appeared with hammers, nails and saws. Had we not told the architect that tonight was the Christmas party, that we were hosting it 'at home' and that Tessa had big plans for how the agency should look? And anyway, whose responsibility would it have been to tell him?

Tessa and the team did a great job. The office was laid out like a local general hospital – St. Luke's General Hospital. The walls sported signs in that bland but readable hospital-type style which read 'Patients this Way' and 'Accidents and Emergency'. There were hospital beds, intravenous drips and X-rays everywhere. The invites were the plastic bands you wear in hospitals around your wrist to keep track of who you are. We invited everyone we knew – partners, clients, suppliers, friends, journalists from *Campaign* magazine, *Marketing* magazine, Roger Alexander and Andrew Johnston – you name it. I think had Fred Meyer been in town, we would have invited him, too.

The evening of 19 December, a mere week after moving in, we held our opening party. That night everyone had something to celebrate either together or individually. The place was heaving. The party was the best we had ever had.

It was a big 'Hello' to the world and an even bigger 'Thank You' to everyone who had helped get us to where we were. We all hobbled home that night buzzing with excitement. We had launched and moved and argued and tripped up and picked ourselves up again. We had made it.

Two days later, I was in a Sainsbury's supermarket in a small market town, near where I live. It was four days to Christmas and I was doing battle with ferocious shoppers who like me left this crucial, specialist shopping right to the last minute. (This Christmas shopping trip is always my major contribution to the family's Christmas planning. I relished it in a strange, sado-masochistic kind of way.)

I was by the 'Eat-Me' dates, mixed nuts and clementines stall when my phone went (I was keeping it on me at all times, of course!).

'Hi, Andy, it's Hilary from IKEA.'

'Oh, Hi.'

'Sorry about the delay. We want you to pitch for our advertising account. It'll be against BBH, Mellors Reay and AMV. We thought you were, um, great, well, a bit odd actually. We liked that.'

'That's great news, Hilary. I'll call Charlotte and we'll get the ball rolling.'

'Nice article.'

'What?'

'The *Financial Times*. Good stuff. Who does your PR?'

'We do. I haven't seen it yet. I'll pick one up.'

'By the way, Andy,' Hilary added, 'where are you? It sounds like you're in a supermarket.'

'I'm in a supermarket.'

'You really are an odd company, aren't you?'

I moved my trolley to the dry pasta and specialty ragu – always quieter at that time of year – and phoned Charlotte on her mobile.

'That's fabulous,' she said. 'I knew we'd done well.'

I heard shouting and metallic scraping sounds in the background. 'Where are you?' I asked.

'I'm in a supermarket,' she replied, 'by the fresh fish.'

'So am I!' I was unnaturally excited by the news that this was a supermarket-to-supermarket call.

'I suppose this is a new way of working,' she said.

'Yes. Yes it is. Odd though.'

I grabbed a copy of the *Financial Times* on my way home. It was a huge article, much bigger than I had expected or hoped – and not a packing crate in sight. The headline ran:

Making a Name for Itself

Dianne Summers visits St. Luke's – a new advertising agency that has set out to be different

It was perfectly written and any worries we had that the chaos of packing crates and broken furniture would diminish the article disappeared fast as the story of what we had achieved began to unfold.

It was a perfect ending to a most extraordinary year.

㉒ In The Bleak Mid-Winter

'The computer network is playing up, e-mail is down, the phones don't work and no one knows where to put their stuff. People aren't moving around, they're getting into habits and routines; they're nesting and they won't budge. Everyone's saying this no-desk business is stupid and won't work. Clients can't get hold of us and are complaining that no one has the right documents to hand when they do. Suppliers are chasing us for late payment of invoices – we've mislaid a batch. Everyone's pissed off.'

An update with Smudger can be an experience.

'But I'm not worried,' he continued, the whole thing in one breath, 'we can sort it.'

'I'm not sure you're talking to the right person, Smudger. In the old office I'd be hearing all this, holding court and dispensing solutions. But that's the old paradigm. Me, at the top, everyone in a place, with controlled powers and a readiness to take orders. We all know we don't want that. I'm not Andy Law the boss, I'm, um, well, just Andy, and you're just Smudger. There's been a revolution, a paradigm shift. We're in uncharted water.'

'Fair enough,' said Smudger. 'Also, the gents' loos don't flush properly and have no air vents. It's like the Black Hole of Calcutta down there. But don't worry, I've got a team of plumbers on the case.'

You can say anything to Smudger and he won't bat an eye-lid.

'Smudger, I saw a mushroom cloud just now, we have three seconds to live.'

'I know. I've got it sorted.'

What I was trying to communicate was something that had been eating away at me over the Christmas break. We had successfully mutinied. We had broken away from the Establishment. We had outmanoeuvred a far greater business than our own. We had invented a new company. We had revolutionised the workplace. We were off.

But to where? And why?

And if we were revolutionaries, what had happened to our vanquished foe? More's the point, who exactly was our vanquished foe?

And what was my role? If history tells us anything, it seemed to me, it tells us that those who lead revolutions, particularly those built on dogma, either rule by iron will (and so cement and crudely enforce the dogma – for example, Lenin, Castro, Thatcher) or so liberate their forces that in the process they liberate themselves out of a job and are at some point seen as *persona non grata* (for example, Churchill, Gorbachev).

I was adamant that our revolution must not simply replace an old hierarchy with a new, more modish one. Everything had to change. The Lenin model was wrong. And there had to be real symbols of change. We had been under fire from Day One from people who felt all we were doing was 'rearranging the deck-chairs', that it was all a PR stunt.

At a dinner before Christmas, I had been accosted by someone I had worked with 15 years earlier. He was now a senior figure in advertising. 'I hate what you've done,' he said. 'You've set up a joke scheme in which you hoodwink your staff into thinking they own something, and they work their nuts off, when really you're still the boss and creaming it.'

It seemed imperative to me that we communicate to the outside world that a fundamental rethink of business management had taken place here and that we all were transformed by it in some obvious, tangible way.

If there was a model to follow, it was more like the Gorbachev one. He changed his country irrevocably. Perestroika was a real agent of transformation. But then again, he was made a scapegoat for all the things that went wrong and was ultimately outcast.

My solution was to take myself out early. It was not a wonderful solution.

You see, it didn't occur to me that no one else saw the situation the way I did. And I didn't really publicly confer. I just felt it was right to behave in the polar opposite way from my previous conventional working life.

On the first working day of January, I issued a manifesto. To myself.

I would not make any decisions, I decided.

I would not run any meetings, I moved.

I would not be the boss, I decreed.

It was a silly thing to have done. The company went into a directional tailspin. But it wasn't the silliest. Or the stupidest. That happened later when I began to step in at random either on request or because I instinctively felt I had to. When things spun out of control, I would miraculously appear and proclaim the solution, then step out again. It was like the captain of a ship helicoptering in to change course, then helicoptering immediately out again.

I did it with the best of intentions of course. I wanted others to find the right way to manage the company. I wanted to create spaces and encourage people to walk into them.

I made big gestures. I should be reviewed like everyone else, I stated. I was no different. If reviews weren't for everyone, then we were not operating a true democratic process.

Duly, Naresh and Charlotte reviewed me. But I didn't hear properly what was being said to me in the review. Although I was seeking to avoid management, others were actively trying to lead me back into it. Not as a power play, but as a recognition of my skills. It was to take until July of the following year before it was finally, happily and profitably solved in a way that convinced me we had a radical solution and others that my talents were being put to best use.

At that time it was a problem in my mind, but thankfully not one that affected the operational running of the company.

I learned Rule 1:

Revolution is not the same as transformation. The former is predicated on a negative, the latter on a positive. The latter is how to change positively.

We were transforming, not revolting. The only real enemy was how we used to be.

I learned Rule 2 as well:

Change everything. Including the colour of your hair, if you like. But don't devalue yourself. Everyone is brilliant. Including yourself. You are a wonderful institution in your own right.

In my mind, I was making everyone else valuable except those I thought already had value, including myself. I was treating conventional value with disdain, without properly appreciating that it was still an asset.

To mock the inbred, ageing, doddering, out-of-step old Senate, the Roman Emperor Caligula made a horse Consul. I guess in my mind I was doing the same. To mock the established institutions of company life – directors, management meetings, closed-door gatherings, control of information – I preferred to strip conventional power of its operating mandate (and with it, a lot of innate ability) and throw a new mandate wide open to anyone (or any group) who had an innovative or just plain interesting idea of what to do with it.

This was a time when many testing ideas that were put to the experiment failed. But it was also a time when we learned a great deal about what the effect of the failures were.

We seemed woefully ill-equipped to handle the day-to-day management issues that arose. David made it clear that he wanted to take operational control as Managing Director. He had served his time as Marketing Director, he had launched the company, he needed newer, fresher challenges that matched his ambitious nature. But that seemed a backward step to me. I knew his skills made him ideal for the job but it just wasn't an innovative move. I was trying to divest myself of power; I thought David should as well.

To make matters worse, in January 1996, we had a whole heap of management issues to deal with: financial, personal, operational and managerial. Neil Thomson and others clamoured for a formal assembly – a Treasury – in which to conduct the financial affairs of the company. In the past, for example, I and a small hand-picked group had taken the seemingly detrimental decision not to try to hang on to First Direct. Now it had to be a wider, more collaborative decision. We were not as financially strong as we could have been had we fought hard for, and retained, First Direct. Some group needed to understand the money – it was wrong, they said, to let shareholder money float aimlessly.

Smudger and others pursued the rights of 'the ordinary shareholder' to know everything about the company and to have a hand in its running. Naresh and others wanted a forum to agree the allocation of resources and to decide fundamental things like how the creative product was to be produced. The Operations Group was reinstated to handle this everyday business. Overriding all of this was an ever-present desire by everyone to exercise their rights as owners of the company.

We all knew that an all-agency vote on everything, say once a week, was crazy. We did not want an overbearing, slow process to hinder the growth of the company. In the first instance we agreed that the QUEST would represent all shareholders and maintain the innovative culture. Who agreed? I can't remember, but it wasn't an all-agency decision.

The QUEST met.

'What's our mandate?' asked Sarah Sanderson.

'Well, I don't know,' I answered. 'This is virgin territory. I guess we just make it up as we go along. What I do know is that you can't look to me to tell everyone what to do. It's not like the old days. I'm no one's boss. I'm just a co-owner like everyone else.'

'So what are we going to do?' Naughty patiently added.

'Everyone has to be personally responsible. There is no spoon-feeding. With ownership comes a high level of responsibility,' I said.

'So?' said Smudger.

'I don't know,' I said.

It didn't work well at all in the first few months. I was seeing it as a kind of 'People's Board' to check and challenge the Operations Group, which I thought was too conventional, and the Treasury (which was quickly established soon after the QUEST first met). Consequently, the company had three almost identical decision-making teams, each flying under a different flag.

I began to scribe little expressions to explain the company's co-ownership in relationship to its management. Some I posted as manifestos around the walls of the company.

'We are co-owned,' I would say, 'but not co-run.'

'Why not?' Sally asked me.

'Why not what?' I answered.

'Why aren't we co-run?'

'Too labour intensive,' I responded. 'It would make us too slow. It's impracticable.'

'We could do it electronically.'

It was an idea I couldn't digest. 'Present it to the agency,' I said. 'It sounds interesting.' She didn't. She was not fond of public presentations.

I learned Rule 3:

A great idea may come from one source but to live on and be accepted, it might be presented by an entirely different one. Find time to recognise and sponsor great ideas.

The Treasury was established with the other ex-managers of Chiat/Day. It was a meeting of department heads, to agree on expenditure. In reality, it was a 'Board'. And everyone saw it as that. The agendas were tedious. The meetings too long. I hated them. I knew I was sitting with the wrong people, but didn't know how to get out of the management box I was in. These meetings were as confining as the QUEST ones were too loose.

Operationally, the company was run by the Chiat/Day Operational Heads – Dave, Naresh, John Grant and Charlotte.

In one innocent fell swoop we had consigned the office to be run by its previous managers. What had changed? The words we used had changed. The QUEST was new. The shares meant something. Other than that there was not a significant shift from the past regime.

To make matters worse, there was no agreed relationship between the Operations Team, the Treasury and the QUEST, and soon they started to run into each other. Personnel issues were discussed by the QUEST, but the Treasury felt it should advise and the Operational Heads felt they had ultimate responsibility for human resources.

When things got messy or confusing, I would soar above everything and play my ace. 'As Chairman, I think we should do this.' It solved the problem, of course, but it was not a new system of democracy.

In truth, the QUEST was a surface-only manifestation of the new age of democracy we had engendered. We had a long way to go before we understood fully how it was all going to work (almost two years in fact). And oddly, against all management wisdom, the answer was to come as we got bigger. It did not surface while we remained the tight entity we were at the time of the mutiny against Omnicom, now over a year ago.

I learned Rule 4:

In times of change, individual motives change, too. The more time, the more change, the more different individual actions there are.

We were not aligned internally. That is to say, we were not as aligned as we expected or wanted to be. But none of us was about to self-destruct. We all retreated into our skill sets and set about with great industry to manage our clients and our lives in as fulfilling a way as we knew how. Deep down, we all knew we had our new company's interests at heart, we just hadn't spent enough time up front scoping out the constitution. This seemed crazy when you think we had from February 1995 to get it right.

㉓ Icebergs Ahead

Neil Thomson aligned us all fast.

'We have three months left to win some new business.'

'Then what?' enquired Naresh.

'Then we are severely low on both income and reserves and if we take the slightest hit, we're going to have to cut staff or salaries, or both.' The decision not to pursue First Direct vigorously was beginning to take its toll.

'We'll win new business,' said Naresh.

'We're back in the bunker again,' observed David. 'One year on and we're almost dead in the water. We can fight our way out of this.'

Round the table sat the Departmental Heads who made up the Treasury. David, Naresh, John, Bono, Charlotte, Neil, Tessa, Smudger and me. Of course we had all known what the impact of losing First Direct meant, but at the time we could do anything, go anywhere. Somehow, in unfamiliar and untidy offices and in the middle of winter, we didn't feel so brave after all.

'It's all hands to the pumps,' I said reaching out for the most obvious Chairman-like comment. 'There is a difference between now and a year ago. Now we all have to do something to save us all. We've all committed to launching St. Luke's, now we have to commit to saving it.'

And we found commitment. Often, when asked about how human capital can be viewed as an asset, I refer to this time. It was a time when the potential of the company doubled with no added ingredient or cost except the desire to save our skins.

The energy the company put into saving St. Luke's drove the company forward faster and harder than at any time in its history. It was present from January right through to December. It blew away complacency and it sidelined smaller internal issues. In fact, it masked our organisational problems and even gave us a confidence to hire at levels often beyond our budget and to commit to ventures that were way beyond our knowledge or experience.

Neil's three-month warning was our *casus belli*. Here was something to kick against. Protection. Survival. Wonderfully base instincts, but ones which would provide focus and alignment, just when we needed it most.

The work of the architect continued unabated alongside the day-to-day operational requirements of the company. I had briefed him to create a spectacular space (one I suppose that we thought Jay would have approved of), and on reviewing his plans, soon learned he wanted to cut a hole through the centre of the company and install a massive metallic spiral staircase. He also had numerous other schemes to improve the overall complexion of the company. It was time to say goodbye to Jay. I was handling company money – money which belonged to Naughty, Smudger, Tessa and Robbie, for example. I was not free to make grand architectural gestures. But I persisted.

Rachael Plant would have been a trusty aid in the building process were it not for her fast promotion into account management. She took to heart the company's maxim of personal transformation and fought hard, successfully, to reinvent a new career for herself. Undeterred, I set about the building project myself, although Tessa was to help out with the overall design brief in response to a scathing personal assessment of the interior décor by Naresh.

Work on the building seemed never ending and provided a permanent, noisy, dusty back cloth for all the real work that St. Luke's was expected to do for its clients and itself.

And there was much to do for ourselves if we were to tackle the mounting backlog of ideas generated at awaydays and various smaller internal brainstorms. The QUEST set about delivering something tangible and started with a maternity policy that would reflect our belief in the value of home-life and would stand as a shining example of how to treat your human capital with decency and respect. With a new lease of life, Rachael, with Libby and Sarah Sanderson, put together the policy. It took the position that a female owner of a company would want time and choices and, although it would cost the company much more than its legal obligation, we all wanted it because it was a blow against outdated thinking that treated women as cripples because of their bio-logical requirement to produce children. Maternity money was aid money to minimise as much as possible. And they stood up for men, too. Twinned with the Maternity Policy was a Paternity Policy that would give men the chance to be on hand when needed and not castigate them or deprive them of their annual holiday allowance just because they wanted to be with the mother and baby.

IKEA decided they should, indeed must, visit our offices. They had seen the *Financial Times* article and felt it was worth experiencing it for real. When they came they were impressed despite the Heath Robinson furniture. Their interest in us gave us something to focus on beyond ourselves. It gave us a specific, localised external war to fight; a pitch to win, against true, competent enemies.

And win it we did. After a long two-month, hard-fought battle, which went to the wire and demanded hourly persistent salesmanship from David Abraham, we were awarded the account.

It was the end of February when Hilary came into the agency and broke the news herself to everyone in the cafeteria downstairs. We had gathered the entire company to witness St. Luke's first major win. We went wild. It was a vindication of so many things. It proved that we could operate efficiently in the workspace. It proved that an odd name and ownership structure wouldn't frighten clients away. It proved that the remodelled spirit of Chiat/Day was not dented by the dramatic cold bath we had taken – with new technology and new internal systems. We drove our demons into a corner and celebrated a totemic victory.

Standing at the back of the café were two Italian gentlemen, Franco Buonaguidi and Bruno.

Franco was Bono's father, who we had coaxed out of early retirement to cook lunch for us. He and Bruno cooked Italian, family meals every Monday to Thursday which we ate seated around large wooden tables. You served yourself, sat at the nearest available space and cleared up afterwards, too. Franco and Bruno's lunches have become legendary. Yes, the food is wonderful, but more than that they provide a hearth for the company, a warm familial kitchen which then, as now, served always to soothe fractious spirits. They know everyone, know about everyone and smile at everyone. And the fact that he's Bono's father makes his connection with us that little bit more meaningful. He stands as a permanent reminder that we are not two-dimensional cut-out figures with no background or history.

Indeed, Franco reminds us that we have full lives and that work must recognise that fact. (Two years later Al Young organised a Parents' Evening at St. Luke's. The office was filled with Mums and Dads eager to see where their child worked and to put a face to the hundreds of names they are regaled with over Sunday lunch. It was one of the best 'bonding' exercises we have ever undertaken.)

At this time there were other developments which also presaged later events.

We pitched for and won the Rock The Vote business. It was a non-partisan political account, encouraging apathetic youth voters to register their vote. A similar campaign had been run in the USA and was credited with bringing thousands more (youth) votes to Clinton. It was a first brush with politics and one we felt chimed neatly with our earnest, democratic, youthful political motives.

We participated in a TV documentary in the *World in Action* series, producing ads for both sides of the argument about whether the UK should be a republic or a monarchy; and we were briefed by a Sunday newspaper to sell the Euro to a sceptical public. Suddenly, hot on the heels of the *Financial Times* article, we found we were operating in other, wider, media.

We were also asked to create a music video for the UK's biggest dance-techno act, DJ Carl Cox. It was outside of our normal scope of work, but we had all discussed many times that we would take the company onto a broader creative canvass as soon as we found the right opportunity.

In March, John Grant launched an attack on linear thinking. It was an early green shoot, which for many who read it (in *Marketing* magazine) may have passed over them as just another view on how to conduct consumer research. It was more than that. It was an overt attempt to discredit sequential production-line thinking and, as such, added another colour to a growing palette which was painting St. Luke's into an entirely different corner.

They were extraordinary, illogical times. Crippled by a lack of a workable textbook, bruised by internal wranglings, giddy from a heady cocktail of 'hot-desking' and 'technology overload', and breathless from a constant focus on our clients and output, there remained a strong and compulsive heart to our movement which swept us almost unconsciously into new creative arenas, challenging intellectual ideas, fascinating political debates and very contemporary cultural issues.

Things were beginning to hot up.

No sooner had IKEA appointed us than we were invited to pitch for the Eurostar cross-channel passenger train. It was (is) a fabulous product that many confused with the tunnel it travels through, Eurotunnel, or with the car-train, Le Shuttle. The marketing was being handled by Richard Branson's Virgin company and yet again we were up against high-quality competition.

The Virgin executives clearly loved the agency concept as much as IKEA did. We were getting a strong impression that the way we worked, with ourselves and our clients, was a powerful selling tool. Our hunch that it was time to work in a less rigid, linear way with clients seemed to be paying off.

We took a risk. The night before the presentation, we discarded all our beautifully typed charts and walked into Richard Branson's Holland Park house armed only with a large sketch pad, thick felt-tip pens and a photograph of Eric Cantona, the maverick French soccer player.

The bravado worked. We were the perfect teammates for the Virgin marketeers who shunned convention and uptight office lifestyles. They signed up almost instantly.

David Abraham was overjoyed. That night in the café, he announced an astounding statistic. We had achieved the year's new business target in the first quarter of the year. We needed more help to handle all this business and he was pleased to announce the imminent arrival of a co-producer for Tessa – Kate Male – and an Account Director for IKEA – Ben Bilboul.

Neil Thomson was never to know what the three-month financial deadline he outlined earlier would have actually looked like.

To cope with the increasing demands of creative control, Dave and Naresh hired a set of co-creative directors. It was unusual for an advertising agency to have more than one creative director, but to announce that we were to have four perplexed many outsiders who refused to believe that Dave and Naresh would simply hand 50 per cent of their creative control over to two new faces.

For us, though, it made perfect sense. We were following a non-pyramidical growth plan. If one set of people felt they were becoming over-burdened paper-pushers instead of creative makers, handing over some of their responsibilities was the right thing to do. The new faces were Tim Hearn and Kate Stanners. As tight and together a creative duo as you could imagine, yet chalk and cheese on the face of it.

When I first met them, they were only a signature away from joining. Dave and Naresh suspected they had a roguish creative streak that they felt could be opened up to become a powerful new force at St. Luke's. They were already famous for their work, in particular, the Jeff Goldblum Holsten Pils ads and the naughty Cadbury's Flake commercial featuring a woman in the bath taking an unusually long time to savour the product between her lips!

Tim Hearn looked as it he had just stepped off a Harley-Davidson. In a faded black leather jacket and bandana tied round his head, he could have passed himself off as a mean and meaty Hell's Angel (some of whom, I later learned, were indeed his friends). He looked as if he was happier with a torque-wrench in his hand rather than a pen, yet it was well known that his copywriting was exquisite. He hardly spoke.

Kate Stanners made up for that. She spoke ten to the dozen and carried boundless enthusiasm for St. Luke's on behalf of both of them. She was raring to go and emitted such energy that even when addressing them both you ended up focusing entirely on her. Where Tim was big and burly, Kate was slender and petite. Tim looked like he had sunk a bottle of Wild Turkey and cruised the highway all night. He sported a resplendent blue-black stubble. Kate was stunningly good-looking, with long blonde hair and vivid, dancing eyes that watched every part of you as you spoke. She was immaculately dressed and looked as if butter wouldn't melt in her mouth.

They were an odd couple. We hired them immediately.

Kate Male, Ben Bilboul, Tim Hearn and Kate Stanners represented something we hadn't come across before. One hundred per cent St. Luker's. They joined with no experience of Chiat/Day, just with the excitement of being a part of something new. They were a new breed and the vanguard of a huge intake of people during 1996 that would swell our numbers to almost 60.

I now know that it was in this formative, blooming spring of 1996, when we suffered cruel growing pains, that St. Luke's was really born. It was one year after our agonising wrench from Omnicom, but from now on it was only St. Luke's. Nothing of Jay, or Chiat/Day, counted for anything.

It was time for us all to move on.

A year after David and I had met with Fred Meyer in the ludicrously priced Hotel Crillon, we were back in Paris again. This time with 40 other people from St. Luke's.

We had travelled *en masse* by Eurostar to celebrate our amazing new business success and held a flag meeting in the basement of a café somewhere near the Boulevard Saint Germain. It was to be followed by lunch – a welcome break and treat for Franco and Bruno who came with us – and a walkabout in Paris, before we returned late that night.

The trip was dominated by one conversation only.

An independent TV production company called Insight Films wanted to make a documentary about us. It was to be a fly-on-the-wall film looking at the way we were running the company and following individuals as they contended with a totally new way of working.

The Directors were a husband and wife team – Debbie and Adam – and they had shown us films they had previously made. David and I liked them. They were taking documentary film-making into a new area. They wanted to make films about humans and the struggles they faced and how they overcame them. They specifically didn't want to ridicule or use the camera to create cheap laughs.

David and I felt the film would be a brilliant project for the company. And for different reasons. As Marketing Director, David Abraham thought it would be newsworthy and would create more interest in us. We were totally new, and needed a lot of explaining. A documentary would be the perfect medium. My reasons were based more in the desire to put the company through some kind of therapy, or self-evaluation. I feared that growth without reason or understanding would devalue the company and that a constant camera would provide a third-party enquiry and stimulation. We would have to live up to what we set out to do, because the cameras would be alongside us like a mirror constantly reflecting our actions and seeing them for what they really were.

The documentary caused a furore. Half the company didn't want to do it and half did. Of those that didn't, some felt that we were giving away our trade secrets needlessly and others felt that the cameras would cramp their natural creative style. In the bars and boutiques of Paris in that late spring afternoon the issue was debated and argued over until most of us were lost in a sea of pros and cons.

The issue was not resolved by general discussion and we all limped home back to England, exhausted from talking and drinking and talking and shopping and talking and travelling.

Debbie and Adam made presentation after presentation to anyone who would listen, trying to persuade more and more people to accept that they were going to be as innovative with their style of documentary as we were with our style of company. The Treasury opted out of the argument, because it wasn't going to incur costs. The Operational Heads were split down the middle. The QUEST became besieged by differing views. The lack of a formal, focused, forceful decision-making body led the idea to eventually, slowly soak away like dirty water down a blocked drain.

Eventually, after weeks of roundabout discussion, I was asked to adjudicate (the helicopter flew in). I was not prepared to say a simple yes or no, since either would have demoralised at least 50 per cent of the company. Yet, something had to be done because 100 per cent of the company was demoralised by the debate itself.

Since the issue was not able to be resolved by the owners (employees), I took it out of general ownership and placed it with a skill set. The documentary was something that would affect the image of the company and, therefore, I felt the decision belonged with Marketing. I assembled the company and told them just that, and that we should trust David Abraham to make the right decision.

He thought about it again, and soon reiterated that he wanted to do it. He felt it was right from a professional point of view.

'OK,' I said, 'I guess you'd better let Debbie and Adam know. The only provisos are that it doesn't affect the flow of work and that those who don't want to participate can totally opt out.'

David phoned Debbie. 'We're on,' he said.

'Wrong,' she replied. 'We're off. As of two days ago. Our sponsor at Channel 4 has moved on. The project has no patron at that TV station, or any other.'

Rule 5:

Every group of humans, formal or informal, in whatever sphere of conduct, must appoint and trust decision-makers to make every kind of decision; even those that the group itself might not agree with. Otherwise you slow down, stop and possibly never start up again.

In parallel with the documentary ran another incident.

The ever-present architect, designers and builders, who were creating havoc and urgently pressing regular radical rethinks on the design, weighed everyone down. Just like the time when I nearly committed us to the Oxford Street office, I sensed a silent revolt. I soon learned that the giant staircase linking all our five floors in one open, dramatic, expansive way, was a bridge too far. No one really had the stomach for it. It was expensive and disruptive.

I ditched the idea and we parked one-third of the staircase that had already been constructed in a storage yard. Later, the following year, as we conducted our Social and Environmental Audit, the incident became known as our 'Brent Spar'. It was a huge, costly object that almost everyone didn't really want.

Rule 6:

You can't make people do what they don't want to do.

㉔ A Creative Company In The Creative Age

That late spring and summer of 1996 we flourished.

We had more creative firepower than ever before. Dave and Naresh were working hard on ideas for Boots No. 7, BBC Radio 1 and IKEA; Kate and Tim were overseeing work for Eurostar; and Al and Jules were taking on *The Observer* newspaper and a new campaign for Midland Bank.

The Project Rooms were taking shape, with the clients contributing to how they should look. IKEA designed and constructed their own, and the Boots team installed bunk beds and the bric-à-brac of a teenage girl's bedroom.

'Feel it, breathe it, be it ... then sell it,' ran the headline in the *Independent* newspaper, which ran a half-page story on the Project Rooms. Al Young tipped them a handy quote. 'Working this way is like method advertising,' he told the reporter. 'The moment you enter each project room you enter the world of the product.'

The Project Rooms were the most successful of our early innovations. They stood for a totally different way of working which was collaborative and non-departmental. In the *Independent* article Sophie McLaughlin, then the Marketing Manager at Radio 1, commented: 'What they do smacks of a greater level of commitment. The good thing is that they work totally collaboratively with the client, rather than presenting an idea in a vacuum.'

It was also an incredible gesture. We were handing the physical office space as well as our mental resources over to our clients, who in turn paid us monthly fees. It created a different kind of business bond which was at once transparent, more trusting and highly respectful. We had placed our clients at the core of our business and changed our very working patterns to accommodate them. When visiting us, they were not so much coming to our offices as meeting in their creative communications centre. This was wonderful. This was collaborative. This was co-owning projects with your stakeholders.

It all made perfect sense to a company that had pitched itself squarely in the Creative Age and which made different demands upon the humans that worked within it. We had to work digitally rather than sequentially, and the Project Rooms became nodal centres of networking and team excellence. We had to be able to draw data from wherever we wanted, both purposely and accidentally, and the fact that we constantly roamed achieved all this as well.

We had to allow for chaos, whilst at the same time delivering a high-quality product on time. And indeed there was, and still is, chaos outside of the project rooms, but inside they operate at an incredibly high level of efficiency, containing all the information the team needs to run their account properly.

I felt that we were ready to communicate to the outside world exactly what we were prepared to stand for in our creative age and wrote the following article which was published in the first edition of *Impact*, a new magazine looking at 'the other side of advertising'.

(The following article is reproduced by permission of *Impact* magazine.)

THE CREATIVITY OF CREATIVITY

The advertising industry is a very conservative business. More conservative than many other creative commercial businesses (like architecture, music, broadcast and publishing, for example) and certainly more conservative than the majority of burgeoning service industries (computer software, information systems, direct-delivery services) which advertising works for with its 'fresh thinking', 'innovation' and 'never-been-done-before' ideas to shift product, proselytise value and raise awareness.

The business itself has hardly changed at all since the 50s. In fact I can rustle up only two significant self-induced changes that the industry has taken in the last 45 years; the first at the end of the 50s, when DDB brought art directors down from the attic, sat them next to copywriters and invented the 'creative team'; the second at the end of the 60s, when BMP turned its market intelligence resource onto customers and created Consumer Planning.

Otherwise the business has been simplistic in its response both to technology (TV ads were initially press work on celluloid, then imitation sitcom and are now largely faux-Hollywood) and to new revenue streams (integration, Euro and international networks).

A truly creative business must do more than judge its own work or limit its own canvass (to Film, Print and Radio – all well over a hundred years old) if it is to be a genuine net contributor to the creativity of the society in which we live. And that's not easy. It takes enormous amounts of energy to think outside the box and create afresh. It requires real, lateral brainpower.

In fact the potential of our brain is one of those subjects that resides uneasily between 'amazing but true' scientific discovery and modern myth. Tony Buzan, President of the Brain Foundation, author of 15 books on the brain and therefore, I guess, on top of the latest theories, suggests we use less than one per cent of our brain's one million, million, neuron capacity.

This clearly has to interest me as someone who operates in the sphere of creativity and idea generation. In fact I now have a kind of 'Ladybird Book of Creative Theory' rattling round in my mind that teases me with the notion that if we could access just one more of the 990,000,000,000 unused neurons in our brains we might create something very special.

I attended a meeting recently with architects, writers, movie producers, politicians and business 'gurus'. We were discussing how creativity might be brought into cities to improve the quality of life.

I was asked about my understanding of creativity, in the workplace, in our work and in our lives, and I could only comment that unless I am doing or saying something that makes me feel uncomfortable, that might draw ridicule or might embarrass me, I don't think I am actually doing or saying anything creative at all.

Towing the party line is business anaesthetic. But nevertheless it's endemic to advertising. It's pathetic how many agencies look the same, act the same, have almost the same names, produce the same by the same combinations of staff and suppliers, in the same boardrooms, with the same hierarchies, the same processes and the same spiel.

Hey, I'm guilty too. From Wasey Campbell Ewald, through FCB, to a residence at CDP, I promulgated the same 'Relevant, Distinctive, Effective', litany that some high priest (Bill Bernbach?) taught us all, all those years ago.

But I challenge it all with the irritating zeal of the reformed smoker and I and my colleagues make a decision a day that makes us feel uncomfortable.

I don't for a minute suggest that what we do is 'The Answer'. But it's a darn sight better (and more fun) than 'The Conventional System'.

Creativity for us is neither geography (the creative floor) nor exclusivity (you go away, and come back in three weeks when the experts say its ready). Its 45 million, million neurons that co-own the agency in a partnership that defies conventional management thinking. Everybody can exert themselves to add to the creative process and by giving equal shares to everyone we don't imprison the creative art in the hearts and wallets of a chosen few. There is creativity in the way we work with clients, the way we write briefs, the media and account planning. Creativity is for us the blast furnace that provides energy at the beginning of a project and drives it through to its immensely satisfying conclusion.

There is creativity in our workplace. The office is no longer the post-Industrial Age school classroom (go to your desk at nine, leave at six; eat and play in between). It's a resource centre. Every part of the office has a role and a responsibility to maximise creative expression. We pulled together all the books, CD-Roms, CDs we had amassed over the years and created a communal library; client centres contain all the client ideas we generate; personal belongings belong in lockers; all computers are shared. Soph-

isticated telecommunications keep us in contact, the refectory throws us together.

St. Luke's – the company itself – is an experiment. It is a creative idea that we constantly test as much as we test the creative ideas we produce. And in the chemistry of this experiment, fresher ideas are constantly suggested.

The question I am most often asked is whether we are trying to create some kind of creative utopia. And I can answer neither yes nor no to this. You see, having replaced yesterday's known and conventional management problems with tomorrow's unknown and unconventional ones, I am now even more unable to predict the outcome of what we do. But we thrive in this environment and are now looking for the next half neuron to stimulate . . .

The article summed up everything I believed at that time about what we were trying to achieve and fast on its heels came creative work to prove the point.

Dave and Naresh's work for IKEA caused a sensation. It declared war on that great British institution – chintz. It assumed a lofty position, positioning IKEA as arbiters of taste and so attempted to dislodge the entrenched views about home styling of two or three generations of homemakers, who curled up nice and snuggly with their slippers and hot chocoloate into a large chintzy sofa.

It was the most talked about ad in the early part of that summer, and because it featured legions of women marching against chintz and consigning flowery armchairs to the rubbish heap, it provoked a swell of both positive and negative emotions. Feminist writers railed against it for trivialising and hijacking their movement. Others praised its sheer creative bravado and one newspaper columnist featured a photo of Tony Blair and his family designed, he thought, to show that should the Blairs enter 10 Downing Street after the 1997 election, they would be sure to 'chuck out the chintz'.

The IKEA campaign was followed by the gifted but volatile soccer player Eric Cantona, singing the praises of the Eurostar train. Cantona was a national figure and one of the few Frenchmen to gain a place in the hearts and minds of the ordinary Brit. He was also a part-time philosopher and he dispensed his words of wisdom on the luxurious benefits of travelling by train to Paris. It entered the vernacular of the British consumer almost instantly and, like IKEA, was powerful enough to make a contribution to the various contemporary discussions in pubs and cafés the length and breadth of the United Kingdom. IKEA and Eurostar were like creative bookends of that summer, framing the period in our vivid creativity.

Hard on the trail of these two pieces of work came a powerful new idea for Boots No. 7, the cosmetic brand. Openly flaunting years of convention in this sector, it advertised its glamorous products without the aid of either fashion models (there were no people featured in the ad at all) or indeed highly polished photographs of the products themselves.

The media locked on to all of it. We were featured on TV, in chat shows, on news programmes; radio talk shows debated the work. Newspapers covered our work over and over again. It got to the stage where if we weren't talked about in the national media, we thought we were doing something wrong!

In fact everything we produced was of the highest calibre. We had never produced so much high-quality work, particularly in such a short period of time. The creative experiment was working better than any of us had possibly imagined. Our creative reputation had never been higher.

In the same edition of *Impact* magazine which featured my article, there was a poll amongst London's creative teams posing the question: 'Which advertising agency would you most like to be poached by?' Nine-months-old St. Luke's came third, nestling amongst creative giants of the industry who had been in business since the early 80s or before. We all felt exonerated. We all felt we had created a magic formula that was set to make us achieve every crazy objective we had ever discussed.

㉕ **One Chapter Closes
And Another One Hundred
Open Up**

'We don't want to be Creative Directors any more.'

'Great,' I responded ('Shit,' I thought).

At the apogee of our creative history, our best creative assets, Dave and Naresh, wanted out. They had had enough and were feeling the burden of having managed the company's creative renaissance. They wanted to be liberated to create on a broader canvas, such as writing programmes for TV or creating magazines. Anything but advertising. 'In fact,' Naresh said, 'we never want to step back into advertising again.' They had come to me because they felt that no other decision-making body in the company would authorise their decision.

They were right to be suspicious of the views of others. Their decision came when we thought we had the right system up and running. On paper it was ludicrous to take out your best creative resource just at the moment when we were attracting clients because of their output.

Yet, I warmed to the thought that we would replough this resource into something entirely new. I liked the idea that we would force a change on the company whilst it was at an all-time high. We had talked so often about expanding the company out of pure advertising and into a wider creative field. This was an opportunity to do that.

I advised the Treasury and QUEST of the decision. I helicoptered in.

It met with fierce opposition, not least from David Abraham, who recognised the strategic validity, but questioned the timing and criticised the lack of a clear business plan. There was no commercial planning.

What market were they aiming at? Where was income going to come from? Did they expect to get a commission to write a Hollywood block-buster within a few months? What would they do if they did get such a commission? Would they steer St. Luke's towards Hollywood? Who agrees that is where we want to go?

But I persisted with my endorsement and argued vehemently that pioneers have no detailed maps, just a general sense of the overall direction they want to take. The company looked like it was going to make a major change and I wanted it to happen despite the resistance, which I took as conservatism, or nervousness about stepping out into new fields.

Dave and Naresh did not have to defend their decision with me around. I took up the cause and for months and months fought off the negative views that surrounded their decision. I am glad I defended the idea. Unlike other decisions I have taken which I now know I could have taken with more thought, this one always felt right to me.

Rule 7:

The birth of a new idea comes best when everythinq is going well and will be painful. Don't attempt to tamper with the process and don't deny the pain.

Dave and Naresh stepped back from making conventional advertising with breathtaking speed. They finished up the work they were doing for Radio 1 and they honoured an agreement with IKEA to see through their next campaign. Their 50 per cent of the client creative work was handed over to Al and Jules, who suddenly felt themselves elevated from a creative team to people who would be called upon to maintain the high standards of the company.

I announced the decision to everyone one Friday evening at a flag meeting. The news was not public knowledge and it came as a shock. The new creative leaders, Kate and Tim and Al and Jules, were immediately looked to for signs of their commitment to the company's creative agenda. Dave and Naresh were questioned about their decision. I was asked whether I was allowed to make the decision. Some took it very hard. For many, they were the team that turned Chiat/Day's product promise into a reality. It seemed a sad door to close and sorry chapter in our evolution. Others were nervous and thrilled in equal measure as they looked ahead and saw the company producing a much more diversified creative product. The 'Dave and Naresh' issue provided us all with a huge subject to debate. Was it the right decision? Was it right that I should so openly and aggressively support it? Who do you talk to if you disagree with it?

Who was running this outfit?

No one was really in control.

Things happened to St. Luke's during this period, very little was planned. Sure, our image, philosophy and *modus operandi* were all in place. However rudimentary, the internal management systems clanked on. But in reality the company idea had grown bigger than all of us.

In the end, Dave and Naresh's departure hardly caused a ripple. David Abraham and I briefed all of our clients and kept working internally to keep things on an even course. The sheer volume of work mowed down small parochial issues like what Dave and Naresh were going to do. There was simply too much to do; new business knocked on the door weekly, but we kept to our golden rule of only pitching for one thing at a time. New people were joining each month and some old faces left. The pool of human capital was regenerating.

When her husband was posted to Hong Kong, Sally Kelso left. It was a wrench to see her leave. We joined Chiat/Day on the same day and I saw her grow and mature into someone of incredible ability and self-confidence as she took advantage of the liberating forces both at Chiat/Day and St. Luke's.

New people took their roles and filled the spaces created by new business, including Tim Hunt, David Pemsel and Neil Henderson, a trio of strong, experienced Account Directors who I knew would some day (soon) seek their own route to transformation via the same liberating forces that had changed so many of us. There was Jody Burrows, Jan Martin and Ken Dixon, new faces who in a year or so would become respected Trustees or pioneers in other new fields of creativity. New creative teams were given immense opportunities, the like of which they knew no other agency would give them, producing work that was distinctive and fresh, and free from the shackles of slavishly followed industry rules.

All the new recruits were joining a conveyor belt that would inexorably lead them on to greater things. They would no sooner join than find themselves contributing to debates in meetings that most people make a life-long career trying to attend.

Doors were opening for us everywhere. The media attention increased. Film crews from around the world became interested, and not a week went by without someone filming something. Authors, gurus, academics, researchers, schoolchildren even, visited from Japan, USA, South America and most of the pre-eminent European universities. Steven Alburty, a colleague from Chiat/Day, who was a key player in the Chrysalis Project and now a freelance journalist, flew over to interview us for one of America's top business magazines, *Fast Company*. I found myself in Sweden, Holland, Belgium, Italy and up and down the UK telling the story of St. Luke's.

We won an award for the most innovative share scheme and sat amongst business leaders and politicians at the Guildhall in London as we heard others proclaiming the virtue of our extraordinary idea. We became involved with Anita Roddick's New Academy of Business which was formed to teach the value of socially responsible business; and I was asked to join The Social Venture Network, an international gathering of organisations who demonstrated real commitment in the area of corporate social responsibility.

Teletext awarded us their business: Clark's Shoes and United Distillers literally handed us their accounts without the convention of a pitch. The BBC expanded their relationship, asking us to make presentations on a strategy for BBC 2. Boots asked us to pitch for Natural Collection.

New project rooms were built; old ones moved. The office underwent constant change. It was as if it was undergoing the same kind of biological change that we humans were, and it led me to think that our next move was to challenge the whole way offices were bought, rented, built and used.

A new QUEST was voted in. This time we made sure all the places were elected. I registered my candidacy for the post, not so much because I saw it as an influential policy group, but because I felt it represented the heart of the company and that was where I was happiest being.

The others stood down from re-election and myself, Bono, George Porteous and Lyn Ellis took up the reins. Bono's election success helped allay worries that he and Naresh wanted to back out of the frontline of the company's development. It also helped to dignify somewhat the totally new work that he and Naresh were doing. The greatest thrill for me, though, was to see Lynn Ellis (23) and George Porteous (25) elected. In any other company, let alone an ad agency, Lynn, who had started as a quiet timid girl in the accounts department and George, who was (and still is at the time of writing) the company's first and only graduate trainee, would have had to wait at least ten years for the chance to contribute to important policy-making meetings.

The shareholders elected Lynn and George (and Bono and me) on one simple criterion – that these people could be trusted to conserve the company's specialness and to innovate its output. Fifteen people stood for the four available posts. To be voted onto the QUEST was a real vote of confidence from the fellow owners in your ability to run the heart of a company like St. Luke's.

I knew Bono would have an enormous impact, but George and Lynn were the real heroes. They debated each point that was raised with incredible maturity. At our awaydays, the level of innovation was impossibly high. Personnel issues were handled with a wisdom you would normally expect in people twice their age. They were fabulous.

Rule 8:

Give people all the space and opportunity they need to shine and they will blind you with their brilliance.

With this rule in mind, we offered an art student from the University of Central England the opportunity to become our Artist in Residence for the summer vacation. Natasha Rampley had only one brief – to surprise and stimulate us with art. She had free rein to do whatever she wanted in the office. She could paint on walls, on floors, on lockers, whatever. Creativity was physically to enter the workplace.

With the entire office as her canvas, Natasha set about a number of projects – some were fun, one was rude, another faintly religious. She would work by night and each morning as we came in we would see our office transformed.

We loved the thrill of this kind of constant change and enjoyed seeing ourselves provoked into a debate by the arrival of an army of tiny mice that appeared painted everywhere and which, when looked at closely, built up through clues a picture and view on the role of modern art.

Natasha graduated with a First Class Honours degree in Art and gained national notoriety for her final year's exhibit – an entire dining room made of things you could eat – sugar glass goblets, chocolate napkins, etc. She is now a regular fixture at St. Luke's.

The year careered to an end at breakneck speed. Tipped to be Agency Of The Year (an unheard of feat for such a new advertising agency), we already knew that we were the fastest-growing agency in London and were jam-packed with incredible talent from all corners of the advertising industry – and on some occasions from outside it. Every single piece of work we had done was talked about in the national media – we didn't have to enter expensive and retrogressive award shows to know how good our product was. We had to pinch ourselves to see if it was all a dream. Were we really that good? Was the company that brilliant?

A couple of days before Christmas, a package arrived for me from New York containing a dozen copies of *Fast Company* magazine. Inside was a six-page colour spread entitled:

The Ad Agency To End All Ad Agencies

St Luke's, a rebellious young agency spun out of the once-revolutionary Chiat/Day, practices what it preaches – the gospel of total ethics and common ownership

Just as the *Financial Times* had baptized us at the end of the previous year, this article confirmed us as one of the most innovative companies in the world today. It was full of wonderful photographs of the office and ourselves, and it went into great detail about the way we worked and the work we produced.

The article launched us onto a world stage. I began to receive e-mails from the USA, New Zealand, Australia and South East Asia as the magazine's circulation reached an extensive international readership.

I realised that St. Luke's was a fascinating product in its own right and that next year we needed to ensure we were organised for an avalanche of interest.

PART FOUR

Struggle In Paradise

㉖　**Winter Of Content**

We did not become Agency Of The Year for 1996. We did better than that.

We were runners-up between the UK's mightiest (and biggest) establishment agency Abbot Mead Vickers and its newest – M & C Saatchi. Tiny St. Luke's nestled between two giants whose reputations stretched so far back, few of us could recall their illustrious beginnings. We all knew that we had been set an even tougher task. To outperform a golden year and gain the number one spot. It was an extraordinary achievement after one year's trading.

Campaign magazine wrote:

When St. Luke's launched in 1995, there were many sneers and much sniping from the cheap seats. The pessimists dismissed its innovative working practices as reminiscent of a Moonie-style cult and its co-operative structure as too unwieldy for an agency. Such critics have had to eat their words during 1996...

...St. Luke's appears to be one of the few genuinely new things to have happened to advertising in Britain in recent years.

Out of a possible nine points that can be awarded for all-round excellence, we were given nine. So we were not as surprised as we might have been, when after a head to head pitch against the mighty J. Walter

Thomson, we were awarded the Boots Natural Collection account.

Kate and Tim's work was breathtaking. And risqué. It was a wonderful start to the year and a crowning achievement for two creative people who started the year with one set of creative partners and ended it, unexpectedly with another.

An avalanche of new business enquiries came our way. Being runners-up gave us excellence with an edge. We were a good horse to back. We could have doubled in size in the first three months of 1997, such was the interest.

Instead we closed our doors. We had yet to digest Clark's Shoes and United Distillers and we were in production with a huge campaign for Teletext that required making over thirty different ads. And we had new people to recruit, accommodate, train and befriend.

In the first quarter of 1997 our staff figures grew by nearly 16 per cent from sixty to seventy-two. (Another twenty were budgeted to come in the remainder of the year.) We now knew that each person would take up to six months to acclimatise and at a time when we were bedding down new clients, this represented a risk. Loyalty to our existing stake-holders was our only concern and that meant ensuring the high standards of service they had come to expect. David and I have never said 'no thank you' so often to so much new business before.

To make sense of the agency for the new recruits I was asked at my yearly review (conducted by Bono and George Porteous in January) to write an 'Owner's Manual'. It was to serve two purposes. It would explain how the company works, what it stands for and how you access it. But it would also straighten out some decision-making forums and help resolve the dilemma of leadership which had lived with me throughout 1996. I set about writing it and gave myself a target of Shareholders' Day, 27 March, to finish it. I asked John Grant for some help.

'Everybody wants this owner's manual,' I moaned to him, 'but I need a hook. I need something that explains the way we work and think and that ties in everything we produce.'

'Well, everything points to us wanting to build a better society,' he replied.

That did it for me.

Writing it was hard. There was an irony in it that I, the person who talked so much about change and fluidity had to commit everything we did to paper. It was like writing up an experiment that had yet to be concluded. I engaged the QUEST to help plan it and we spent a day at my house, working out what should go in and what shouldn't. I was keen on a 'warts and all' approach, including an explanation of the Omnicom deal, the actual legal articles of the association and an explanation of what we had failed to achieve.

George, Lynn and Bono were equally as eager and if anything wanted to go further. Why had people left? (One person became a deep-sea diving instructor in the British Virgin Islands – which was understandable – who could turn that down? But others had left for different reasons.) And what will we do with people that don't work out, in this hyper-liberated support culture?

At the end of the day we let our minds roam over other issues that were concerning us.

'Growth,' said Lynn. 'Its the only thing I hear about.'

'Agreed.' said George. 'Everyone's frightened that the bigger we get, the weaker our culture will become.'

'And the worse our work will get,' offered Bono, who had set himself up as a vociferous defender of the standards he and Naresh had established.

'What's the point of growing just for its own sake?' Lynn said. 'Remember all those sessions way back in '95 when we said all we wanted was to be in a company we were proud of?'

'But without growth, we'll stagnate.' I answered. 'I'm not saying grow quickly. I'm saying grow properly. Look at Dave and Naresh, they want to grow into new areas.'

Lynn was adamant. 'Well, people don't like it. Look at how well we've done. And the building. We love the building. If we grow and have to move it'll be another sad loss.'

'Just being positive for a moment.' George piped up, 'If we do move, what's the strategy? The QUEST should be advising on this so we don't have another building débâcle – no offence Andy.'

'None taken.'

'If we move we should help to build a better society,' said Lynn.

'We should buy an old cinema or leisure centre and renovate it. We could become a social centre.' Bono said.

'We could sponsor a school,' George said.

'We could move into a school,' Lynn said.

We all relaxed and dreamt and laughed. It was a long way off, yet an exciting prospect. We had a hundred and one ideas like that to put to the company, but the time wasn't right. Our job was to solve the 'growth problem'.

I didn't like the way everyone was getting nervous about growth and there were rumblings that 'all these new people weren't real St. Lukers'. I presented the Owner's Manual at the Shareholders' Day and ceremoniously threw it away at the same time.

'This book was redundant the moment I completed it,' I announced. 'But you wanted it, so here it is.'

I then launched into a speech, or was it a tirade? about the mood of the company.

'We must think of ourselves as pioneers travelling west on the wagon train. As long as we keep moving, we'll keep exploring. It doesn't matter how long the train is, in fact the more the merrier. If the wagon train stops it will form a protective circle. It'll start a civilising process that would appoint police, create rules. You don't need these when you're on the move. You look out, sure, for yourself and for each other, but that's as far as it goes. Everyone is personally responsible to keep up with the wagon train. But even if you drag behind, someone will help you to keep up. No, if this wagon train circles, it'll socialise itself into stasis.'

This was my theme and I was determined to pursue it. Focusing blindly on growth as the problem was not, to my mind, the issue. Planning it was.

We needed a plan for growth.

㉗ Spring In The Hothouse

itting in on the Shareholders' Day were Simon Zadec and Vernon Jennings. They were in the process of conducting a different sort of audit from the financial one that the meeting was legally observing. I had commissioned them at the end of the previous year to conduct a Social and Environmental Audit of St. Luke's which would establish a framework for ethical, as well as financial and creative growth.

It was the third leg of an unholy trinity of decisions that I was generally castigated for. (The Staircase and Dave and Naresh's Big Adventure being the other two.) All three decisions were examples of my stepping in and out.

The audit would take most of the year to complete, but at this stage they, too, had deduced that decision-making and my role (and David's as well as all the Department Heads) needed to be clarified before any audit could assess the real effect and external impact of the organisational structure we had put in place.

David established a Resource Committee to handle the day-to-day issues that required funding. I was happy not to be involved, seeing my QUEST role as more than enough responsibility. We continued to reject clients who were desperate to work with us, so that we could digest our internal issues and David and I began to set ever higher targets to dissuade prospects from coming in at all.

In one famous incident David outlined so many restrictions that we put on new clients that the client (who wanted anonymity at that stage) was bombarded by a five-minute-long litany of what we were not prepared to do. They left a little bewildered and some weeks later we discovered that we had just sent a division of British Airways packing!

We had more than enough to do. Both sets of creative directors were working flat out and new people streamed in every week. We stuck rigidly to our strategy of engaging with existing stakeholders first and foremost and wined and dined them, delivered and over-delivered and refused to look up over the parapet to see what was coming. New work was emerging for Midland Bank, Teletext and *The Observer* and developmental work for Clark's Shoes was looking really exciting. We seemed in a pressure cooker. Clients were knocking on the lid, work was boiling furiously inside and still the thorny old issue of decision-making remained unresolved. Still, we knew all our clients were happy. Or at least we thought so.

In the late spring, soon after the Labour Party's historic General Election victory, the *Observer*'s Marketing Director rang me up.

'We want to hold a review.'

'You want to do what?' I was stupefied.

'We want to hold a review,' he repeated. 'We feel that in the light of the election and the fact that we have a new editor [Will Hutton], it's time to review our advertising requirements. You'll be invited to re-pitch and defend your position, of course.'

I couldn't believe my ears. We had spent nearly six months concentrating on our clients and nothing else. The last three months had been a period of intensive work. The proposed work for *The Observer* was exciting and different and, we felt, was going to set them apart. We hadn't been in this position for nearly two years.

'Give me a few minutes,' I said. 'I'll call you back.'

I hastily assembled the team. They were horrified.

'Do you think he's seen our new proposals?' Clare Nash asked.

'That's beside the point,' I answered. 'It's New Labour, New *Observer*, New ad agency. It's as simple as that.'

'Well,' said Al, 'we have a rule, don't we? We never re-pitch for existing business.' It was a rule we implemented a long time ago, in the days of Chiat/Day, so strictly speaking it had entered St. Luke's by default rather than as a constitutional point of order. For example, that rule did not exist in the Owner's Manual!

'Well, even if we don't have that rule,' advised Neil Thomson, 'they're labour-intensive and our lowest payer. Losing them won't hurt.'

'It'll hurt our pride and spoil our unblemished record,' said Al. 'We can live with that.'

I called *The Observer*.

'We'll decline to pitch,' I informed him. 'The team wish you the very best of luck with your new arrangements.' Then I went further than I had intended. I had read a great deal of what Will Hutton, the editor, had to say about the potential of the UK to become a super economic power. His thoughts seemed as new and fresh and aligned as the ideals we were developing at St. Luke's. I saw him as a distant ally who would nod to what we were doing, rather than frown as so many observers and pundits had done in the past.

I sent him a fax suggesting his decision was not in the spirit of new stakeholder relations. He replied saying that it was only a review and all businesses were entitled to review suppliers. It enraged me even more and I regretted sending the fax. I was angry because I felt I was learning an unfair lesson. In the Creative Age, co-operation should be forcing a stronger bond between supplier and buyer.

Rule 9:

When you set out on a course and head for the future, not everyone will understand, or care where you're going. You may even end up somewhere people don't understand or like. Explaining every detail of the journey alleviates this condition.

In theory, losing *The Observer* freed up resources, but we were still not prepared to jump into the next opportunity that marched through the door. Particularly Cable & Wireless, who approached us with a whopping great £50 million spend.

It was too big. It would have dominated the company and crushed us. But we offered some thinking from Dave and Naresh (now known as Division 3). They presented programming ideas and some long ads – almost 'Infomercials', designed to establish Cable & Wireless as a major provider of phone, TV and Internet services. For a while it looked like they would strike lucky, then their proposals drifted from the client's consciousness as they got involved in the conventional launch of the new service.

I can think of no other advertising agency on the planet that would have turned down the opportunity to go for £50 million worth of Cable & Wireless business. But we did and we felt it was right for the sake of our clients, the spirit of the co-owners and the soul of the company. The pressure was on to resolve the internal resource issue. On paper we had all the people we needed, but we just didn't seem to be able to unlock the energy that potentially existed.

It was five months now since we had taken on a new account. It was eight months since Dave and Naresh stepped aside. Everyone should have been used to the new creative regime and myriad of new faces. How much more time was needed?

I discovered that at the heart of the issue was a nervousness about the quality of the work in the aftermath of Dave and Naresh's decision. Would it be at the same provocative standard? Were the new teams up to it? Weren't Dave and Naresh the one and only – and best – team in the entire UK? Could the others match their standards, let alone surpass them?

This was not gossiping, or politicking. This was an airing of a general concern. It was a no brainer for me. I had seen so many times how evidently skilled people pushed into positions of responsibility rose fast. Kate Stanner, Tim Hearn, Alan Young and Julian Vizard would carry our creative flag more than adequately.

In answer to the question, 'But how do you know the work will be good?', I would answer, 'Because they are passionately determined to make it so.' I always back people. But in the Creative Age I was surely going to back creative people. The company would rally to their support and they would be vindicated. I was sure of it. It was more than a hunch and less than an informed view. But I really believed it and David did, too.

The Social and Environmental Audit played back a grass-roots desire for me to take a postive leadership role and not trust that any spaces I created would automatically be filled. No one saw this as an old paradigm assertion of power. On the contrary, everyone wanted to know that the wagon train had someone at the helm.

David and I needed time to plan how we could innovatively reorganise ourselves and we embarked on a process of one-on-one consultations with as many people as we could to help us. I inserted a breathing space into the process and through the QUEST, declared a Summer of Love. No pitches until the end of the summer. More time for ourselves. Let's cool down and remind ourselves of the core values that got us where we were.

㉘ The Summer Of Love?

In the middle of June, David took himself off to Harvard for a rigorous two-week course in business management. It was something he had wanted to do for a long time and in the spirit of self-improvement, thought it would be beneficial to both him and the company.

We agreed that on his return we would both sit down and work out exactly how we would handle the leadership and growth issues of the company. We, too, were in a time vice. My wife was expecting our third child in September and we wanted to make sure the agency was properly tuned for success before I took advantage of our wonderfully generous paternity leave. The thought of coyly entering the autumn with no new business fire in our bellies seemed likely if we didn't work out how to organise ourselves. It was only a *Summer* of Love after all.

On his return, armed with a library of pertinent books and his head ringing with strategic advice, David booked the two of us onto the Eurostar train to Paris for what was to become a watershed in the company's development.

For eighteen solid hours we retrod every inch of the company's past and reminded ourselves of the *a priori* philosophical tenets at the heart of the company. We reread the notes from every awayday and then discovered that the solution, as had been so often the case, was staring us in the face.

We would split the company like amoeba (as two or three of the groups at the last St. Luke's awayday had recommended), thus forming self-contained entrepreneurial groups managed by whatever structure suited them and led by creative people with a creative mission. No group would be bigger than 35 and in this way new entities would be born at the rate of least one a year. The groups would be small enough for everyone to really know and understand each other and would together form a creative confederacy under the flag of St. Luke's.

We analysed each other's strengths and weaknesses and agreed to work as a team balancing each other elegantly. I would define the vision of the company and David would see that every mission we went on was in search of that vision. I was to cajole and support and stimulate, David was to make things happen operationally. We agreed in a bar in Paris that David would return to St. Luke's as the Operations Director and that together we would formally announce the split and present it in the context of the future of the company.

The ramifications were enormous. Setting aside the detailed implementation that would be required to forge two distinct entities out of one and the strain that might place on some of our clients (who had already ridden one trauma with us two years earlier), we were placing the company's creative future in the hands of one team who had been with us for barely a year and another with precious little experience of creative management. There could be no going back without dire consequences on the motivation and morale of Al and Jules and Kate and Tim. There was no possibility of The Return Of Dave And Naresh.

The amoeba system altered the operational and organisational DNA of the company and would therefore play a defining role in the evolution of the idea of St. Luke's. Furthermore, it would establish leadership roles for me and David and would reunite us as a functioning team. With staff numbers creeping towards ninety, it was make or break. Either this was the solution that would carry us forward and establish The Movement, or we would limp awkwardly like a lame plump duck, towards an unfocused and undynamic destiny.

We were utterly confident in what we wanted to do and on our return set about talking to those individuals who might be most affected. Every single person took a different and unique stand. The responses ranged from anger to relief, suspicion to conviction, hate to love. I felt like a surgeon hovering over a bruised and exhausted soldier, clamping random spurts of lifeblood as fast as new ones appeared. It was messy and ugly but both David and I knew that it was ultimately life giving.

We presented it to the company *en masse*. It met with silence.

'You've got a result,' said Smudger.

'I'll live with it,' said Naresh.

'Thank you.' said George. 'We can all get on with our jobs now.'

The Summer of Love ended the instant we made the amoeba presentation. In truth it only lasted a few weeks. The effect it had took every single one of us by surprise. Far from being a piece of subtle internal reorganisation it released an energy source that must have been banged up behind bars for months.

We flew out of our cage like a bat out of hell.

With four months to go until the end of the year and a hundred 'no thank yous' to a torrent of new business since January we let rip. In the closing hours of the Summer of Love, Fox's Biscuits invited us to pitch for their account. It was just what we were looking for. It was an everyday product, from a well-established British company, which had a long history of social responsibility. The pitch was assigned to the Al and Jules group with Clare Nash and Phil Teer providing the management and strategy.

We presented an idea which would place Fox's at the heart of the community and used the biscuits as a currency for socialising, particularly with people you don't know. It flew in the face of decades of advertising in this sector which saw biscuits as trifles, incidental items.

We were a couple of weeks into the pitch when the Department for Employment and Education paid us a visit. They were drawing up a long list of advertising agencies to handle the Labour Government's first big communications drive – to persuade businesses to take on unemployed people under a new financial arrangement called 'New Deal'.

When they asked us our views on unemployment they opened a floodgate of beliefs and values. Work was important to us. We felt it could be liberating. To be unemployed gave you no possibility of fulfilment. David made it clear that this was personally important to every single person at St. Luke's. Given what we'd all been through working on the nation's 'World At Work' would be a dream come true.

At first our nomination was not widely accepted. We were a new company without the track record of big established London ad agencies. But after endless phone calls and persistent badgering, our position on the shortlist prevailed. They asked us to pitch and David led the charge.

It was to be the most complex pitch we had yet undertaken.

When Fox's awarded us their business you could have heard the cheering for miles around. It was like rain after a long drought. We had spent the year organising ourselves and paying attention to our clients and this was now a demonstrable sign of dynamism. Fox's loved the approach and were willing and able to take the idea to the heart of their company.

We had barely caught our breath when Coca-Cola asked us to work on some long-term strategies for new brands. They had seen a booklet produced by John Grant entitled 'Sensorama' about the culture and climate of communicating to the youth market and were intrigued by the thinking. It was a collection of essays by various members of the company, including our Artist In Residence Natasha Rampley, and encouraged a lateral view of what young people were thinking and doing in the mid- to late 90s. We relished the thought of working with such a famous name.

Then Disney approached us to handle an international assignment that was in need of creative input. They were assembling children from all over the world for a 'Children's Summit' and felt the concept needed more imagination. It wasn't conventional advertising. Were we interested? Of course we were, for that very reason. We snapped it up.

The assignment went to a fourth group, which we code-named Barcelona in memory of the city in which we dreamt up the idea. Just as we had agreed at one of our re-invention processes in one of our awaydays, an amoeba split had taken place. Andrew Hill, previously our Media Director, Ken Dixon, previously a planner and Smudger had opted to throw in their old roles and recreate themselves in 'creative media'. They would think beyond conventional TV and print and find communication solutions in new media. With Disney to kick off (as well as assignments from existing clients) they were off with a bang.

Just before Christmas we heard we were down to the final two for the Government account. We had beaten off agency after agency. We had emerged as one of the favourites although we had started as rank outsiders. Throughout we knew that there were worries about our size, our zaniness, our credibility. You name it, someone somewhere had a problem with some aspect of St. Luke's. It was uphill all the way. Kate Stanners and Tim Hearn had never worked so hard for something they so believed in. Winning this would make them, in every possible way.

Now, all that stood between us and winning was a successful presentation to the Chancellor of the Exchequer, Gordon Brown and Minister without Portfolio, Peter Mandelson. We were desperate. We passionately wanted this. Two years ago we'd have envisioned this situation and laughed at ourselves for our ludicrous presumptions. But it was real. It was really happening. And it was within arm's reach.

Just about the whole company was involved in one way or another. Hubsters worked through the night, Gidon, the Head of IT was at one point to be found on all fours in the Cabinet offices setting up a professional multimedia show. Eventually, after a presentation in the Cabinet offices behind 10 Downing Street and an ominous silence for a couple of days, Helena Rafalowska, a bright, young civil servant who had pushed boundaries and cajoled the sternest ministers on our behalf rang to say she would be coming in for a chat.

An expectant crowd gathered and she addressed everyone.

'Well, I am pleased to announce St. Luke's has been awarded the "New Deal" business. You have beaten the competition against the odds. Well done. The team did a brilliant job. Now you have only one job to do. Make sure you sell the idea to every business in Britain.' Kate and Tim fell off their chairs. The agency whooped in uncontrollable delight.

We couldn't help but savour the sweetness of such a victory as that. Since 1992 David and I had been investigating the world of work, its ethics, its purpose, its effect. After the mutiny of 1995, 35 people had all stuck together despite being offered lucrative positions elsewhere to form a totally unique company that put its humans first and encouraged work itself to be liberating and fun. We valued the opportunities work could bestow on people and saw the beginnings of a new economic order which steered profits away from the hands of a tiny minority, who needed the assistance and sweat of others to achieve their goals and rechannelled it towards a wider constituency of stakeholders, including the community at large. We weren't communists or Marxists or Moonies (although we were labelled as such), we were Creativists, at work, in work, and suddenly, after all these years, after months and months of tortuous self-enquiry and potential failure, we were awarded £18 million to persuade every businessman in Great Britain to address the loathsome spectre of unemployment, to solve it as a shared duty and to put vigour and pride back into the jobs of thousands, possibly millions of people all over the country. It *was* a dream come true.

If I were writing a book, people would think I'd made it all up.

Epilogue

S t. Luke's was voted Agency Of The Year by *Campaign* magazine. 'Love it, or hate it,' the magazine wrote, 'St. Luke's as a co-operative has managed to create something different in business.'

We knew we were in the running and the QUEST had met to discuss how we should handle the award, were it to come our way.

This was a different QUEST. During St. Luke's Day (held at The Anugraha, a curious mosque-like hotel set in acres of English country-side) it was agreed that there would be six places – all voted – and a QUEST Secretary to record the meetings. Kerry Newman, recently returned from maternity leave, was the Secretary and the Questors were voted in from the widest possible spectrum of skills, ages and experience. I decided not to stand. I was relaxed with how and when I would be contributing.

There was Robbie Sparks, The Father of the House we call him, a typographer by trade, and Andy Palmer, an Account Director who worked on Clark's Shoes and would go on to handle the New Deal campaign. Andy Lockley, a copywriter who would cajole the group into taking risks and Jan Martin, a controller in Finance. They were joined by Jody Burrows, a TV producer, and Ben Bilboul, who you may remember was (with Kate Male) the first St. Luker.

I'm telling you who they are because you have to realise that in any other company these people would be years away from any management post. Some would never be considered management material. But to the shareholders of St. Luke's that year, they were skilled enough to be entrusted with the soul of the company.

It was this soul that they debated when the Agency Of The Year award was made to us. Some argued it would be wrong to accept it, since we eschewed all other awards and were not keen on being embraced into the advertising community. Others felt it would be churlish to 'send it back'. We hadn't entered for it or contrived in any way to get it. Anyway, what harm had *Campaign* magazine ever done us? Why would we be rude? There was a vocal contingent who were wary of an agency party on the evening of the eighth – they had booked seats at the International Darts Tournament in Frimley Green, 25 miles south of London.

This QUEST would not reject the award, but it would not revel in it either.

To celebrate Agency Of The Year, following on from the runner-up position the year before, and to recognise the second successive 9 out of 9 rating, 25 per cent of the company went to the International Darts Tournament and the rest of us went to a pub nearby and enjoyed a quiet ale.

When the news was announced that we had beaten last year's performance and been voted best agency in the UK, we were inundated with requests for a documentary from a number of TV stations including the BBC and Channel 4. David and I felt it would be improper to open negotiations without speaking to Debbie and Adam of Insight Films, who had tried in vain for nearly two years to make a film.

When we contacted them, they were in Australia. 'We're agency of the year,' I told them, 'and now everyone wants to make a film about us.'

'We knew it,' Debbie said. 'This would have been a great film; we could have followed all your struggles until eventually you emerge as the best ad agency in town. Shit. This is a disaster. The film would have been wonderful. Shit.'

'We'll still go with you guys if you want to do it,' I said.

One week later, with a commission from Channel 4, they were in the agency filming everything we said and did.

'We could be here for six months,' Adam said.

'Fine,' I said.

Scene:
The inside of 10 Downing Street.

In attendance:
Various New Deal dignitaries, Prime Minister Tony Blair, Gordon Brown and St. Luke's very own David Abraham.

Civil Servant to Gordon Brown:
'Gordon, it appears our agency St. Luke's has been voted Advertising Agency Of The Year.'

Gordon Brown to Civil Servant:
'I know. This Government never makes mistakes.'

Business Matters

Yesterday I went down to the Ristorante San Luca with my colleagues. Being a Monday, I wanted to enjoy Franco and Bruno's free English breakfast and to see how this Monday's Open Mind session was received. There had been two before. The first week we all gathered our personal happiness into imaginary rubber balls and threw them at Ben Bilboul. The following week we formed triangles of affection with two people we didn't know that well. This week we gained in stature by stretching and massaging each other. Over the years we have performed and discussed things that make these seemingly curious, even embarrassing, moments seem somewhat regular and ordinary.

I was going to walk upstairs to The Egg when I saw John Grant sitting eating his breakfast.

'I'm glad I caught you, I want to ask you about happiness in your work life. Bill Gates is very successful, but I wonder if he is very happy?'

'We've spoken of this in the past,' John said, 'and you must accept the concept of fulfilment before you can properly determine whether happiness exists or whether it has a role at all. Bill Gates is fulfilling a life's ambition. He might not have known it when he was a child and events may have affected his trajectory, but he is constantly fulfilling ambitions and objectives. Fulfilment is infinite, but measurable. In a sense the scale of fulfilment can have a negative aspect. You can be unfulfilled and you can move from that state into an experience of fulfilment which is incremental. Happiness is a static point along the path of fulfilment. At any one stage I can declare myself happy, but still feel there is more to fulfil.'

John continued: 'I am happy now, because I am eating my breakfast, but my day is, right now, unfulfilled.'

At this point we were joined by David Abraham, Clare Nash, Mari Cortizo and Sally Kelso.

'Can work be a happy and fulfilling experience for everyone, or do you have to have certain characteristics?'

David answered: 'Aristotle developed his own philosophical view of happiness, *eudaimonia*, which more exactly equates to "human flourishing". For Aristotle, human beings must choose between living a harmonious life that accords with everything they stand for, physically, emotionally and spiritually, or a disharmonious life that fits purely with only what they are physically, just an animal with only flesh and blood.'

John agreed: 'Human flourishing is a happy state. Nowadays we would quote Noël Coward who felt that "Work is more fun than fun". We have created a state whereby we encourage personal transformation. It is a gift that comes from ownership. As owners – equal owners – we can fulfil our ambitions. When Smudger wanted to leave the production department he recreated himself as a Creative Media Producer, someone who creates events and affairs that communicate a client's strategy in an unconventional way. He and others created a new business for St. Luke's.'

'I am worried that we have just created a good life for ourselves. We are self-contained, unlikely to suffer devastating bad luck and engaged in a permanent process of self-awareness. In our attempt to break down the walls between business and society have we not simply created a Garden of Eden, just for ourselves, which is every bit as different from ordinary life as any other workplace?'

Sally chipped in: 'We have to get things right internally before we can effect things externally. If we are a confused force then we will emit signals of confusion. We must know exactly why we are doing what we are doing. Only then should we allow ourselves the opportunity to affect people outside. That's why we talk about ourselves so much. That's where self-awareness comes in. When you join St. Luke's you wear two hats. You do the job you were hired to do or which you have been transformed into – in my case I was hired as a secretary, but I have changed and become the Head of IT and you also do the job of inventing and refining St. Luke's. Mind you, we are more aligned now than ever before. When

Sustainability conducted our Environmental and Social audit they discovered that 86 per cent of us felt that our own personal values chimed with the values of St. Luke's. We are getting our own house in order.'

'But self-awareness is good,' Clare replied. 'Aristotle argued that we humans should do what is naturally and fundamentally human. The Greeks had a word for this – *ergon*, meaning "function" or "characteristic activity". Thinking is a characteristically human function. I think that if you bother to think about whether something is right or wrong, or good or bad, you have answered the question almost before you ask it. You will know that good is better than bad. Asking the question simultaneously provides the answer.'

Mari added, *Homo sapiens* is a rational species. *Homo sapiens* understands that expressing virtue is right rather than wrong.'

To which Sally asked, 'But can you be virtuous at work? There are so many times when people are forced to behave uncharacteristically in order to meet the obligations of their employers. Recently, of 40,000 US businessmen surveyed, 95 per cent said they lied at work. And look at us in advertising. A 1995 Gallup poll asked Americans to rank more than twenty occupations in terms of honesty and ethics. The only jobs to score lower than advertising executives were members of Congress and second-hand car dealers.'

David wanted to add to this point: he had made a speech to the advertising industry in 1994 about how advertising was publicly portrayed via the movies. Advertising executives had never been treated kindly by Hollywood and businessmen in general did not fare well. Of all Hollywood movies featuring businessmen, 75 per cent portrayed them as evil. 'The impression of business in the UK is the same as in America,' he said. 'When consumers are asked who is trusted (there are many surveys on this conducted by MORI), they choose not to trust businessmen. They place businessmen very low down. Doctors and the clergy are ranked the highest. The only professions less trusted than businessmen are politicians and journalists.'

Al Young came over. 'That's curious, because if you ask people which institutions they trust, they will place companies like the Royal Mail, the Post Office, building societies and banks way above trade unions, Parliament and the press. The former are at the top of the league, the latter at the bottom.'

Kola Ogundipe had been listening. 'Yes, that fits, there's nothing wrong with business *per se*, it's just the business leaders and managers that are less trusted. It's the human element. When Sally talked about getting our own house in order, she meant aligning the true virtuous beliefs of humans – human nature – with the business entity itself.'

The conversation grew in a number of directions. More people came to the discussion and sometimes there was more than one conversation at a time. Small groups began to debate different issues amongst themselves. In the background there was a clatter of cooking as Franco and Bruno prepared lunch.

'I am surprised that trade unions and politicians are ranked so low,' said Andrew Hill. 'Trade Unions were defenders of human rights in the workplace and politicians, if you look at the landslide Labour victory, can be positively voted in, as well as rejected.'

Neil Henderson replied, 'The 20th century has moved people emotionally away from large institutions. You can see it everywhere. Successive governments in all citizen-literate countries around the world have been withdrawing from state intervention and control when it comes to the rights of the consumer. Twenty years ago if my mother discovered a drawing pin in a can of sardines she would just throw it away and think nothing of it. If she found more and more strange objects she might talk to the grocer who sold her the sardines, or possibly the Ministry of Agriculture and Fisheries. No way would she write to the Chairman of the company who actually produced the sardines. The effect is an incredible rise in localised consumer groups and TV watchdogs who give vent to individually expressed complaints. One single consumer feels he or she has the right to challenge anyone in business who affects what they do, say or eat. Look at the raging debate about biotechnology and genetically altered foods. Iceland, the big frozen-food chain, will no longer take genetically altered food because they feel the customer is not fully informed. Customers are powerful lobbyists, they vote with their wallets. In the USA today, 75 per cent of consumers deliberately boycott certain products. In the UK, 65 per cent of consumers say they would take real action against a company if they disapproved of its actions. Individuals have taken control.'

Al took up the point: 'In other areas we have taken control as individuals and shunned large institutions. We were urged to contract out of the State Earnings-Related Pension Scheme and now a hundred or more financial institutions are urging us to create our own, self-administered pensions. The National Health has been slowly giving way to more effective "over the counter – OTC" remedies, private health plans and even "doctors by phone" concepts which create an immediate personally organised treatment service. Trade unions have lost their teeth as workers look after their own parochial issues and re-evaluate their role in the labour market. Maybe one day most companies will be employee owned, like ours, negating the need completely for an organised body to defend the workers. They will need no Big Brother because as co-owners they will be enabled to run the company without bosses creating a sour environment with secrets, hidden agendas and a general air of mistrust.'

Kola returned to the discussion about virtue at work. 'I believe you can be virtuous at work if it is your own company. You will care about the actions of a company you own. You will ask yourself questions and you will be ashamed when you discover bad practice. But bad values creep in all the time. We don't submit our time sheets to Neil Thomson when we should. We don't always clear away our dishes.'

Neil heard this, from across the room. He came over, with Phil Teer, Robbie Sparks, Rachael Plant and Smudger.

Robbie said, 'It's not right that Rose clears up our mess. She is the Housekeeper not the human keeper. But we are still somewhat institutionalised. We still see Rose as the cleaner who will clear up after us. Some here will still see her as "just the cleaner" in their minds, although they will have the social grace not to make it known to her. Actually this is her company as much as ours.'

Neil Thomson agreed. 'People are not snubbing me personally when they don't hand in their time sheets, it's just that they have not fully understood personal responsibility and how it conjoins with ownership. For many, in their minds, their jobs are still ranked lowly. They tend to behave more like employees because that is what they are used to.'

Phil wanted to explore this point. 'There is a relationship between mutual need and personal aptitude. In this society, St. Luke's, we need each other to behave properly or else all our lives will fall into disarray and our clients will find us slovenly, untidy and ill-tempered. But the problem is that some people think their job makes them less able to help and at the same time more vulnerable if things go wrong.'

'But we talk about personal responsibility, community and co-operation all the time,' I answered.

'Yes,' replied John, 'but not everyone has experienced these things. Life here is good now. No one envisages a major problem. It's not complacency so much as satisfaction. It's easier to stick together if we think we are going to fall together.'

'Should we deliberately create a fall – impose some real business threats and problems?' David asked.

'We have short-term problems, then we overcome them and we celebrate them as if they were great victories,' I commented.

'But that is an incomplete feeling of reward,' said Mari. 'One swallow does not a summer make. No, we don't need to create a fall, we need to encourage perpetual personal transformation. That is the creative mandate of St. Luke's. Then life here will be made up of a series of individual achievements – personal "summers" if you like and overall the company will grow.'

Kate Stanners was nearby. She had finished talking with Tim Hearn and made a comment on what Mari had said. 'I just wonder how this group that has grown so quickly and which could grow even faster, can make provision for a series of personally fulfilled ambitions. Not everyone can do what they most want to do. Isn't there a common consensus that determines we must all do things that are interrelated to each other?'

Robbie answered, 'A business based on the development and deployment of human capital must take note of what the humans can achieve. But there must be limitations. The review process acts as a guiding principle, but we can never limit our potential.'

Rachael added, 'The opposite is also true. We won't do things which run counter to the characteristics and desires of the human capital. Just because we see a competitive business successfully trading in one market – and making heaps of money – does not immediately mean that we, too, trade in that market. We grow by what we most want to do and by what we can agree together. After all, there are no ventures that involve only one person.'

David was keen to develop this point: 'For sure, a business in pursuit of money alone will not grow in the direction of the ambitions of all the humans within it. Most businesses are obsessed with the bottom line. As Henry Ford said, "A business that makes nothing but money is a poor kind of business." If a business is privately owned it will exist to enrich the owners who set it up. Even if they set it up many years ago and have received ten-fold a financial reward to offset the personal risk they had taken. If a business is publicly quoted it will be driven by shareholder value. Often managers of the business will never meet the shareholders. You might work all your life for a company delivering a 20 per cent margin year on year to stock market fund managers. You will retire and and recoup the investment made by the selfsame fund managers. This will go on for as long as you live. But when you and your partner die the money stops. Who takes that money? Well, it is deemed to belong to funds that hold shares in your company. Sometimes people work so hard to achieve the 20 per cent that they die within a few years of retirement. What of their sweat equity then?'

Jan Martin came into the discussion: 'We make money, of course, we should be proud of that. But there is a difference here. Money is so open, so much a part of our everyday life it is like air. In our industry and many, many others finance is located out of sight. "Out of sight, out of mind" as the saying goes. In fact the finance department is usually in the basement or another building altogether. It does not interact with the rest of the company and often maintains its own deeply depressing culture.'

Kate added, 'In companies where finance is hidden, you end up believing there is something to hide. It is my understanding that the John Lewis Partnership issue the week's trading figures to every partner (employee) every week. That openness treats everyone as adults. And you have to admit it is a very successful retailer, with a high level of consumer trust.'

'Yes, that's right,' said Andy Palmer from the back of the group. 'In a conventional company the main responsibility of finance is either to report the financial results to a corporate holding company, or to assist the small number of company owners in maximising their individual wealth before they sell out to a corporate holding company or become one themselves.'

Jan agreed. 'Agency profitability is not disclosed to clients or the majority of staff. In fact it is not unusual for individuals in the finance department itself not to know financial information such as turnover and client income.'

'In a company predicated on human capital, humans will need to know,' John said.

'There is no company pride in the financial performance of many companies,' Jan continued. 'If anything, it is hidden in case the "troops" might want a greater share.'

Mari said, 'There is no transparency of information with clients and many advertising agencies make hidden profits via undisclosed mark-ups. That's not right. We wouldn't feel right if we did that.'

'No, not at all. I don't remember, when we sat in the Room With No Windows, that we agreed to create a company that made profits via undisclosed mark-ups,' Robbie said.

Phil commented, 'At St. Luke's, the finance function is an integral part of the revolution and people in it have a very high profile both internally, and with our clients. Financial results are widely available and discussed. As shareholders, everyone in the company is affected by the financial performance and can have an influence on improving income levels or preventing unnecessary costs. This increases our profit.'

Neil Thomson, Finance Director, said, 'Profit is like health. We need it, but it is not what we live for. Plato observed that just as poets are fond of their own poems and parents of their own children, so money-makers become devoted to money, not because like other people (like you and me), they find it useful, but because it is their own creation. So they are tiresome company, as they have no standard but cash value.'

The crowd round the breakfast grew. Ben Bilboul and Kate Male were listening in.

'Our creation is St. Luke's,' said Ben. 'That's what we are most fond of.'

'Yes, my heart is lifted when I see newer people showing someone round and I hear the pride they have in the company as they describe it in the tiniest detail,' I replied.

'You are proud, Andy, because you hear people speak of the company that was born years ago but which has resonance today,' said Kate Male.

James Wood and George Porteous were talking to Lynn Ellis about the history of the company when someone reprimanded them.

'You're right,' George said. 'Yesterday doesn't matter, it is today and tomorrow that matter. Nostalgia is like an eating disorder, it's addictive and pleasurable, but empty, all at the same time.'

'Nostalgia defines motives in a past context,' added Lynn.

'And makes you sad, rather than happy,' James remarked.

'Are we ignoring the past,' asked Tim Hearn, 'and all it has to teach us?'

'Only the good parts,' answered Robbie. 'The failures are worth noting.'

'If we are just living for today and tomorrow, we are always moving forward. Isn't it reckless to never stop and settle with what we have?' asked Jan Martin.

'The unexamined life is not worth living,' Al replied. 'Taking risks brings its own rewards. Like discovery, for example. It brings mistakes too, but if you know you will make mistakes and not be fired for making them, then you will proceed fearlessly. Bravery is important, but permission is more important still.'

'Who gives us the permission to be brave?' asked Lynn.

'We all do.' And, indeed, Ben spoke for us all.

'Bravery is a fundamental part of the creative process.' Bono was always saying this.

'It allows us to look round corners we wouldn't normally look round and peer over cliffs which seem precarious,' added Naresh.

Julian Vizard agreed, 'Without bravery we'd be wallowing in mediocrity. Our work should thrive in the extremes.'

The crowd dispersed to Project Rooms, The Womb, The Egg and The Hub. I turned to John who had finished his breakfast.

'We have met with so many people with whom we have had the good fortune to debate philosophies within St. Luke's. Each has added something to our knowledge of what a service concept in the creative age might look like. People like Charles Handy, Vernon Jennings, Charles Leadbeater, David Mills, Geoff Mulgan, Richard Pascal, Anita and Gordon Roddick, Steve Russell, Elaine Sternberg, Franceska van Dijk, Simon Zadek and Theodore Zeldin. And there will be more influences. I wonder if together they make a philosophy?'

John Grant looked at me and said, 'Maybe, but as Wittgenstein wrote in his *Tractatus Logico-Philosophicus*, "Whereof one cannot speak, thereof one must be silent." It is a highly metaphysical remark that attempts to convey the unsayable, unthinkable doctrine that we must accept that there is a realm about which one can say nothing. Perhaps this is just a way of life.'

'I don't think we are in that realm. Conversation is our mentor. It is like air in a soufflé. Communication builds the company. It is creating what we are. Without conversation, communication, challenge and debate, the soufflé will sink. It's hard. But then we created this. And now these are the times we are in.'

Some Books Which Have Made Me Think

Aristotle, *Nichomachaen Ethics*, Oxford University Press, 1980

Barker, Joel, *Future Edge*, William Morrow and Company Inc., 1992

Bennis, Warren, *Organizing Genius*, Nicholas Brealey, 1997

Block, Peter, *Stewardship*, Berrett-Koehler, 1993

Buzan, Tony & Keene, Raymond, *The Age Heresy*, Ebury Press, 1996

Cameron, Julia, *The Artist's Way*, Souvenir Press, 1994

Cannon, Tom, *Corporate Responsibility*, Pitman, 1992

Chopra, Deepak, *The Way of the Wizard*, Harmony Books, 1995

de Geus, Arie, *The Living Company*, Nicholas Brealey, 1997

Dyson, George, *Darwin Among the Machines*, Addison-Wesley, 1997

Elkington, John, *Cannibals with Forks*, Capstone, 1997

Gibson, Rowan, *Rethinking the Future*, Nicholas Brealey, 1997

Gilder, George, *Life After Television*, Whittle Books, 1990

Hamel, Gary & Prahalad, C. K., *Competing for the Future*, Harvard Business School Press, 1994

Handy, Charles, *Beyond Certainty*, Random House, 1995

Handy, Charles, *The Hungry Spirit*, Random House, 1997

Jackson, David, *Dynamic Organisations*, Macmillan Press, 1997

Jacobs, Jane, *Systems of Survival*, Random House, 1992

Kao, John, *Jamming*, HarperCollins, 1996

Koestler, Arthur, *The Act of Creation*, Hutchinson & Co., 1964

Lala, R. M., *The Creation of Wealth*, Padmini Mirchandi for IBH Publishers, 1981

Leadbeater, Charles, *A Piece of the Action*, Demos, 1997

McLuhan, Marshall & Powers, Bruce, *The Global Village*, Oxford University Press, 1986

McLuhan, Marshall, *Understanding Media*, Routledge, 1964

Mulgan, Geoff, *Connexity*, Chatto & Windus, 1997

Nalebuff, Barry & Brandenburger, Adam, *Co-opetition*, HarperCollins, 1996

Nash, Laura, *Good Intentions Aside*, Harvard Business School, 1990

Peters, Tom, *Liberation Management*, Macmillan Press, 1992

Plato, *The Republic*, Penguin, 1955

Plender, John, *A Stake in the Future*, Nicholas Brealey, 1997

Stacey, Ralph, *Managing the Unknowable*, Jossey-Bass, 1992

Stack, Jack, *The Great Game of Business*, Bantam Doubleday Dell, 1992

Sternberg, Elaine, *Just Business*, Little Brown, 1994

Zeldin, Theodore, *An Intimate History of Humanity*, Sinclair-Stevenson, 1994

Index